DENTAL MORPHOLOGY FOR ANTHROPOLOGY

This work provides a new, comprehensive update to the Arizona State University Dental Anthropology System (ASUDAS). Drawing upon her extensive experience in informatics, curating data, and dental morphological data acquisition, Edgar has developed accessible and user friendly standardized images and descriptions of dental morphological variants. The manual provides nearly 400 illustrations that indicate ideal expressions of each dental trait. These drawings are coupled with over 650 photographs of real teeth, indicating real-world examples of each expression. Additionally, trait descriptions have been written to be clear, comparative, and easy to apply. Together, the images and descriptions are presented in a standardized form for quick and simple reference. All of these modifications to ASUDAS make it more usable by students and professionals alike. In addition to these features of the manual, the text makes a brief but strong argument for why dental morphology will continue to be a useful tool in biological anthropology through the 21st century.

Heather J. H. Edgar is Curator of Human Osteology for the Maxwell Museum of Anthropology and Associate Professor of Anthropology at the University of New Mexico, USA. Her research focuses on the ways in which historical events and cultural trends shape the biology of populations, especially in the U.S. and Mexico.

DENTAL MORPHOLOGY FOR ANTHROPOLOGY

An Illustrated Manual

Heather J. H. Edgar
Illustrations by E. Susanne Daly

Routledge
Taylor & Francis Group
NEW YORK AND LONDON

First published 2017
by Routledge
711 Third Avenue, New York, NY 10017

and by Routledge
2 Park Square, Milton Park, Abingdon, Oxon, OX14 4RN

Routledge is an imprint of the Taylor & Francis Group, an informa business

Library of Congress Cataloging-in-Publication Data
A catalog record for this book has been requested

ISBN: 978-1-62958-511-6 (hbk)
ISBN: 978-1-62958-512-3 (pbk)
ISBN: 978-1-315-30083-2 (ebk)

Typeset in Bembo
by Apex CoVantage, LLC

Printed and bound in Great Britain by
TJ International Ltd, Padstow, Cornwall

For Bruce, my traveling-through-life companion.

CONTENTS

Foreword *ix*
Acknowledgments *xi*
Photo Credits *xiii*
A Note About the Use of the Words "Race" and "Ancestry" *xvii*

1 Rationale: Why Study Dental Morphology, and Why Use This Book to Do It? 1
Problems Collecting Dental Morphological Data 2
Dental Morphological Data Are Useful 3
Hominin Evolutionary Relationships 4
Worldwide Patterns of Variation 4
Intraregional Variation 5
Intracemetery Relationships 6
Individual Level Analyses 7

2 How to Study Dental Morphology 8
Data Collection 8
Scoring Types 10
Breakpoints 10
Weighted Frequencies 13
Data Analysis 14
Biological Distance 14
Individual Estimation of Group Membership 16

3 Dental Morphology Manual 18

4 Data Collection Pages 148

5 Root Traits 153

6 Arch and Tooth Reference Pages 155

Glossary *162*
Trait Expression Summary Pages *166*
References *175*
Index *182*

FOREWORD

When I was an undergraduate at Arizona State University in the late 1960s, dental morphology was the last thing on my mind. My heart was set on becoming an archaeologist with a focus on the U.S. southwest (how unique, right?). Sometimes, the best-laid plans go awry. In 1967, Christy G. Turner II came to ASU as a recent PhD out of the University of Wisconsin who had just defended his dissertation titled *The Dentition of Arctic Peoples*. I knew little about the Arctic and even less about teeth, but Dr. Turner was young, enthusiastic, and charismatic. He somehow convinced me to make casts of Easter Island dental casts borrowed from a Canadian dentist. After five years, I defended my dissertation with the cumbersome title *Dental Morphology: A Genetic Analysis of American White Families and Variation in Living Southwest Indians*, thus becoming the first PhD in physical anthropology to graduate from ASU. When I defended my dissertation, I had no clue about its significance, seriously believing it could easily be relegated to the dustbin of history.

In 1968, dental morphology was largely the province of dentists such as Albert A. Dahlberg, P. O. Pedersen, and C.F.A. Moorrees. Stimulated by these researchers and his mentor, Bertram S. Kraus at the University of Arizona, Turner wanted to build on their foundation and use tooth crown and root morphology to address bigger anthropological issues. The first one he tackled and pursued for two decades was the peopling of the New World. His 1971 paper on three-rooted lower first molars led to the development of the three-wave model for the settlement of the Americas that has been the centerpiece of discussion and debate for over 40 years. Slowly but surely, the physical anthropological world began paying attention to research on dental morphology. Plus, more and more students were focusing on morphology in their pursuit of MA and PhD degrees.

I maintained a lifelong relationship with Turner, and during many of my visits to his unique home on Campo Alegre, we would discuss anthropology and morphology and hope this area of research would continue to blossom and expand. In

1991, Turner codified the methodology that he had developed in conjunction with graduate students, and the Arizona State University Dental Anthropology System was born. To the two of us, ASUDAS was a methodological foundation but not an end point. We hoped students and researchers would identify more traits and find more applications for morphology.

That leads us to the current volume. Dr. Edgar has developed a manual that will help researchers fine-tune their observations on crown and root morphology in either bioarchaeological or forensic contexts. Her research focusing on ancestry assessment using morphology has jump-started an area long ignored. I have suspected morphology would be useful in this area, but I lacked the statistical skills to take it on by myself. Forensic anthropologists either ignore entirely or pay little heed to how morphology could be used for evaluating ancestry. She and I both share a goal of combating the 'fear of teeth' in the forensic arena (excluding identifications based on restoration). Hopefully, this volume with its excellent illustrations of graded trait expressions will stimulate many workers to dip their toes into the morphological arena. Reducing levels of intra- and inter-observer error in studying morphology has long been a concern of mine and one that is clearly shared by Heather. Once an individual has mastered the fundamentals of dental anatomy, this manual will be a tremendous aid in increasing interest in and enhancing the reliability of dental morphological observations.

G. Richard Scott
Professor of Anthropology
University of Nevada Reno

ACKNOWLEDGMENTS

My thanks goes to the staffs of the many fantastic institutions that have permitted me to collect the dental morphological data that has allowed the crafting of this manual: American Museum of Natural History; Arizona State University School of Evolution and Social Change; Berliner Gesellschaft für Anthropologie, Ethnologie und Urgeschichte; Centro INAH Yucatán; Case Western Reserve University Dental School; Central Michigan University Department of Sociology, Anthropology, and Social Work; Cleveland Museum of Natural History; Escuela Nacional de Antropología e Historia, Instituto de Investigaciones Antropológicas, UNAM; Instituto Nacional de Antropología e Historia; Jikei University Medical School; L'Institut Fondamental d'Afrique Noire Cheikh Anta Diop; Maxwell Museum of Anthropology; Musée de l'Homme; Národní Muzeum; National Museum of Health and Medicine; National Museum of Natural History; New York University Dental School; Nova Southeastern University Dental School; Ohio State University Anthropology Department; Pima County Office of the Medical Examiner; Sapienza Università di Roma; Servizio di Antropologia, Tivoli; Texas Archaeological Research Laboratory; the Natural History Museum; Universidad Autónoma de Yucatán Dental School; Universidad de Granada School of Medicine; University of Southern California Dental School; State Museum of New York; University of Tennessee Health Sciences Center Dental School; University of Tokyo University Museum; and the University of Washington Dental School. Thank you also to the sources of funding for the travel to these institutions: the Forensic Anthropology Center at the University of Tennessee, the National Science Foundation, the Ohio State University, and the University of New Mexico.

Thank you to my students and former students, especially Corey Ragsdale, Anna Rautman, and Katelyn Rusk, for working with me on this endeavor. Thanks to Marin Pilloud and the staff of the Joint POW Accounting Command for being guinea pigs for the first version of this manual. Thank you to my friends and colleagues, especially Cathy Willermet, for your support. Finally, thanks go to Sheilagh Brooks, Raymond Rawson, Paul W. Sciulli, and, most importantly, to Christy G. Turner II, for teaching me how to collect, analyze, and interpret dental morphological data.

Heather J. H. Edgar

PHOTO CREDITS

See the manual pages for trait abbreviations.

American Museum of Natural History

LM2GP +, LP4LC 5, UM1C5 5, UM1CB 4, UM2PR 0, UM3PEG 0, UM3CA 0, UMEE 2, UP3M MXPAR 3, LM2C5 1, LM2C5 0, LM2C5 0, LM1AF 2, LP3LC 6, LM1PS 1, LM2C5 1, LM2C5 0, LM2C5 0, LM1AF 2, LP3LC 6, LM1PS 1, LM1C5 1

Arizona State University School of Human Evolution and Social Change

UM1MC 0

Berliner Gesellschaft für Anthropologie, Ethnologie und Urgeschichte

LCDR 3, LCDR 5, LM1AF 2, LM1AF 3, LM1C6 2, LM1C7 1, LM1C7 2, LM1C7 2, LM1C7 4, LM1CN 6, LM1DW 1, LM2C7 1, LM2C7 3, LM2PS 6 M3, LM3PEG 0, LP3LC 3, LP3LC 9, LP4LC 6, LP4LC 7, UCMR 3, UI1DS 0, UI1TD 4, UM1C5 1, UM1CB 1, UM1CB 4, UM1CB 6, UM1HC 4, UM1HC 6, UM2CB 1, UM2CB 2, UM2CB 3, UM2CB 5, UM2CB 6, UP3AC2, UP3D MXPAR 4, UP4AC 3, UP4D MXPAR 0, UP3M MXPAR 0, UP4M MXPAR 1, MAX ARCH, MAND ARCH

Escuela Nacional de Antropología e Historia

LM1C6 5, UI1IG 4, UI1SS 6

Centro INAH Yucatán

LCDR 1, LCDR 2, LM1AF 4, LM1PS 2, LM2PS 1, LM2PS 2, LP4LC 5, UI2MB 1, UM1CB 2, UP4D MXPAR 3, UI2SS 6, UI2SS 7, UI2TD 5, UI2TD 6

Instituto de Investigaciones Antropológicas, UNAM

LCDR 4, LI1SS 3, LI2SS 3, UCSS 6, UM2MC 5

Instituto Nacional de Antropología e Historia

LM1C6 4, LM1C6 4, LM1GP +, LM1GP X, LM1PS 5, LM1PS 7, LM1TC 1, LM2C6 4, LM2CN 4, LM2GP +, LM2PS 1, LM2PS 2, LM2PS 3, LM2PS 4, LM2PS 4 M3, LM2PS 5 M3, LM2TC 0, LM2TC 0, LM2TC 1, LM3CA 1, LP3LC 2, LP3LC 3, LP4LC 6, LP4LC 7, LC 2 ROOT, LP3 3 ROOT, LM PEARL, UM PEARL, ODONTOME, SUPER, UI2 TALON 1, UCSS 2, UI1DS 5, UI1DS 6, UI1IG 0, UI1IG 2, UI1IG 2, UI1IG 4, UI1SS 3, UI1TD 2, UI1TD 4, UI1TD 6, UM1C5 0, UM1CB 3, UM1CB 3, UM1PR 1, UM1PR 1, UI2 PEG 0, UI2CA 1, UI2DS 4, UM2CB 2, UM2PR 4, UM2PR 5, UP3AC 2, UM2PR 1

Jikei University Medical School

LM2CN 5, LMEE 0, LMEE 1, LMEE 3, LP3LC 7, UCSS 0, UCTD 1, UI1DS 6, UI1SS 1, UM1C5 4, UM1CB 0, UM1PR 0, UM2CB 0, UM2HC 6, UM2PR 6, UM3PEG 1, UP3D MAXPAR 0, UP3D MXPAR 1, UP3M MXPAR 0, UP4D MXPAR 0, UP4D MXPAR 1, UI2IG 4, UI2SS 2

L'Institut Fondamental d'Afrique Noire Cheikh Anta Diop

LM1C5 3, LM1GPY, UM1CB 7, UMEE 1, LP4LC 2, UCSS 5, UM2C5 3, UM2C5 1, UM2MC 6

Maxwell Museum of Anthropology

LCDR 2, LCDR 0, LM1AF 0, LM1GP +, LI2SS 3, LCDR 3, LI1SS 0, LM1C7 4, GEMMATE I, LCDR 5, LCDR 4, LI1SS 1, LP3LC 4, ODONTOME, LI1SS 3, LI1CA 1, LI2SS 0, UI1WING 2, UI2 TALON 1, LM1PS 4, LI1CA 1, LI2SS 1, UM1C5 4, UP3TC 1, Li1SS 2, LM1AF 0, LI2SS 1, UM1CB 1, UCDR 3, LM1PS 5, LM1C5 2, LM1AF 1, UM2C5 1, UCSS 5, LI2SS 0, LM1C6 3, LM1C6 0, UI2 PEG 1, UCTD 3, LP3LC 5, LM1CN 4, LM1CN 5, UI2CA 1, UM1MC 3, LM1DW 0, LM1TC 0, LM1DW 0, UI2DS 0, UI2 PEG 1, UCSS 6, LM2C5 5, LM1PS 0, UI2DS 1, UM2CB 1, UCTD 2, LM2C6 4, LM1TC 0, UM2CB 3, UM2CB 7, LM1AF 1, LMEE 2, LM1TC 1, UMEE 1, UM2MC 5, LM2C7 1, LP3EF 1, LM2C5 3, UMEE 2, UP4D MXPAR 3, LP3LC 8, LP4EF 1, LM2C5 3, UP3M MXPAR 2, DECID MAX, LM1PS 3, LP4EF 1, LM2CN 3, UP4M MXPAR 4, LM1AF 4, LP4 LC 1, LM2CN 4, LM1DW 2, LP4LC 4, LM2GP X, LM2C5 4, LP4LC 8, LM2PS 0, UCTD 4, UI2MB 1, LM2PS 0, UI1DS 1, SUPER, LM3PEG 0, UI1DS 1, UCMR 0, LM3CA 0, UI1DS 2, UCMR 3, LM3CA 1, UI1DS 2, UCSS 4, LMEE 1, UI1DS 4, UI1WING 3, LMEE 3, UI1DS 4, UI1DS 3, LP3EF 0, UM1HC 2, UI1IG 0, LP3LC 0, UM2C5 3, UI1SS 5, LP3LC 0, UI2DS 1, UI1TD 1, LP3LC 1, UM2HC 0, UI1TD 5, LP3LC 5, UM2MC 6, UM1C5 0, LP3LC 6, UM1C5 2, LP3LC 8, UM1C5 2, LP4EF 0, UM1C5 3, LP4EF 0, UM1CB 0, LP4LC 3, UM1CB 5, LP4LC 3, UM1MC 2, LP4LC 8, UM1MC 6, LP4LC 9, UM1PR 4, UI1DIAS 0, UI2 PEG 0, UI1WING 2, UM2C5 4, UM1HC 6,

UM2CB 0, UM1MC 4, UI2CA 0, UM1MC 4, UI2DS 2, UM1MC 5, UI2DS 3, UM1MC 5, UM2HC 3, UM2C5 2, UM2HC 4, UM2CB 0, UM2PR 0, UM2CB 1, UM3PEG 1, UM2HC 0, UM3CA 1, UM2HC 1, UMEE 3, UMEE 0, UMEE 3, UP3D MXPAR 0, UP3AC 3, UP3M MXPAR 1, UP3D MXPAR 4, UP4AC 2

Musée de l'Homme

LP4LC 1, UI2DS 0, UM2MC 0, UM2MC 0, UM3PEG 0, UM3CA 0, UM3CA 1, UP3M MXPAR 4, LM2C6 2, LP4LC 0, UI1WING 1, LM2C6 0, LM2GP X, LM2CN 6, LM2GPY

Národní Muzeum

UI2 PEG 2, UI1DS 5, UCSS 4, UCDR 5, UM1HC 4, UM1HC 5, LM1C7 0, UCSS 3, UI1SS 2, UCTD 6, LM2C5 2, UCTD 0, UI2SS 2, LM2C7 0

National Museum of Natural History

LM1C6 3, LM1GP X, LM2C6 0, LM2C6 5, LM2CN 6, LM2PS 3, LP SUPER, UI1DIAS 1, UI1SS 5, UM1C5 5, UI2CA O, UM2HC 5, UM2PR 2, UM2PR 4, UP3AC 0, UP3AC 0, UP3M MXPAR 1, UP4AC 0

National Museum of Natural History Repatriation Office

LM1C5 0, LM1C5 0, LM1C5 2, LM1C5 3, LM1C5 4, LM1C6 1, LM1C6 2, LM1C6 5, LM1CN 4, LM1DW 3 M2, LM1PS 6, LM2C6 1, LM2C6 1, LM2C6 2, LM2C6 3, LM2C7 4, LM2GPY, LP4LC 2, UCDR 4, UCMR 1, UCMR 1, UI1WING 1, UI1WING 4, UM1HC 0, UM1PR 2, UM1PR 3, UM2CB 6, UM2HC 2, UM2HC 3, UM2HC 6, UM3PEG 2, UP3D MXPAR 3, UP3DS 1, UP3M MXPAR 0, UP4M MXPAR 3, LMEE 0, UM2HC 4, UM2PR 3

Nova Southeastern University Dental School

LP4LC 0, UP4TC 1, UM1CB 7, LM2C6 2, UM1HC 3, UCSS 2, UCDR 5, UCDR 3, UCDR 4, UM2C5 2, LM1C7 3, LM1PS 0, LI1SS 0, UCTD 5, UM1HC 5, UCTD 5, LCDR 1, UM1CB 2, UCTD 6, UCTD 3, LM2C7 2, LP3LC 1, LM1C7 1, UM1C5 1, LM1DW 1, LP3LC 2, UI2TD 6

Anna L. M. Rautman

LCDR 0, LM1AF 3

Universidad Autónoma de Yucatán

LI1CA 0, LI1SS 1, LI1SS 2, UP3M MXPAR 3, UP4D MXPAR 1, UI1DIAS 0, UI2TD 2

Universidad de Granada

LI1CA 0, LM2CN 3, LP4LC 4, UCDR 0, UCDR 1, UCSS 1, UCSS 1, UI1DS 0, UI1SS 0, UI1TD 0, UM1PR 0, UM2C5 0, UM2C5 5, UM2HC 2, UM2HC 5, UM2HC 1, UM2MC 1, UM2MC 2, UM2MC 2, UM2MC 3, UM2MC 4, UMEE 0, UP3AC 1, UP3AC 2, UP4AC 1, UI2IG 1, UI2SS 0, UI2SS 0, UI2TD 0

University of Washington Dental School
LM1C5 5, LM2C6 3, LM2PS 6, LM2PS 7, LM2TC 1, LM3PEG 1, LP3EF 0, LP3EF 1, LP4LC 8, LM1 C 8 9, LM2 CREN, UCMR 2, UI1DIAS 1, UI1WING 4, UI1SS 6, UI1TD 5, UI1TD 6, UM1CB 6, UM1HC 1, UM1HC 3, UM1MC 3, UM1PR 2, UI2 PEG 2, UM2CB 4, UM2CB 5, UM2CB 7, UM2HC 1, UP3D MXPAR 2, UP4AC 1, UP4D MXPAR 4, UI2SS 1, UI2TD 1

A NOTE ABOUT THE USE OF THE WORDS "RACE" AND "ANCESTRY"

For the purposes of this manual, "race" refers to the social race a person is ascribed to by other people. This ascription is based on a number of factors, both cultural (such as accent and style of dress) and biological (such as skin color and facial features), and it is time and place specific. Dental characteristics can provide important clues for estimating what this ascription would have been during a person's life. This is because biological characteristics, such as genetic markers, cranial variation, and dental morphology, provide indicators of genetic ancestry. Because of the demographic history of our species, numerous dental characteristics vary in frequency in different geographic regions of the world. An individual's dental morphology varies at least in part depending on the geographic area(s) from which their ancestry derives. A researcher interested in estimating the race of an unknown individual can examine a dentition for clues about the ancestry of that individual. However, ancestry does not equal race, and the error of the estimate between the two is unknown.

1

RATIONALE

Why Study Dental Morphology, and Why Use This Book to Do It?

The purpose of this manual is to modernize and democratize dental morphological research in biological anthropology. It is intended for use by professional and future professional biological anthropologists who collect dental morphological data to learn something about human population history and variation, and by forensic anthropologists who want to include dental morphology in their estimations of ancestry. The manual also will be useful for documenting human remains in cultural resource management and similar situations. Finally, students taking dental anthropology and other classes can use it to learn how to collect dental morphological data.

A few years back, I was at my first-ever meeting of the Society for American Archaeology (SAA) when I heard a presentation by two advanced graduate students who were working for a contract archaeology firm. The firm had excavated a cemetery that was being moved, and the students were reporting the results of their analysis of the dental morphological data they had collected. I knew something about the populations from which their samples derived, and I was totally shocked by their results; they made no sense to me. After the session was over, I went to talk to the students to ask them more about their findings. However, we mostly ended up talking about their data collection, which they were upset about. As the only crew members with any osteological course work under their belts, they had been assigned the task of collecting the dental morphological data. However, they had no previous experience with dental morphology and had never had a class in dental anthropology. Their only firsthand knowledge of teeth came from what they had learned in their general osteology class, and what they had taught themselves. The students told me that they found the data very difficult to collect and that they had low confidence in their own findings.

I wrote an open letter about the issues I foresaw with nonspecialists collecting dental morphological data, especially from skeletal material that was likely to be reburied unseen, by anyone but the original investigators (Edgar, 2008). My hope was that I could work with several individuals to develop "dental anthropology standards for the 21st century," something like Standards for Data Collection from Human Skeletal Remains (Buikstra and Ubelaker, 1994) for dental morphology. Of course, there is some information about dental morphology in "Standards" but it seemed inadequate for thorough analyses. This manual is my attempt to address the issues.

I am optimistic that this manual will alleviate the specific problems those students encountered, which are described in more detail in the following section. However, I would like to make clear that this manual is not a critique of previous work. Each previous effort at standardization has been a groundbreaking improvement over what preceded it. Starting with Aleš Hrdička, and continuing with Albert Dahlberg, Kazurō Hanihara, Melvin Moss and Paul Sciulli (working with deciduous teeth), and, of course, Christy G. Turner II, the method of dental morphological data collection has become more standard, more sophisticated, and more complete.

Problems Collecting Dental Morphological Data

In talking with the students at the SAA, I realized there are three major issues for newcomers to dental morphological data:

1. The plaques and descriptions associated with the ASUDAS require a high level of familiarity with teeth. For those of us who work with teeth every day, it can be hard to remember looking at a tooth and not knowing immediately whether it is maxillary or mandibular, left or right, or first or second, or which surface is mesial or distal.
2. Despite the reliance on the original chapter (Turner et al., 1991) or later publications that refer back to it (i.e., Hillson, 1996), the ASUDAS is a living system, meaning that there have been changes and additions that are not reflected in the article, the plaques, or both. Metacone and hypocone variation provide clear examples. For these traits, Turner et al. (1991) describe a level of expression intermediate between the scores of "3" and "4" that is not shown on the plaques for either trait, and which is called "3.5," although it doesn't really represent a half step in expression. Clearly, this additional level of expression causes problems in statistical analyses. Additionally, several traits have been described since 1991. Some of these have plaques, such as maxillary premolar accessory ridges, while others, such as talon tooth or elongated form premolars, do not.
3. The ASUDAS system as it is only really works for professionals who have seen at least hundreds of dentitions from a variety of populations. This is due to the way variation in many traits is described. Take, for example, the descriptions of cusp 5 (Turner et al., 1991). A score of "1" is assigned when cusp 5 is "very small," "2" is "small," "3" is "medium sized," "4" is "large," and "5" is "very large." Of course, these descriptions are almost meaningless unless one is already familiar with overall variation in cusp 5 size.

One could argue that only researchers thoroughly familiar with normal tooth morphology should collect dental morphological data. One could also argue that all the traits that are standardized are available in the literature and that a good researcher will find out about all of the traits relevant to the samples with which they are working. Finally, one could argue that experience with a large number and variety of dentitions makes data collectors trustworthy. However, I would argue that (1) the data is going to be collected by the less experienced anyway, so it is better to help them collect data that is useful; (2) it always is better to democratize science; and (3) modernizing techniques for dental morphological research does not degrade previous research, but hopefully improves future work by students and professionals.

Dental Morphological Data Are Useful

The problems described earlier are serious, but dental morphological data are so useful that it is incumbent upon us to continue to refine and improve its collection. Teeth are the hardest substance in the body, so they are the material most apt to preserve and the most commonly found fossils. Dental morphological characters can be studied relatively quickly, so population-level analyses are possible. The observation process is completely nondestructive, meaning that museums are more likely to give permission for these analyses than for other methods such as stable isotope or DNA analyses. Another useful feature of dental morphological data is that they can be compared across time and space: Neandertals from 50,000 years ago in Iran can be compared to Neolithic Italians, Jomon in Japan, Bantu in Africa, and casts of living individuals in Detroit, if the research question requires it.

None of these factors of convenience would be important if dental morphology did not provide the information anthropologists want, phenotypic evidence of genetic relationships (phenetics) among species, regional and local populations, and individuals. Assertions that dental morphological characteristics are neutral, slow to evolve, and heritable have been presented many times before (Larsen and Kelley, 1991; Hillson, 1996; Scott and Turner, 1997). The neutrality of dental morphology is indicated by the fact that dental wear has obliterated it throughout much of human evolution and the fact that most traits do not affect overall tooth size (Scott and Turner, 1997). Evidence for the slowness of change in dental morphology comes from the observation that many dental traits can be observed in other primates (Skinner and Gunz, 2010; Hardin and Legge, 2013; Irish et al., 2014). Heritability, the degree to which genetic variability affects trait variability, has been shown for many dental traits in many populations at several points in time (Harris, 1977; Scott and Potter, 1984; Nichol, 1989). Dental traits have been shown to mirror genetic relationships, although perhaps without as much resolution (Ricout et al., 2010; Hubbard et al., 2015). Recent studies in dental genetics (i.e., Thesleff, 2006; Bianchi et al., 2007; Tan et al., 2014) and development (i.e., Jernvall and Jung, 2000; Brook, 2009; Moormann et al., 2013) help us to slowly start to understand how and why tooth morphology comes to be, and what can be reasonably inferred about populations from its expression. See Townsend et al. (2012) and recent edited volumes on dental anthropology (Irish and Nelson, 2008; Scott and Irish, 2013; Irish and Scott, 2016) for more discussion of these subjects. In the next section, there are examples of dental morphological data applied to addressing anthropological questions at various population levels.

Hominin Evolutionary Relationships

Dental morphology has been informatively applied numerous times to questions of relationships between and among modern humans and various fossil hominin species (i.e., Stringer et al., 1997; Irish and Guatelli-Steinberg, 2003; Hlusko, 2004; Guatelli-Steinberg and Irish, 2005; Irish et al., 2013). Studies of dental morphology of early hominin taxa are consistent with other fossil and genetic evidence indicating Africa as the homeland for modern humans (Stringer, 1997; Irish and Guatelli-Steinberg, 2003). Dental morphological analyses have examined relationships among the various named Australopith species (Guatelli-Steinberg and Irish, 2005; Irish et al., 2013). Such studies have been greatly aided by increasing knowledge about the genetics and development of dental morphology, which allows trait frequency similarities to be interpreted as either primitive (symplesiomorphic) or shared derived (synapomorphic) characteristics. However, they remain hampered, as do most paleoanthropological analyses, by small sample sizes and great time depth.

Bailey and colleagues (Bailey et al., 2009; Bailey and Hublin, 2013) summarize differences in dental morphology between Neandertals and modern humans in a simple table. In the maxillary dentition, Neandertals show shovel-shaped incisors at higher frequency, commonly co-occurring with labial convexity. Additionally, Neandertals have small relative molar occlusal polygon areas and crown shapes that appear skewed when compared to modern human crowns. In Neandertal mandibular molars, trigonid crests are common, and the first molar crown outline is more round than is commonly seen in modern humans. Bailey and Hublin (2013) further compare the ranges of expression for 13 traits in modern humans to the ranges of expression in six premodern species from *Homo erectus* to late Neandertals. From this comparison, they discuss a "modern human dental morphological pattern" (Bailey and Hublin, 2013, p. 237), identifying all the caveats that come with pan-species generalizations. They describe several morphological traits seen only or mostly in modern humans, especially nonshoveled maxillary central incisors and canines and four cusped mandibular first and second molars.

Worldwide Patterns of Variation

Dental morphology has been used to explore human variation on a global scale. These analyses have been further used to draw inferences about large-scale migration and *in situ* evolution (i.e., Sofaer et al., 1972; Greenberg et al., 1986; Irish and Turner, 1990; Scott and Turner, 1997; Hanihara, 2008; 2013). The major work exemplifying such analyses is Scott and Turner's *The Anthropology of Modern Human Teeth* (1997). This work draws on what is likely the largest collection of dental morphological data amassed, representing more than 30,000 individuals and describing regional variation in each dental morphological characteristic studied. The authors conducted a mean measure of divergence biological distance analysis and applied a number of methods to examine interpopulation and interregional relationships. These methods include the unweighted pair-group method with arithmetic mean, multidimensional scaling, neighbor joining, and "starburst" form dendrogram. This final tool is a tree rooted in Africa, which shows somewhat unexpected, relatively short branch lengths to Australia, Melanesia, Micronesia, and Southeast Asia, along with expectedly long branch lengths to several American samples.

Hanihara (2008) drew on data from 15 dental variables in 12 worldwide geographical samples to examine patterns in amounts of inter- and intraregional variation. An analysis of F_{ST}, a measure of variation within groups, indicated that the greatest amount of variation in dental morphology exists in Sub-Saharan Africa, and that F_{ST} decays with distance from Africa. This reflects a global population structure determined by serial bottlenecks as populations migrated across the world, in agreement with craniometric (Relethford, 2001; Roseman, 2004) and genetic (Manica et al., 2005; Serre and Pääbo, 2007) studies. However, Hanihara (2008) shows greater-than-expected, intraregional variation in Melanesian, Micronesian, and Polynesian samples, as well as Northeast Asian samples. The island populations' greater-than-expected variation is interpreted as resulting from gene flow coupled with small populations and genetic drift, while the Northeast Asian variation is explained as evidence that many sources of gene flow contributed to population variation in the region.

In further research, Hanihara (2013) combined dental morphology with dental metrics to argue that at least some of the original migration out of Africa came through the Horn of Africa along the coast of the Indian Ocean. This counters previous research that emphasized migration out of Africa into Europe through the Levant (Underhill, 2001; Luis et al., 2004). In a related finding, Hanihara (2013) reasons that dental morphology and metric data are relatively selectively neutral, because the global patterns in variation in these characteristics mirror those of neutral genetic variation.

Several authors have also described patterns of variation in dental morphology that portray general tendencies in several regions. These "dental complexes" list relatively high and low frequency traits seen in regions different from complexes seen in other regions. While interesting, such complexes are difficult to apply in any statistical analyses. These dental complexes are summarized in Table 1.1.

Intraregional Variation

It is at this level that most dental morphological analyses have been made. This research dates to almost the beginning of biological anthropology (Hrdlička, 1911; 1921; Gregory, 1922). Reference plaques and research by Albert Dahlberg (1951) increased the comparability of dental data across researchers. Research greatly increased in use

TABLE 1.1 Dental Complexes Described in the Literature. Numbers in parentheses indicate grades for specific traits.

Dental Complex	*Region*	*High Frequency Traits*	*Low Frequency Traits*	*Reference*
Sinodont	North Asia, Native Americans	UI1DS, UI1SS, UMEE, UM3PR, LM1DW, one-root UP3, three-root LM1	LM2CN (4)	Turner, 1979; 1987
Sundadont	Southeast Asia	LM2CN (4)	UI1DS, UI1SS, UMEE, UM3PR, LM1DW, one-root UP3, three-root LM1	Turner, 1979; 1987
Afridont	Africa South of the Sahara	UCMR, UM1CB, LM2GP (Y), two-root UP3, three-root UM2, two-root LM2	UM1DS, UM3CA, UMEE	Irish, 1997; 2013
Eurodont	Europe, North Africa	UM1CB,LP4LC (2+), UM2HC (0), Two-root LC	UI1WING, UI1DS, UI1SS, UCMR, UMEE, LM1DW, LM2GP (Y), LM1C6, LM1C7, LM1PS Three-root LM1	Hanihara, 1967; Mayhall et al. 1982; Scott et al., 2013

after the publication of "Scoring Procedures for Key Morphological Traits of the Permanent Dentition: The Arizona State University Dental Anthropology System" (Turner et al., 1991), the paper that still represents the core of dental morphological data collection today. Papers since then are too numerous to name, but they present analyses set in all regions of the world, from the subcontinental to the village-to-village level, from the earliest humans to contemporary peoples. Questions that can be addressed focus on local and regional migration and population admixture, which are research areas central to anthropological inquiry across the subfields.

Intracemetery Relationships

Stojanowski and Schillaci (2006) outlined the methods and value of using phenotypic characteristics, including dental morphological characteristics, in intracemetery analyses. They argue strongly that such characteristics reflect enough genetic variation to be applicable to examining relationships at this scale. Such small-scale analyses can provide evidence about familial relationships, mortuary practices, social structure, post-marital residence, inequality, hidden heterogeneity of health risk, and several other features of anthropological interest (Stojanowski and Schillaci, 2006).

Dental morphology has been frequently applied to determining and analyzing kinships in cemetery settings (e.g., Alt and Vach, 1991; 1998; Christensen, 1998; Jacobi, 2000; Corruccini and Shimada, 2002; McClelland, 2003; Pilloud and Larsen, 2011). Paul and Stojanowski (2015) have showed that, in addition to characteristics of the permanent dentition, deciduous morphology can also be useful for detecting familial relationships. Ricout et al. (2010) showed that dental nonmetric characteristics identified familial relationships in an ancient Mongolian cemetery; these relationships were correlated with those determined using DNA analysis.

Individual Level Analyses

The primary application of studies of individual dental morphology has been in forensic anthropology (Schmidt, 2008; Scott et al., 2016). Here the goal is to estimate the ancestry of an unknown individual by comparing his or her dental characteristics to appropriate samples of known ancestry. As a method that makes use of probability-based statistics, forensic dental morphology is still in its infancy. Recent research has focused on American subpopulations (Edgar, 2005; 2013) and undocumented migrants to the U.S. (George, 2015). However, the methods currently being developed could be applied anywhere in the world.

Likewise, Ragsdale et al. (2016) present a method to estimate group membership in individuals from archaeological contexts using multidimensional scaling (MDS). Unknown individuals and individuals in groups of known ancestry from which the unknown individuals derive are mapped together on a scatter plot that emphasizes morphological variation. The unknown individuals are thought to be associated with the group with which they most closely plot. This method has been successfully applied in paleoanthropology, where sample sizes often preclude other methods, but MDS can be informative (Grine et al., 2013; Stratford et al., 2016). While this is a promising method for future analyses, perhaps forensically, as well as bioarchaeologically, the need for a thorough understanding of the putative ancestral populations cannot be emphasized enough.

2

HOW TO STUDY DENTAL MORPHOLOGY

Data Collection

Most often, dental morphological data is collected in a museum setting. In this case, the process of data collection is relatively straightforward in theory, but can become complicated by the realities of working with human skeletal or dental cast collections. One hopes the process begins by settling down at a table in a museum, lifting a pristine skull and mandible out of a box that has been brought to you by a collections assistant, and finding all of the teeth present, clean, free of pathology, unworn, and in place. Then one simply refers to this manual, and perhaps to the ASUDAS plaques, and records the scores onto paper, or directly into a computerized spreadsheet or database.

I am happy to say that such a data collection experience is possible. However, it is extremely rare. I have worked in collections where there was no table. Commonly, there is no collections assistant. Usually, teeth are dirty, worn, or carious; partially absent; glued into the wrong sockets; or all of the above. These are not insurmountable problems.

As the researcher, you are likely a guest using collections supervised by others, undoubtedly with limited resources. It is important to keep this in mind throughout your interactions with curators and collections managers. In addition to this rule of thumb, here is some basic guidance to be sure that the data you collect is the best possible data:

- If you have loose teeth, identify each tooth and then arrange them in an order that will facilitate data collection. Hillson (1996) provides excellent guidance on tooth identification. Some researchers use an arch shape to keep loose teeth in order during analysis. I use Lucite plaques with small amounts of oil-based clay to hold the teeth with their crowns up and in numerical order (see Figure 2.1.)

- If you have teeth in sockets, be sure that each tooth is in its correct place. It is not at all uncommon to find previous workers have placed or glued teeth in incorrect anatomical order.
- Gently remove surface dirt from the areas of the teeth you will be observing. The collections manager may prohibit you from removing more than surface dust and will likely prohibit you from removing calculus. Be sure to discuss this before making any alterations to the tooth surface.
- Be aware that tooth wear, breakage, and pathology obscure dental morphological observation. If you are not sure whether you can reliably score a tooth, it is better for your analysis to mark it as unobservable.

As more researchers recognize the value of dental morphological data, its collection occurs in more varied settings beyond the museum. These settings might include a field lab near an excavation, at the site of an excavation itself, or in forensic situations such as a medical examiner's laboratory or even perhaps at a death scene investigation. The more exotic the data collection location is, the greater the challenge for researchers to be systematic in gathering the data.

Before any statistical analyses, dental morphological data is almost always converted to frequency data. However, it is useful to understand that not all observations inherently consist of the same type of data. See the manual pages for an explanation of the abbreviations used in the following section.

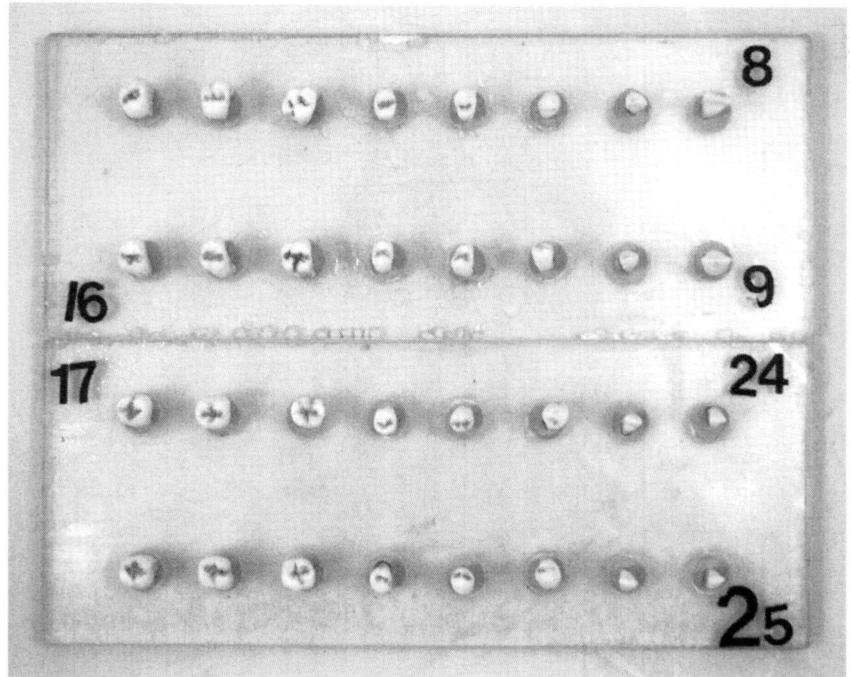

FIGURE 2.1 Lucite Plaques for Organizing Loose Teeth

Scoring Types

- Count: Some dental traits consist in all or in part of counts of tooth features. These traits include UP3AC, UP4AC, LP3LC, LP4LC, LM1CN, and LM2CN.
- Presence/Absence: Many dental traits are observations of whether a characteristic exists on a tooth. These traits include UI1DIAS, UI2CA, UM3CA, UP3DS, LI1CA, LM3CA, LP3EF, LP4EF, LM1TC, and LM2TC. The rare traits described in the manual also fall into this category.
- Ordinal Grade: Many dental traits are quantified so that higher scores represent larger or more complex expressions. These traits include UI1LC, UI1DS, UI2DS, UI1SS, UI2SS, UCSS, UI1TD, UI2TD, UCTD, UCMR, UP3M MXPAR, UP4M MXPAR, UP3D MXPAR, UP4 MXPAR, UM1MC, UM2MC, UM1HC, UM2HC, UM1C5, UM2C5, UM1PS, UM2PS, UMEE, LI1SS, LI2SS, LCDR, LM1AF, LM1DW, LM1PS, LM2PS, LM1C5, LM2C5, LM1C6, LM2C6, LM1C7, LM2C7, and LMEE. LP3LC and LP4LC might be considered in this category rather than as counted expressions. On the other hand, ordinal grade scores are higher for UI2PR and UM3PR when the tooth is smaller or of simpler morphology.
- Other: The form of expression is unclear for a few traits, including UI1WING, LM1GP, and LM2GP. An increasing score might represent increasing complexity for these traits, or it may also represent the presence of different but equally complex expression.

Breakpoints

For purposes of statistical analysis, arbitrary "threshold levels" have been used for many of the characteristics to account for their quasicontinuous nature. The first major description of breakpoints for "key" teeth came from Turner (1987). Many later authors have drawn on this work. However, these same authors also sometimes included traits not covered by Turner (1987), or sometimes deviated from the breakpoints described in that work. Often, the breakpoints used to discern population relationships in one part of the world are not as applicable in another part of the world. For example, shovel-shape teeth are much more common, and much more commonly seen at higher expressions, in Asians and Native Americans than in European and African populations (Scott and Turner, 1997). A low breakpoint might be useful in studying relationships among Spanish, French, and English medieval samples, but would be useless in examining population history among Mayans, Mexicans, and Tlaxcalans in Mexico. Breakpoints can be customized by either looking for natural breaks in frequencies of expression or by finding the greatest difference in expression frequencies between the samples of interest.

Table 2.1 lists breakpoints as described by some of the works most commonly cited as providing them, as well as my own work.

TABLE 2.1 Breakpoints for Data Analyses Using Dichotomized Scores. Italics indicate alternatives when different breakpoints have been described by multiple authors.

Trait	*Absent*	*Present*	*Citation*	*Note*
WING	2–4	1	Turner, 1987	
DIAS	0	1	Irish, 1993	1 = > 0.5mm
UI1LC	0–1	2–4	Irish, 1993	
UI1DS	0–1	2–6	Turner, 1987	
UI1DS	*0–2*	*3–6*	*Hanihara, 2013*	
UI2DS	0	1–6	Edgar, 2007	
UI1SS	0–2	3–7	Turner, 1987	only scores 0–6 defined
UI1SS	*0–1*	*2–6*	*Haeussler et al., 1989*	
UI2SS	0–2	3–7	Hanihara, 2013	
UI2SS	*0–1*	*2–7*	*Haeussler et al., 1989*	
UCSS	0–1	2–7	Edgar, 2007	
UI2CA	0	1	Edgar, 2002	
UM3CA	0	1	Turner, 1987	peg/reduced and congenital absence are considered in one observation, with any expression counted as present
UI2PEG	0	1	Haeussler et al., 1989	
UI2PEG	*0*	*1–2*	*Irish, 1993*	
UM3PEG	0	1–2	Turner, 1987	peg/reduced and congenital absence are considered in one observation, with any expression counted as present
UI1IG	0	1–4	Edgar et al., 2015	
UI2IG	0	1	Turner, 1987	scores 2–4 not mentioned
UI1TD	0–1	2–6	Edgar, 2002	
UI2TD	0–1	2–6	Edgar, 2002	
UI2TD	*0*	*1–9*	*Turner, 1987*	only scores 0–6 defined
UI2TD	*0–1*	*2–6*	*Irish, 1993*	
UCTD	0–1	2–6	Edgar, 2007	
UCMR	0	1–3	Turner, 1987	
UCDR	0–1	2–5	Turner, 1987	
UP3AC	0	1–3	Edgar, 2007	
UP4AC	0	1–3	Edgar, 2007	
UP3DS	0	1	Morris et al., 1978	
UP3M MXPAR	0–1	2–4	Burnett et al., 2010	
UP4M MXPAR	0–1	2–4	Burnett et al., 2010	
UP3D MXPAR	0–1	2–4	Burnett et al., 2010	

(*Continued*)

TABLE 2.1 (Continued)

Trait	*Absent*	*Present*	*Citation*	*Note*
UP4D MXPAR	0–1	2–4	Burnett et al., 2010	
UM1MC	0–4	5–6	Edgar, 2002	
UM2MC	0–4	5–6	Edgar, 2007	
UM3MC	0–4	5–6	Edgar, 2002	
UM1HC	0–4	5–6	Edgar, 2007	
UM2HC	0–1	2–5	Turner, 1987	
UM2HC	*0–1*	*2–6*	*Edgar, 2002*	
UM2HC	*0–2*	*3–5*	*Irish, 1993*	
UM3HC	0–1	2–6	Edgar, 2002	
UM1C5	0	1–5	Scott and Turner, 1997	
UM1C5	*0–1*	*2–5*	*Irish, 1993*	
UM2C5	0	1–5	Haeussler et al., 1989	
UM3C5	0	1–5	Edgar, 2002	
UM1CB	0–1	2–7	Turner, 1987	
UM1CB	*0–4*	*5–7*	*Scott and Turner, 1997*	
UM1CB	*0–2*	*3–7*	*Hanihara, 2013*	
UM2CB	0	1–7	Edgar, 2007	
UM3CB	0	1–7	Edgar, 2002	
UM1PS	0	1–6	Edgar, 2002	
UM2PS	0	1–6	Edgar, 2002	
UM3PS	0	1–5	Turner, 1987	
UMEE	0–1	2–3	Turner, 1987	scored on UM1 only
LI1SS	0	1–3	Haeussler et al., 1989	
LI2SS	0	1–3	Edgar, 2007	
LI1CA	0	1	Edgar, 2002	
LM3CA	0	1	Edgar, 2002	
LCDR	0	1–5	Edgar, 2007	
LP3LC	0–1	2–9	Irish, 1993	
LP3LC	*0–3*	*4–9*	*Edgar, 2007*	
LP4LC	0–1	2–3	Turner, 1987	scored as a count of lingual cusps
LP4LC	*0–2*	*3–9*	*Edgar, 2007*	
LP3EF	0	1	Edgar and Sciulli, 2004	
LP4EF	0	1	Edgar and Sciulli, 2004	
LM1AF	0–1	2–4	Irish, 1993	
LM1DW	0–1	2–3	Turner, 1990	
LM1DW	*0–2*	*3*	*Haeussler et al., 1989*	
LM1DW	*0*	*1–3*	*Edgar, 2007*	
LM1GP	+, X (1–2)	Y (0)	Edgar, 2002	

Trait	*Absent*	*Present*	*Citation*	*Note*
LM2GP	+, X (1–2)	Y (0)	Turner, 1987	
LM3GP	+, X (1–2)	Y (0)	Edgar, 2002	
LM1CN	4–5	6	Irish, 1993	
LM2CN	4	5–6	Irish, 1993	
LM3CN	3	4–6	Edgar, 2002	
LM1PS	0	1–8	Turner, 1987	only scores 0–6 defined
LM1PS	*0–1*	*2–7*	*Hanihara, 2013*	
LM2PS	0	1–7	Edgar, 2007	
LM3PS	0	1–7	Edgar, 2002	
LM1TC	0	1	Turner, 1987	described as "distal trigonid crest"
LM2TC	0	1	Edgar, 2002	
LM3TC	0	1	Edgar, 2002	
LM1C5	0	1–5	Scott and Turner, 1997	
LM2C5	0	1–5	Scott and Turner, 1997	
LM3C5	0	1–5	Edgar, 2002	
LM1C6	0	1	Turner, 1987	scored as a count of cusps, with any presence of cusp 6 being counted as present
LM1C6	*0*	*1–6*	*Scott and Turner, 1997*	*only scores 0–5 defined*
LM2C6	0	1–5	Edgar, 2002	
LM3C6	0	1–5	Edgar, 2002	
LM1C7	0	1–5	Turner, 1987	
LM1C7	*0*	*1–4*	*Scott and Turner, 1997*	*1A not scored*
LM1C7	*0–1*	*2–4*	*Irish, 1993*	
LM2C7	0	1–4	Edgar, 2007	
LM3C7	0	1–4	Edgar, 2002	
LMEE	0–1	2–3	Turner, 1987	only UMEE is described

Weighted Frequencies

Instead of using breakpoints to calculate frequencies of presence and absence of trait expression, some authors have suggested using weighted frequencies (Turner, 1985; Bailey, 2002). These steps are involved with computing a weighted coefficient for any trait for each sample of interest:

1. Divide 1 by the number of levels of expression potentially observed for the trait.
2. Multiple each level of expression by the result of step 1.

3. Multiply the frequency of each level of expression by the result of step 2 associated with that level of expression.
4. Sum the results of step 3.

Use the results of these steps in further calculations in the same way as presence/absence frequencies are determined using breakpoints.

Data Analysis

Much of the previous research using dental morphological data has centered on understanding how populations are related to each other through time and space. Such analyses rely on statistics that analyze biological distance, or biodistance. Biodistance statistics measure how related groups are based on similarities in frequencies of morphological characteristics, metrics, or DNA variants. These groups are defined by archaeological, historical, or other anthropological criteria (Buikstra et al., 1990; Pietrusewsky, 2014). Primary methods for calculating biological distance from dental morphological data have been mean measure of divergence (MMD) and a form of Mahalanobis generalized distance statistic modified for categorical data: pseudo-Mahalanobis D^2. Both MMD and pseudo-Mahalanobis D^2 can be used as initial steps in analyses that are either model-free, which can elucidate general patterns of interpopulation variation, or model bound, which are designed using specific evolutionary models (Relethford and Blangero, 1990). Unweighted pair group method with arithmetic mean (UPGMA) and varimax rotation have also been used to analyze population relationships.

More recently, dental morphological data are being used to estimate the affinity of unknown individuals with socially recognized groups, such as races. Statistical approaches for this kind of analysis have included logistic discriminant function analyses, MMD, and simple probability analyses. More sophisticated techniques, such as decision trees, may also hold promise.

Biological Distance

Biological distance measures relative relationships among samples, as indicated by variation in their morphological characteristics (Buikstra et al., 1990). This work is done through the application of statistics that estimate affinity or divergence by measuring the similarity of expression of characteristics in different samples and quantifying average differences between those samples. The characteristics can be metric (continuous) or nonmetric (categorical or ordinal), and the studies can be univariate or multivariate. Using distance statistics, small distances between groups indicate that the groups are more similar in their dental morphology than groups separated by large distances. Statistics that calculate affinity are oppositely interpreted. The assumption is made that similarities and differences in overall patterns of dental morphology indicate degrees of relatedness between the groups being compared.

MMD and pseudo-Mahalanobis D^2 are the most common biological distance statistics. Most studies of biological distance that rely on data from dental morphology use the MMD as the primary, if not sole, biological distance statistic. While both statistics are applicable to the kind of data available in dental morphological studies, they differ in whether they are applicable to correlated or uncorrelated characteristics. A third method that has long been used, albeit less frequently, is UPGMA. There are several additional statistical approaches available, including principal components or coordinates analyses, often paired with other distance measures, such as Nei's, Sangvi's, or other distances (Scott and Turner, 1997), or with varimax rotation (Cucina et al., 2015). An R-matrix modified for nonmetric data (Relethford, 1994) has been used in related studies that examine patterns of variation, rather than biological distance (i.e., Hanihara, 2008).

Mean Measure of Divergence

C. A. B. Smith developed the MMD statistic, and it was first used to look at changes associated with inbreeding in mice (Grewal, 1962; Berry and Berry, 1967). Berry and Berry (1967) first applied it to the study of biological affinities or distance in humans. The MMD estimates biological distance between pairs of samples based on the degree of phenetic similarity (Irish, 1997). The statistic assumes the statistical independence of traits. Small distances indicate that groups are phenetically similar, from which it can be inferred that they share genes and are related.

Like pseudo-Mahalanobis D^2, MMD is useful if trait expression varies between groups, when frequencies are between 5% and 95% (de Souza and Houghton, 1977). Some major benefits of its use are its ability to work with incomplete data and its applicability to samples as small as 10 to 20 observations. Drawbacks to the statistic include its sensitivity to intertrait correlation (Edgar, 2004) and the various errors that have been associated with its calculation in prior publications (Harris and Sjøvold, 2004). Whether the MMD is the best statistic for analyzing dental morphological traits for biological distance has become quite contentious (Konigsberg, 2006; Edgar, 2007; Harris, 2008; Irish, 2010; Nikita, 2015).

Pseudo-Mahalanobis D^2

The pseudo-Mahalanobis D^2 is the sum of squares of differences between corresponding mean values of two sets of measurements weighted by the variance/covariance matrix:

$$D^2 = (\chi_{ik} - \chi_{jk})' \, \Sigma \, (\chi_{ik} - \chi_{jk}),$$

where χ_{ik} is the trait frequency for sample i for trait k, and χ_{jk} is the same for sample j. The middle term (Σ) is a pooled covariance matrix of Z scores for tetrachoric correlations between the k traits (Brown, 1977; Manly, 1994), adjusting for correlations between each pair of characteristics (Mizoguchi, 1977; Konigsberg, 1990) and the threshold nature of dental morphological traits (Scott and Turner, 1997). As with MMD results, small distances indicate that groups are phenetically similar, from which it is inferred that they share genes and are related.

UPGMA

UPGMA uses the averages of differences between pairs of trait frequencies to determine a pairwise similarity matrix (as opposed to a distance matrix, as developed by MMD or pseudo-Mahalanobis D^2). This matrix is then iteratively referred to in order to develop a dendrogram that reflects sample relationships, thus joining the two most closely related samples first and then joining that cluster to the next closest sample or cluster of samples. The resulting tree reflects the assumption of a constant rate of change among samples (Sokal and Michener, 1958). Powell (1993) applied UPGMA to dental morphological data to test hypotheses for the peopling of the Americas. The technique has also been used to examine population history in Southeast Asia (Matsumura and Hudson, 2005); Scott et al. (2013) applied its clustering feature alone to Basque relationships in Europe.

Individual Estimation of Group Membership

While dental morphology has most famously been used in biological distance analyses to understand population relationships through time or over space, it has also long been used to estimate the likelihood with which an individual can be associated with various groups (Lasker and Lee, 1957). For many years, this estimation was nonstatistical, amounting to statements such as, "Well, this person has shovel shaped incisors, so they must be Native American" (Hinkes, 1990). More recently, several statistical techniques, including the development of discriminant functions and logistic regression analysis, have been applied to the question of individual ancestry (Edgar, 2005; 2013; Alsoleihat, 2013; Irish, 2015).

Discriminant Analysis and Logistic Regression

Logistic discriminant function classifies individual data into sample data sets. Logistic regression relates an individual set of data for dependent variables (i.e., dental traits) to sample data independent variables (i.e., races) (Press and Wilson, 1978). Both are for applications where at least one variable is qualitative, and the different uses of these two methods can be subtle for the nonspecialist. Most often, the question of group/ethnicity/ancestry/race is asked in forensic anthropological casework, where race is part of the biological profile, along with age, sex, and stature, that helps narrow the range of possible missing persons to which an unknown individual must be compared in order to make a positive identification. I used probabilities based on logistic regressions and Bayesian regression to develop a series of tables that could be used to estimate whether an unknown person was African American or European American based on dental morphology

(Edgar, 2005). While classification accuracy is high using this method, around 90%, error rates are unknown. Subsequently, I developed logistic regression equations that could be used to estimate whether an unknown individual was African American, European American, Hispanic American from Florida, or Hispanic American from New Mexico (Edgar, 2013). Accuracy varies with the equation applied, but is generally high for estimating whether the unknown individual is African American, European American, or Hispanic American, and generally low in estimating the geographic origin of Hispanic Americans. One positive improvement of this method is that error estimates are provided for each equation. However, because only a relatively small number of equations were provided, the method is limited to samples where specific variables are observable (Pilloud et al., 2016). This means that the method cannot be applied to a specimen that has many traits observable, but not the single most informative trait.

Other Statistical Methods

Irish (2015) proposed a method wherein an observer notes the frequencies of trait presence and absence in populations from which an unknown individual potentially derives from. The unknown's trait scores are assigned the frequency seen in each population, and then all frequencies for each population are summed. The unknown individual is estimated to derive from the population with the highest number. In a similar but somewhat more complicated proposed method, Alsoleihat (2013) suggests representing an individual in an MMD analysis by the highest frequency associated with trait presence or absence (whichever an unknown has). The unknown is then estimated to derive from the sample with which there is the smallest distance. In a bioarchaeological application, Ragsdale et al. (2016) used MDS to place individuals (in this case, Aztec skull masks) in a scatter plot with individuals representing the possible groups from which the unknown individuals may have derived. This method may be especially useful in cases where all the possible groups are closely related and morphological variation is likely to be subtle, because it can draw on a large number of variables. While these methods are intriguing, they are as yet unverified and do not provide estimates of error.

3

DENTAL MORPHOLOGY MANUAL

The following pages provide all the information needed to score dental morphological traits, 63 common and six rare dental morphological characteristics. Each common trait is described in its own matrix—one pair of facing pages for each tooth for which the trait is scored. Each pair of pages provides the same standardized information in a standard format. Information on each page includes the following:

- the trait name, including the tooth to be scored
- the abbreviated trait name
- a description of the characteristic
- a drawing indicating where on a tooth to look for the characteristic
- the name of the ASUDAS plaque that shows the trait, if one exists
- a list of other teeth for which the trait is scored
- a description and drawing, as well as two photographs of each grade possible for the trait.

Exceptions include cases where two drawings are provided to indicate that a particular grade may exist in more than one form, and cases where no or only one real-world example of a grade was available to photograph. Rare traits have not been drawn, but references are provided to the original works where they are described.

Trait descriptions are based on those by Turner et al. (1991). Modifications to those descriptions were made only to improve clarity, add detail, and simplify statistical analysis of the resulting observations. Many of the descriptions compare the size of a crown trait, such as cusp size, relative to other factors that can be observed about a tooth, such as size of another cusp. In general, the drawn images are intended to illustrate ideal expressions of traits at each level. Photographs show real-world examples of the same levels of expression. Maxillary teeth are shown as right-side antimeres; mandibular teeth are shown as left side. Score both left- and right-side antimeres.

The manual pages contain empty shaded boxes, which represent cases where no grade is observable for a particular trait.

The data entry sheets following the manual pages can be copied and used for data collection. Alternatively, a basic, Access-based database specific for this method can be downloaded free from http://anthropology.unm.edu/people_faculty_heather_edgar.htm.

<table>
<tr><td colspan="3">Full Name of Trait (Abbrev.): Maxillary Incisor Winging—First (WING)</td></tr>
<tr><td colspan="3">Detailed Trait Description: This observation concerns the orientation of the two maxillary central incisors relative to each other and to the rest of the dental arcade.</td></tr>
<tr><td></td><td>1. Winging: both maxillary central incisors' distal margins are anterior to their mesial margins so that their labial surfaces form a "V" with the apex pointing in toward the palate. 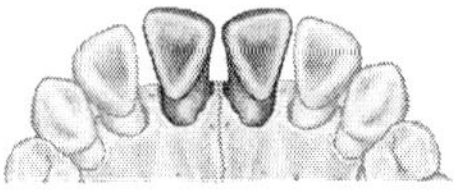 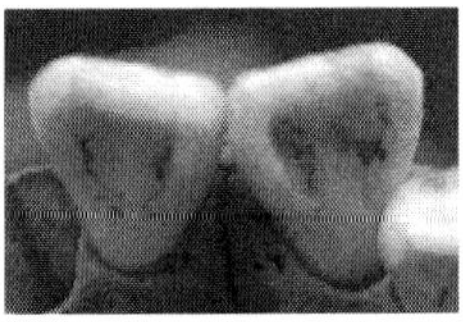 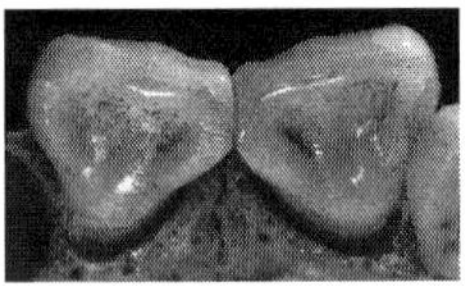</td><td>2. Unilateral winging: one maxillary central incisor's distal margin is anterior to its mesial margin. 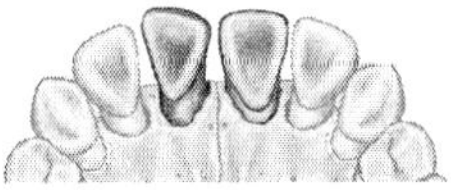 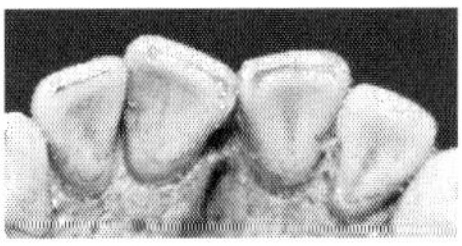 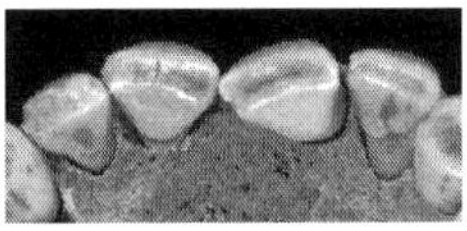</td></tr>
<tr><td></td><td></td><td></td></tr>
</table>

		ASUDAS Plaque: None
		Other Teeth Scored: None
3. The maxillary central incisors are straight in relation to each other, or follow the curve of the rest of the arch. 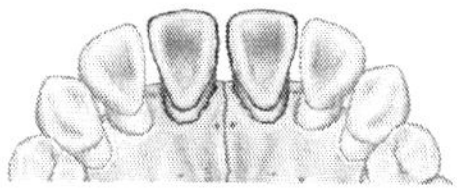 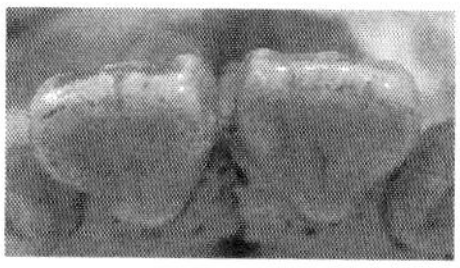 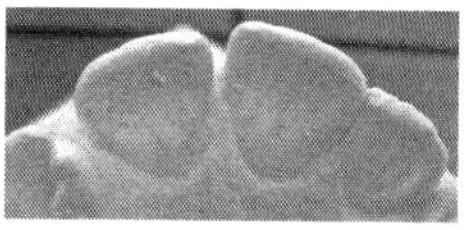		4. Counter-winging: one or both maxillary central incisors' mesial margins are abnormally anterior to their distal margins so that their lingual surfaces form a "V" with the apex pointing away anterior from the palate. 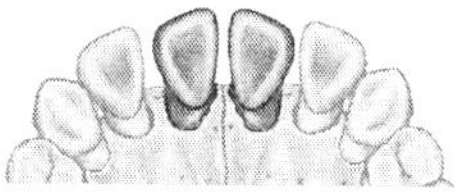 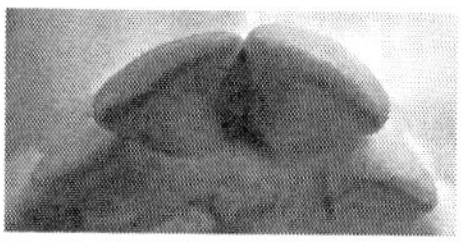 

Full Name of Trait (Abbrev.): Maxillary Incisor Diastema—First (DIAS)

Detailed Trait Description: A gap of at least 1 mm between the two central incisors. Orthodontic treatment may remove this gap, so it should not be scored on individuals who may have had braces.

0. There is no gap or a gap of less than 1 mm between the two maxillary central incisors.
1. A gap of more than 1 mm exists between the two maxillary central incisors.

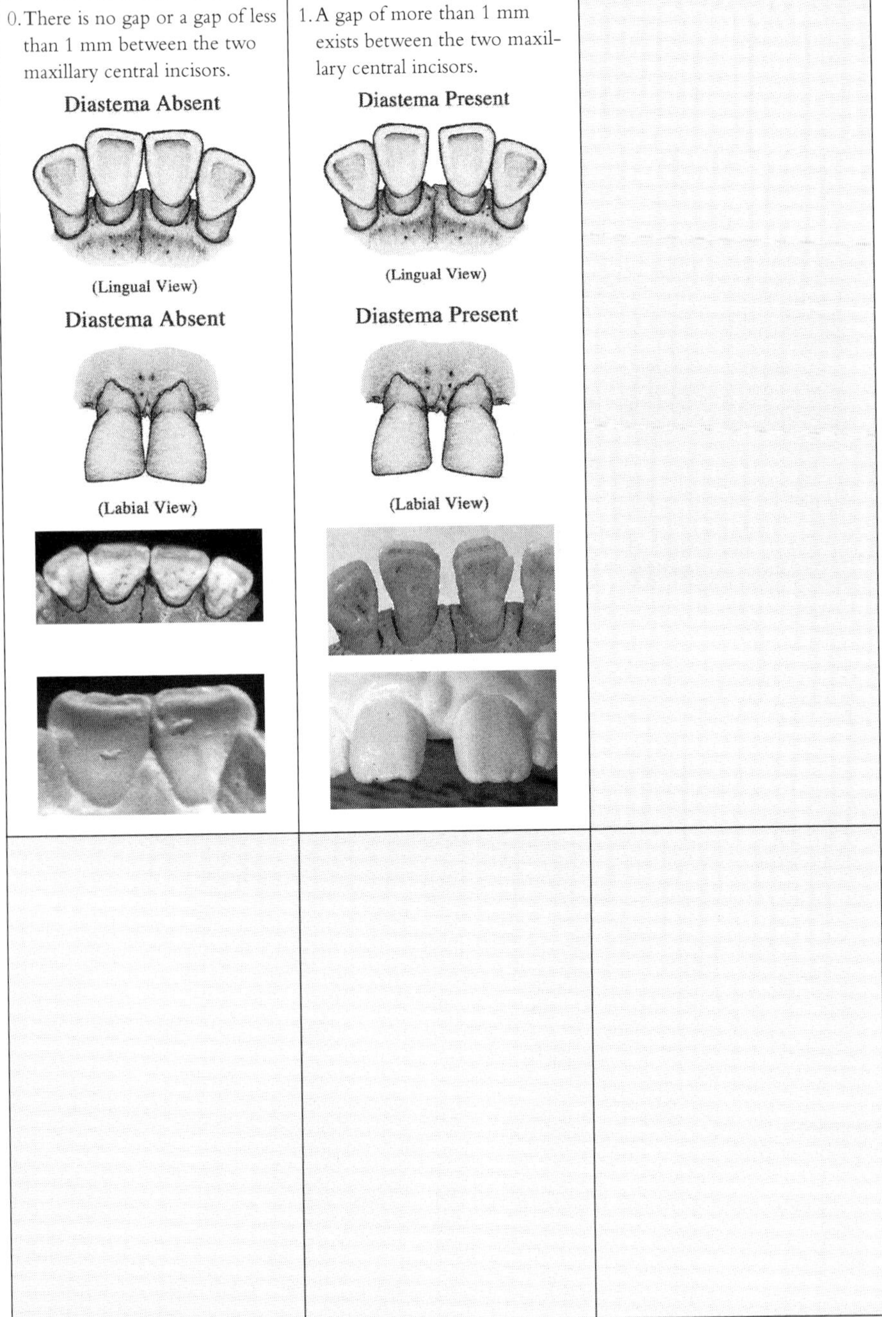

		ASUDAS Plaque: None
		Other Teeth Scored: None

Full Name of Trait (Abbrev.): Maxillary Incisor Labial Curvature—First (UI1LC)		
Detailed Trait Description: The observation concerns the flatness or convexity of the labial surface of the maxillary central incisors. Make the observation looking at the tooth from both the labial and occlusal views. The area two-thirds of the tooth's length from the cervical margin in the middle of the labial surface is the most informative.		
0. The labial surface is flat, with no curvature. 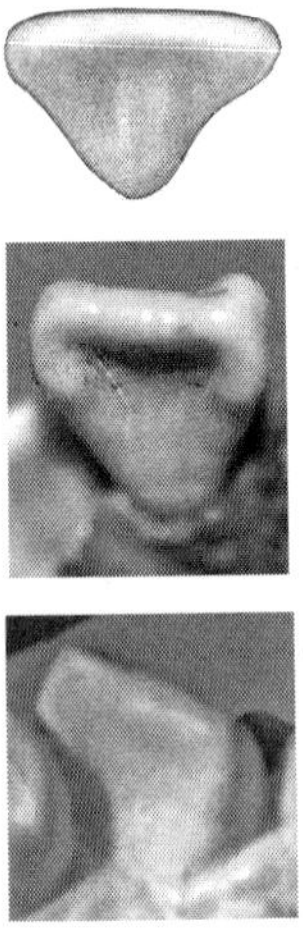	1. The labial surface has very slight curvature, not exactly straight. 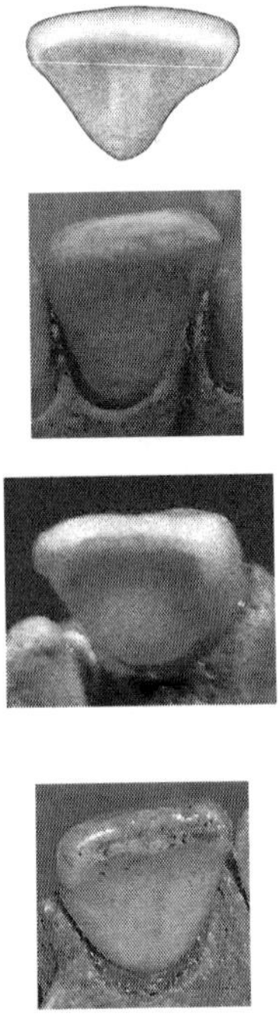	2. Curvature can be seen in the middle of the labial surface when viewed from the occlusal view, but the tooth does not seem curved when viewed labially. 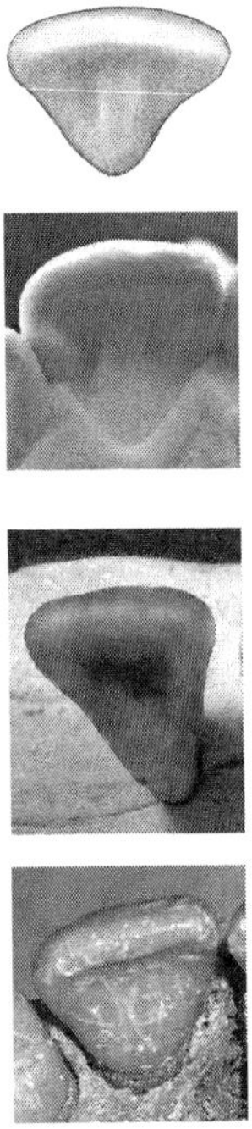

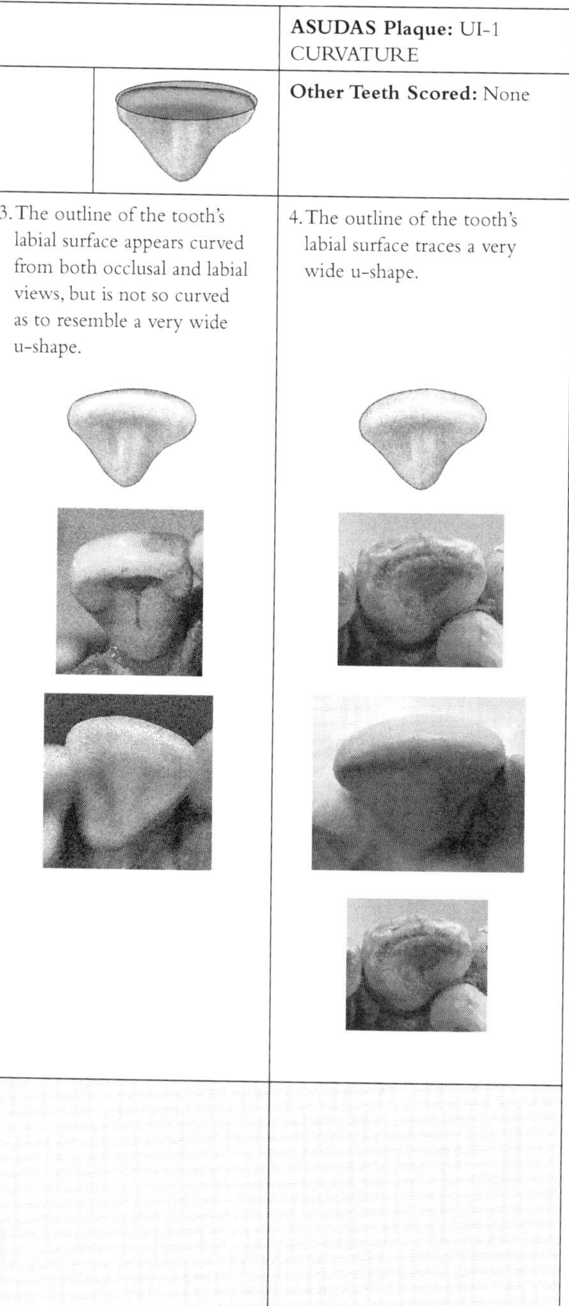

	ASUDAS Plaque: UI-1 CURVATURE
	Other Teeth Scored: None
3. The outline of the tooth's labial surface appears curved from both occlusal and labial views, but is not so curved as to resemble a very wide u-shape.	4. The outline of the tooth's labial surface traces a very wide u-shape.

Full Name of Trait (Abbrev.): Maxillary Incisor Double Shovel—First (UI1DS)

Detailed Trait Description: Of interest are the marginal ridges on the labial side of the tooth. The mesial ridge is more important in determining grade than is the distal ridge. UI1 often has much greater expression of this trait than does UI2.

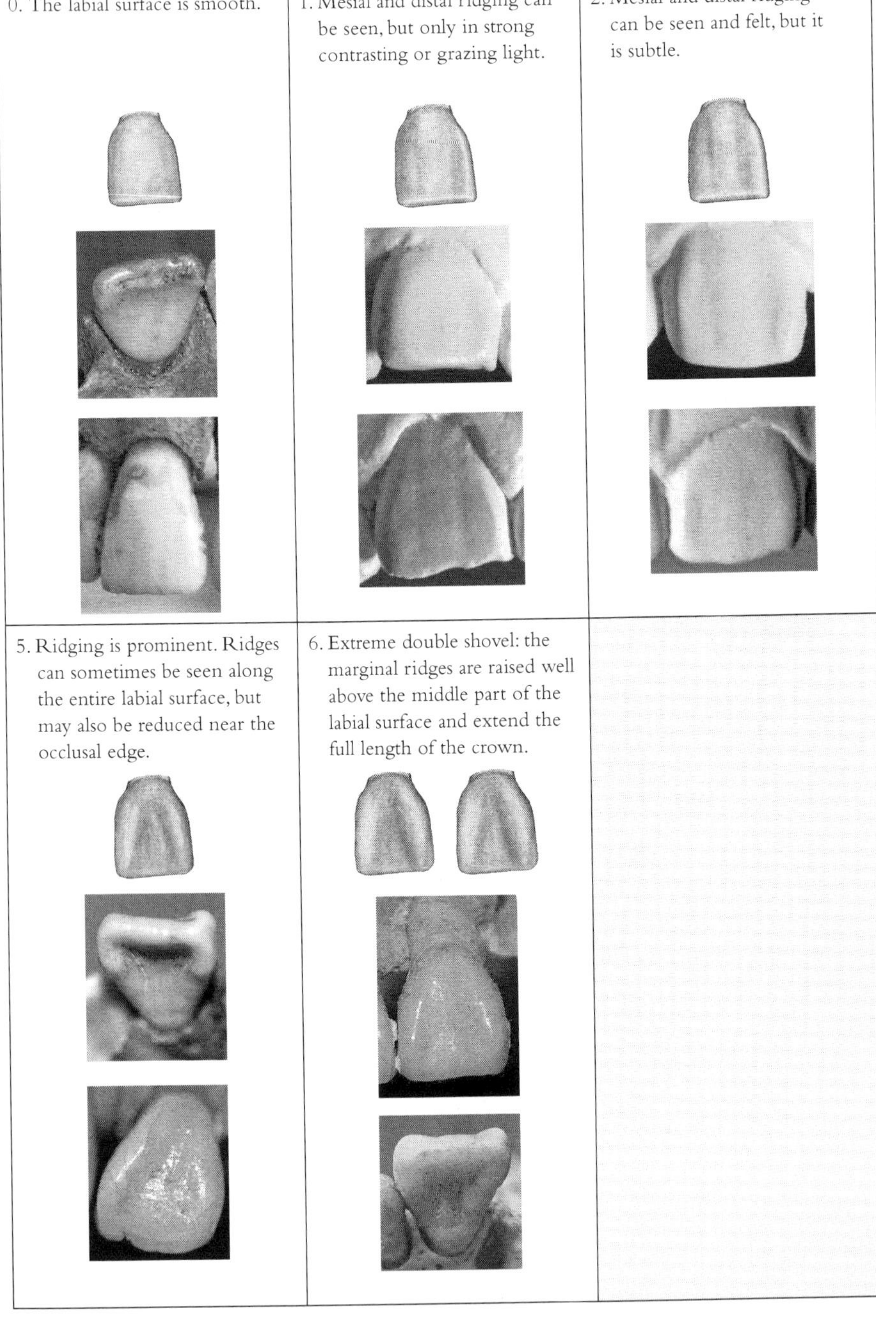

	ASUDAS Plaque: DOUBLE SHOVELING
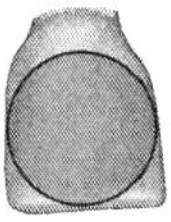	**Other Teeth Scored:** UI2
3. Ridging can be easily felt and seen, but is not prominent over half the total crown height. 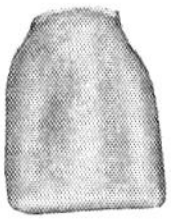 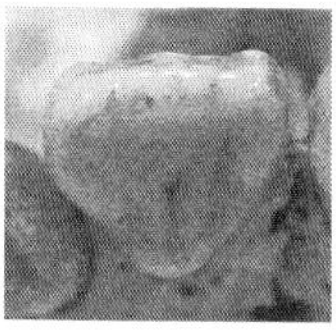 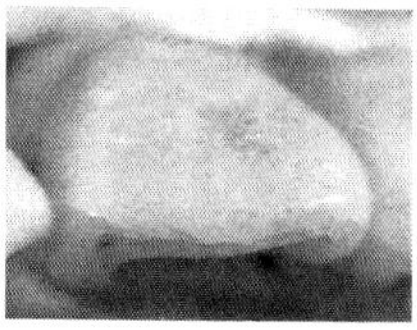	4. Ridging is prominent along at least half the total crown height. 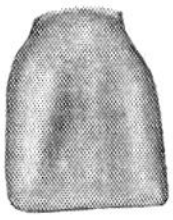 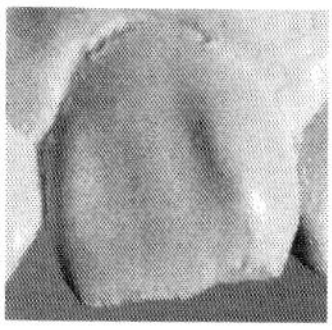 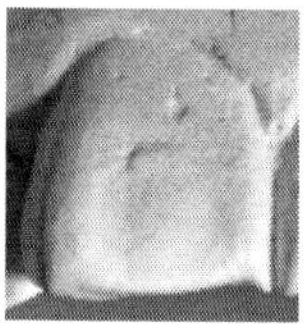

Full Name of Trait (Abbrev.): Maxillary Incisor Double Shovel—Second (UI2DS)		
Detailed Trait Description: Of interest are the marginal ridges on the labial side of the tooth. The mesial ridge is more important in determining grade than is the distal ridge. UI2 often has much less expression of this trait than does UI1.		
0. The labial surface is smooth.  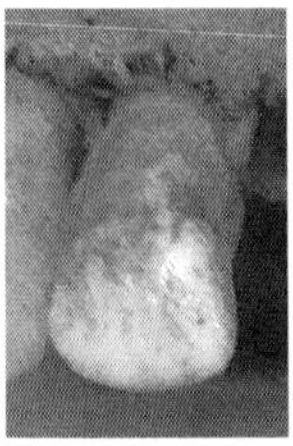 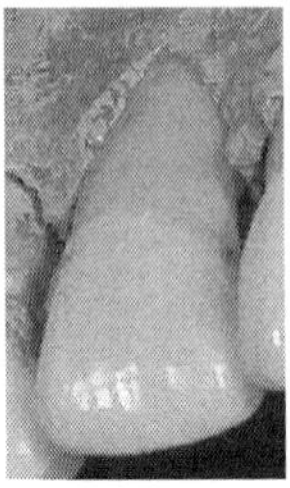	1. Mesial and distal ridging can be seen, but only in strong contrasting or grazing light. 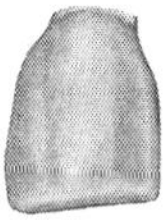 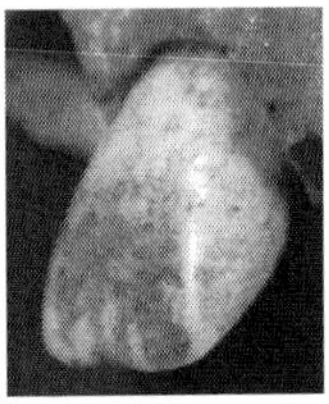 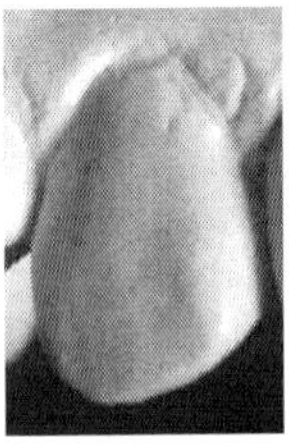	2. Mesial and distal ridging can be seen and felt, but it is subtle.  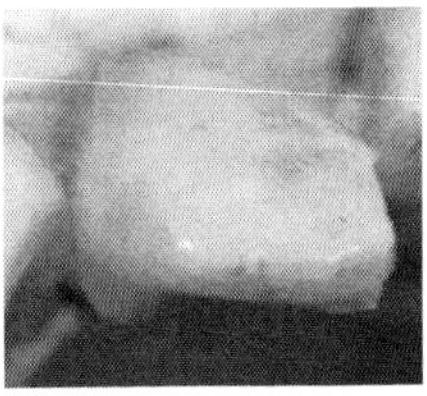 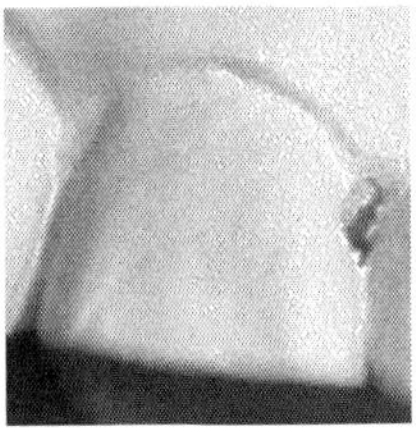
5. Ridging is prominent and may be seen along the length of the tooth crown, although it may fade near the occusal edge. 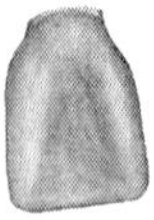 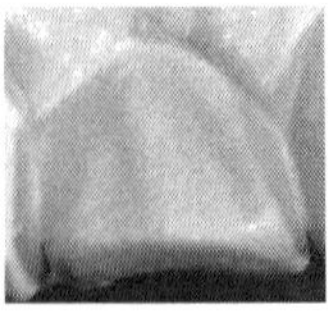 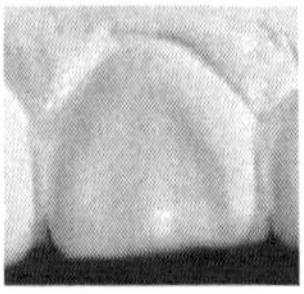	6. Extreme double shovel: the marginal ridges are raised well above the middle part of the labial surface and extend the length of the crown.  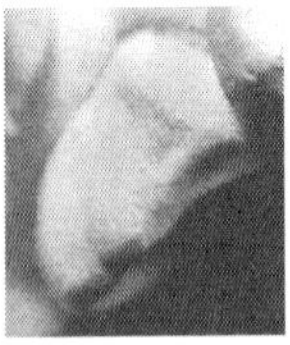 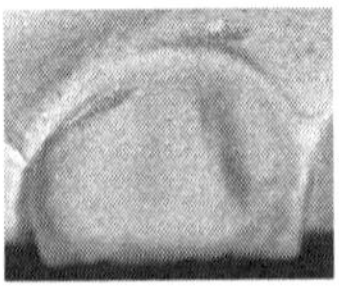	

		ASUDAS Plaque: DOUBLE SHOVELING
	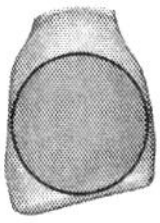	**Other Teeth Scored:** UI1
3. Ridging can be easily felt and seen, but is not prominent over half the crown height. 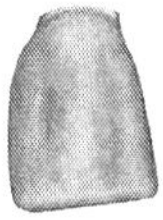 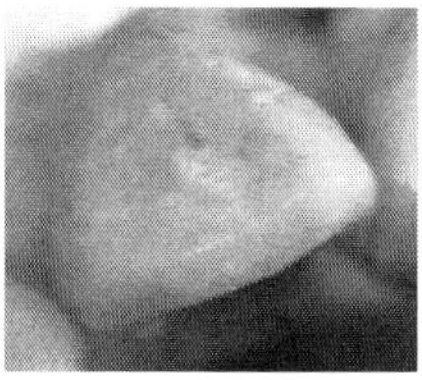 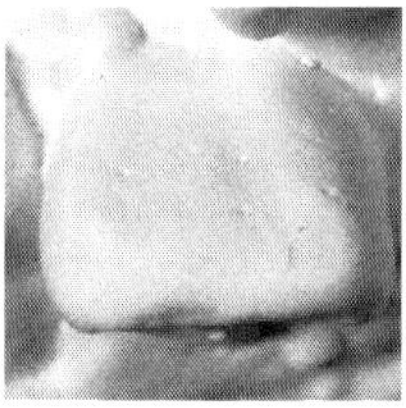		4. Ridging is prominent along at least half the total crown height. 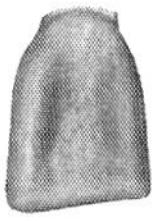 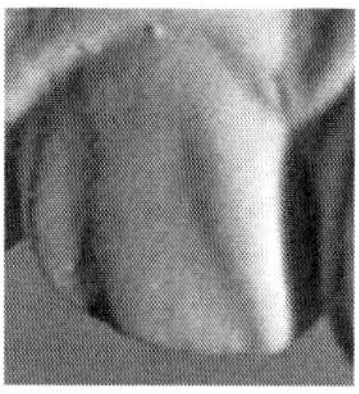 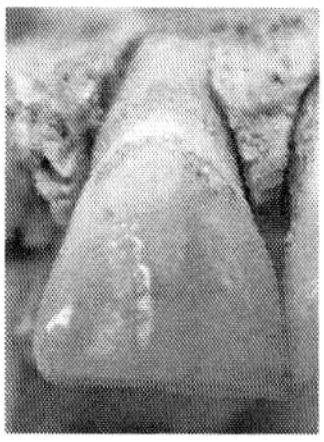

Full Name of Trait (Abbrev.): Maxillary Incisor Shovel Shape—First (UI1SS)

Detailed Trait Description: Of interest are the marginal ridges on the lingual side of the tooth. Lower grades tend to show ridging only near the occlusal edge, while higher scores show longer ridges that may converge at or near the cingulum.

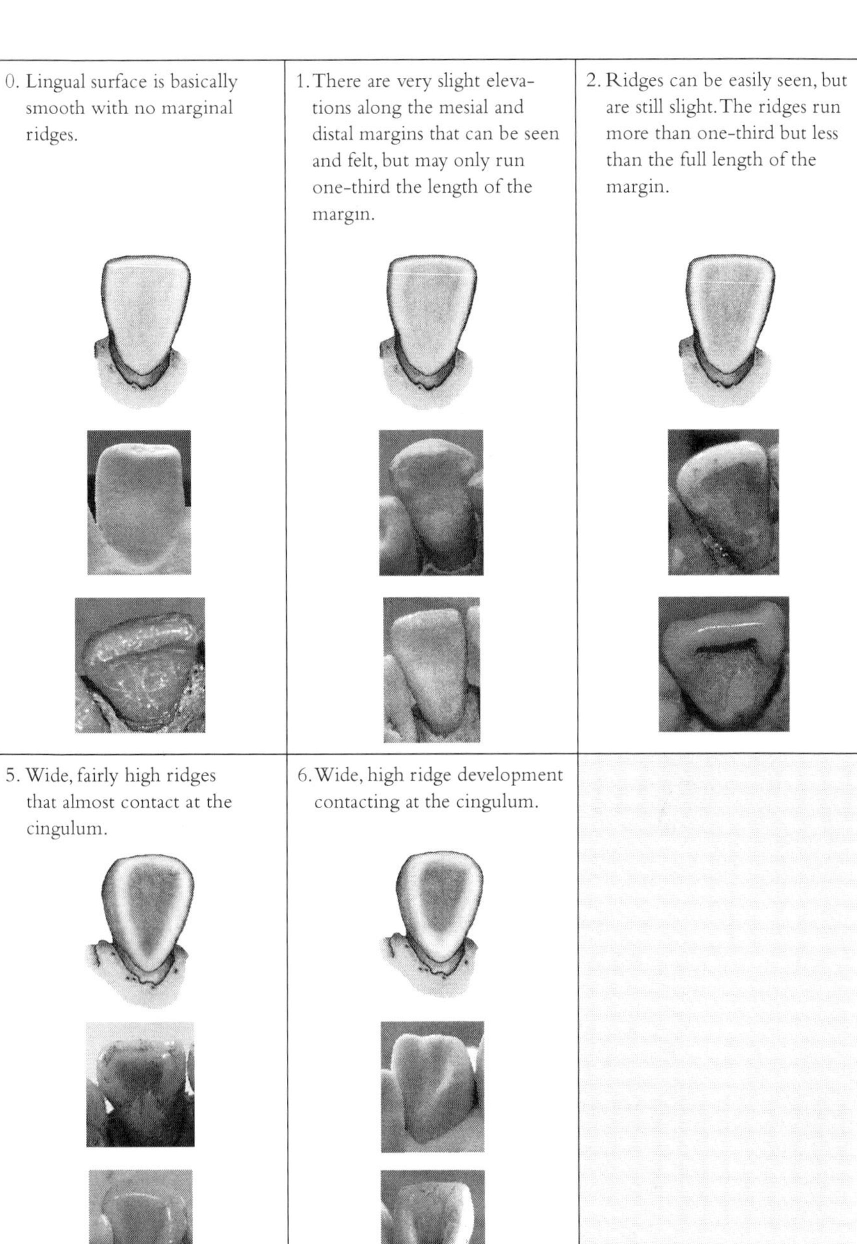

0. Lingual surface is basically smooth with no marginal ridges.	1. There are very slight elevations along the mesial and distal margins that can be seen and felt, but may only run one-third the length of the margin.	2. Ridges can be easily seen, but are still slight. The ridges run more than one-third but less than the full length of the margin.
5. Wide, fairly high ridges that almost contact at the cingulum.	6. Wide, high ridge development contacting at the cingulum.	

	ASUDAS Plaque: SHOV UI1
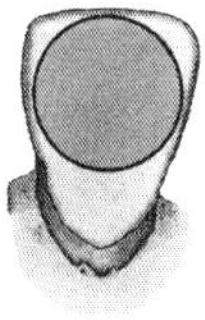	**Other Teeth Scored:** UI2; UC
3. There is stronger ridging present than previous grades. The ridges may converge toward the cingulum. 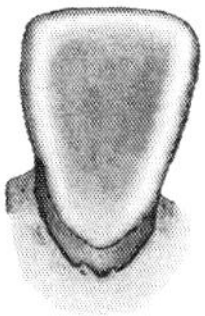  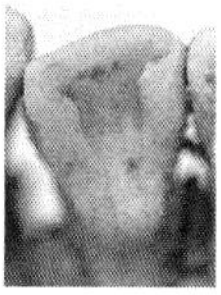	4. Ridges are wider, but not as high as in higher scores. These ridges almost converge on the cingulum. 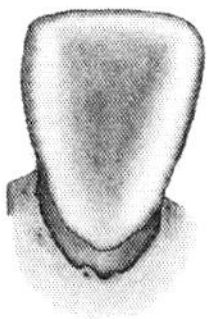 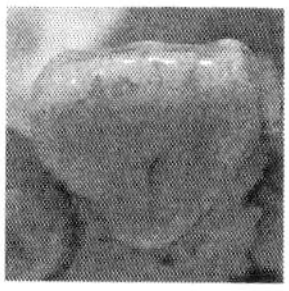 

Full Name of Trait (Abbrev.): Maxillary Incisor Shovel Shape—Second (UI2SS)

Detailed Trait Description: Of interest are the marginal ridges on the lingual side of the tooth. Lower grades tend to show ridging only near the occlusal edge, while higher scores show longer ridges that may converge at or near the cingulum.

0. Lingual surface is basically smooth with no marginal ridges. 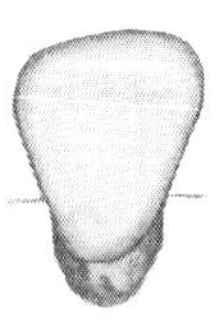 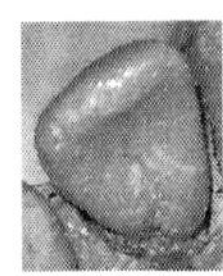	1. There are very slight elevations along the mesial and distal margins that can be seen and felt, but may only run one-third the length of the margin. 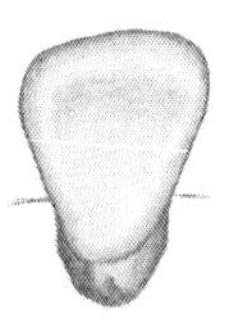 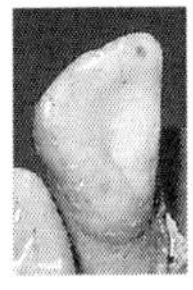 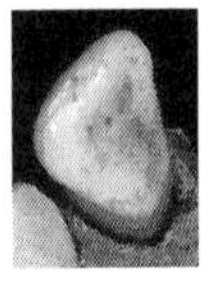	2. Ridges can be easily seen, but are still narrow. The ridges run more than one-third but less than the full length of the margin. 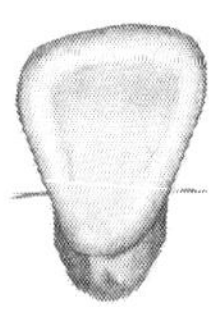 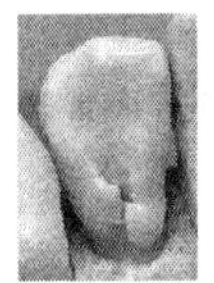 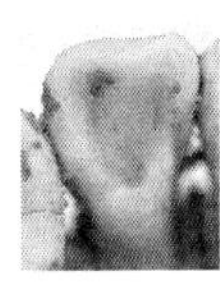
5. Wide, fairly high ridges that almost contact at the cingulum. 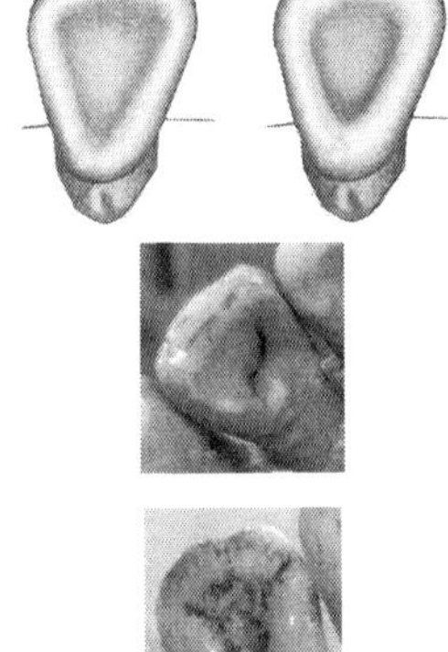	6. Wide, high ridge development contacting at the cingulum. 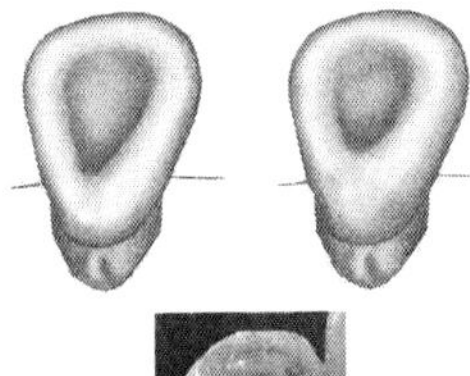 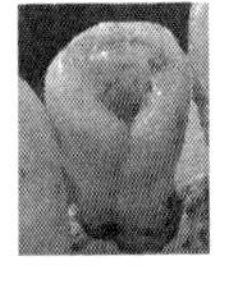 	7. Barrel-shaped tooth. 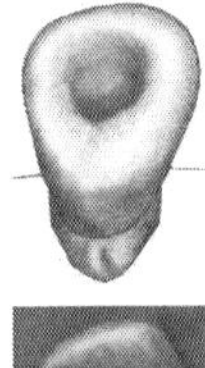 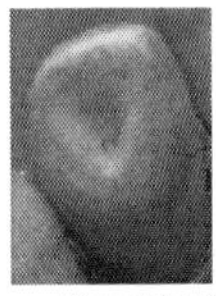 

	ASUDAS Plaque: SHOV UI2
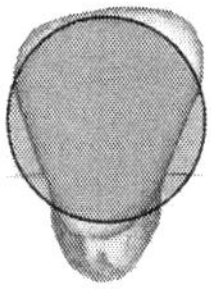	**Other Teeth Scored:** UI1; UC
3. There is stronger ridging present than in previous grades. The ridges may converge toward the cingulum. 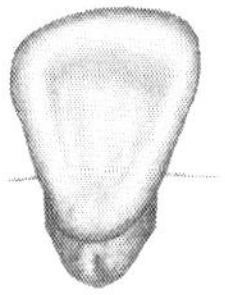 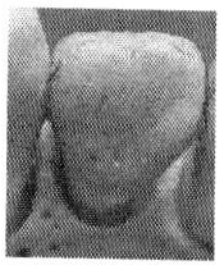 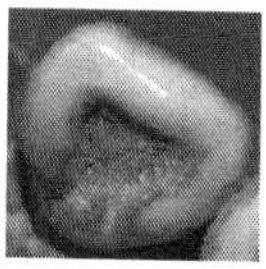	4. Ridges are wider, but not as high as in higher scores. These ridges almost converge on the cingulum. 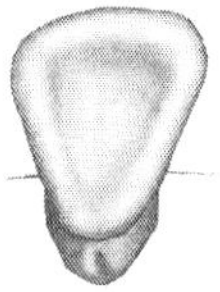 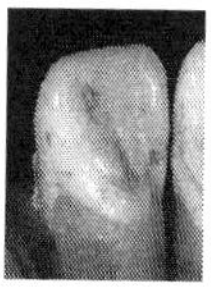 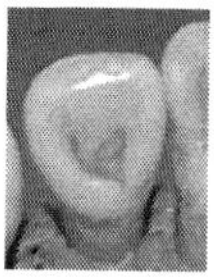

Full Name of Trait (Abbrev.): Maxillary Canine Shovel Shape (UCSS)		
Detailed Trait Description: Of interest are the marginal ridges on the lingual side of the tooth. Lower grades tend to show ridging only near the cingulum, while higher scores show longer ridges that may extend to the occlusal edge that also converge at the cingulum.		
0. Lingual surface is basically flat with no marginal ridges. 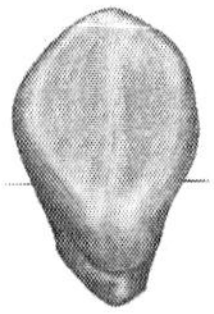 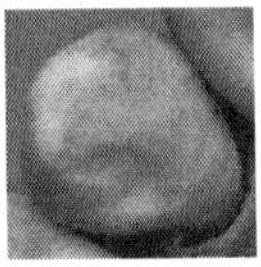 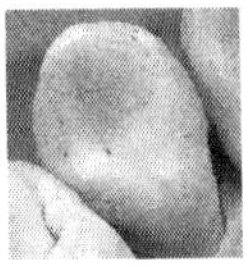	1. There are very slight elevations along the mesial and distal margins that can be seen and felt, but may only run one-third the length of the margin. 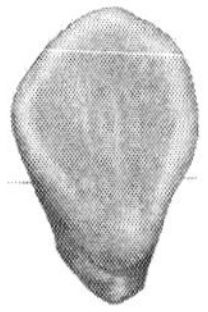 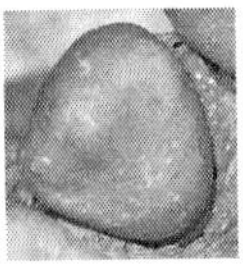 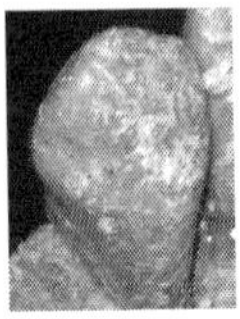	2. Ridges can be easily seen, but are still narrow. The ridges run more than one-third but less than the full length of the margin. 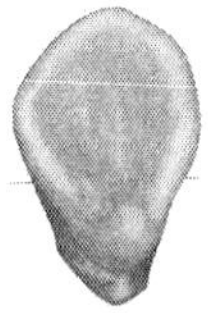 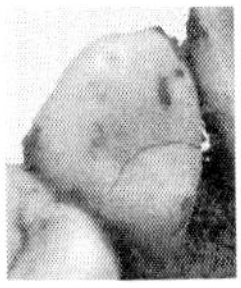 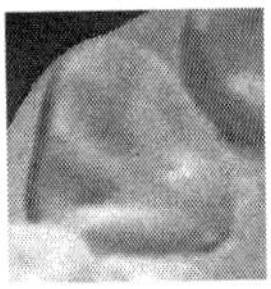
5. Wide, fairly high ridges that almost contact at the cingulum. 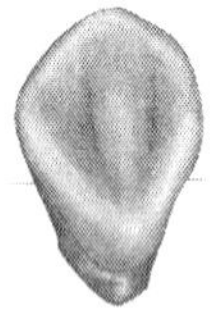 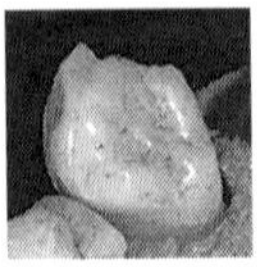 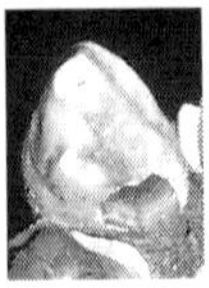	6. Strongest ridge development contacting at the cingulum. 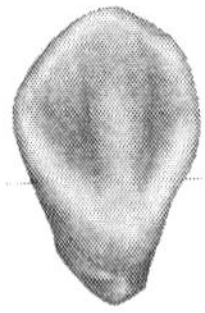 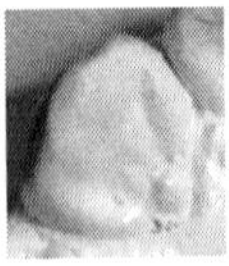 	

	ASUDAS Plaque: SHOV UI2
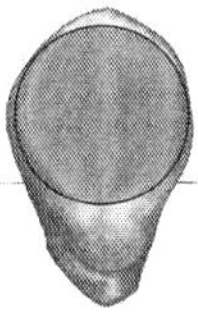	**Other Teeth Scored:** UI1; UI2
3. There is stronger ridging present than in previous grades. The ridges may converge toward the cingulum. 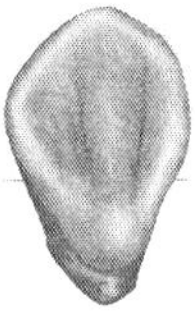 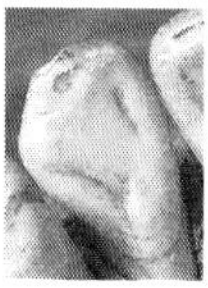 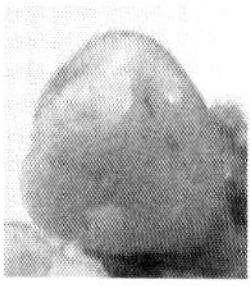	4. Ridges are wider, but not as high as in higher scores. These ridges almost converge on the cingulum. 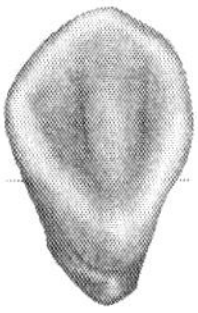 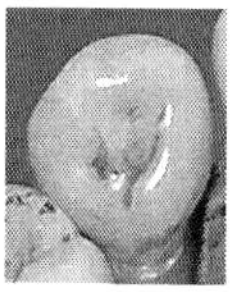 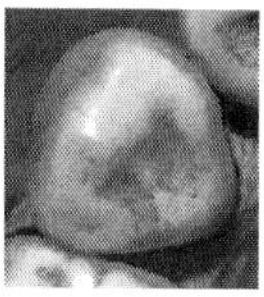

Full Name of Trait (Abbrev.): Maxillary Incisor Congenital Absence—Second (UI2CA)

Detailed Trait Description: There is no evidence of a maxillary lateral incisor between the central incisor and canine. Optimally, this trait is scored using radiographic images. However, it can be scored without them if care is taken not to include individuals who may have lost the tooth because of wear or caries, or who are likely to retain an unerupted lateral incisor. A gap or a misalignment of teeth may indicate tooth loss.

0	1
0. The maxillary lateral incisor is present.	1. The maxillary lateral incisor is absent and there is no evidence that the tooth is unerupted or has been lost because of pathology such as a space between UI1 and UC. 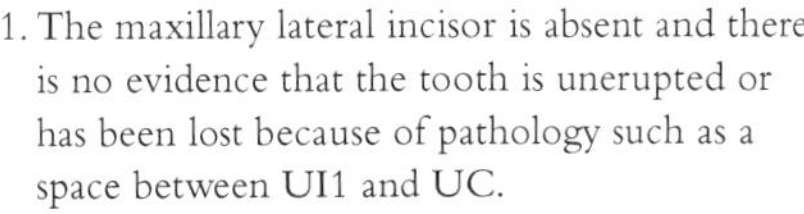
	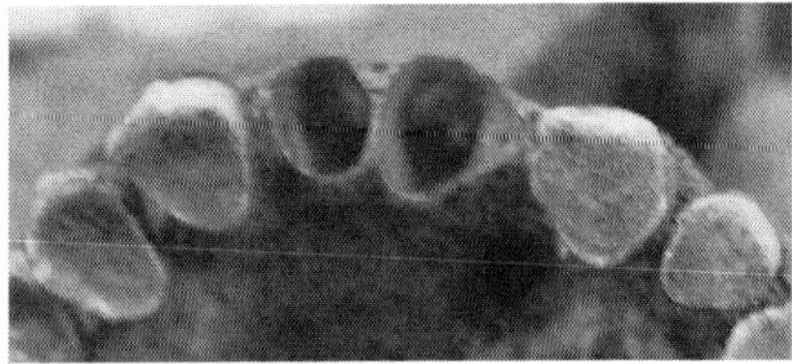
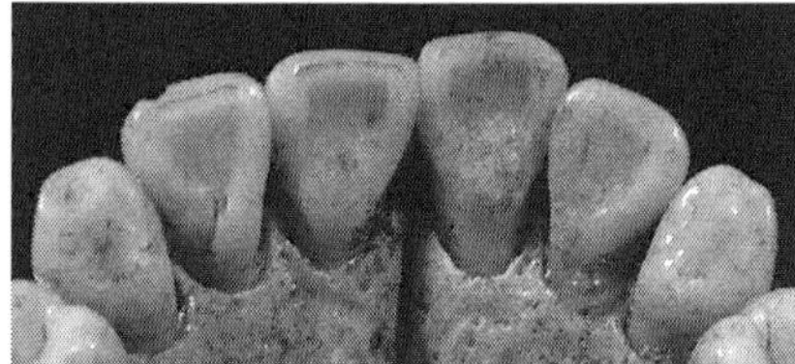	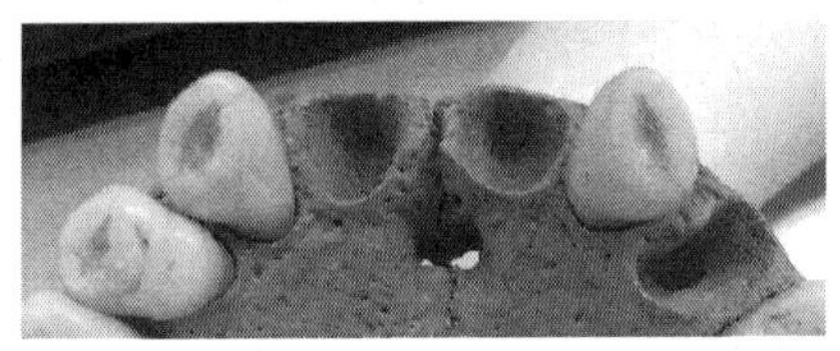

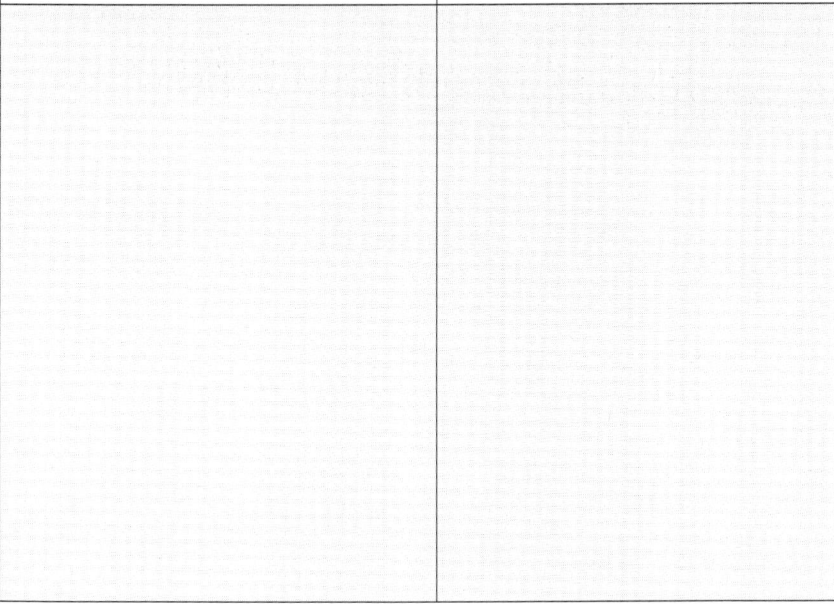

			ASUDAS Plaque: None
			Other Teeth Scored: UM3; LI1; LM3

Full Name of Trait (Abbrev.): Maxillary Molar Congenital Absence—Third (UM3CA)

Detailed Trait Description: There is no evidence of a maxillary third molar distal to the second molar. Optimally, this trait is scored using radiographic images. However, it can be scored without them if care is taken not to include individuals who may have lost the tooth because of wear or caries, or in contemporary western populations where an individual is likely to have had the tooth surgically removed. A gap or misalignment of teeth may indicate tooth loss.

0. The maxillary third molar is present.

1. The maxillary third molar is absent and there is no evidence that the tooth is unerupted or has been lost because of pathology or surgical removal such as a gap distal to UM2.

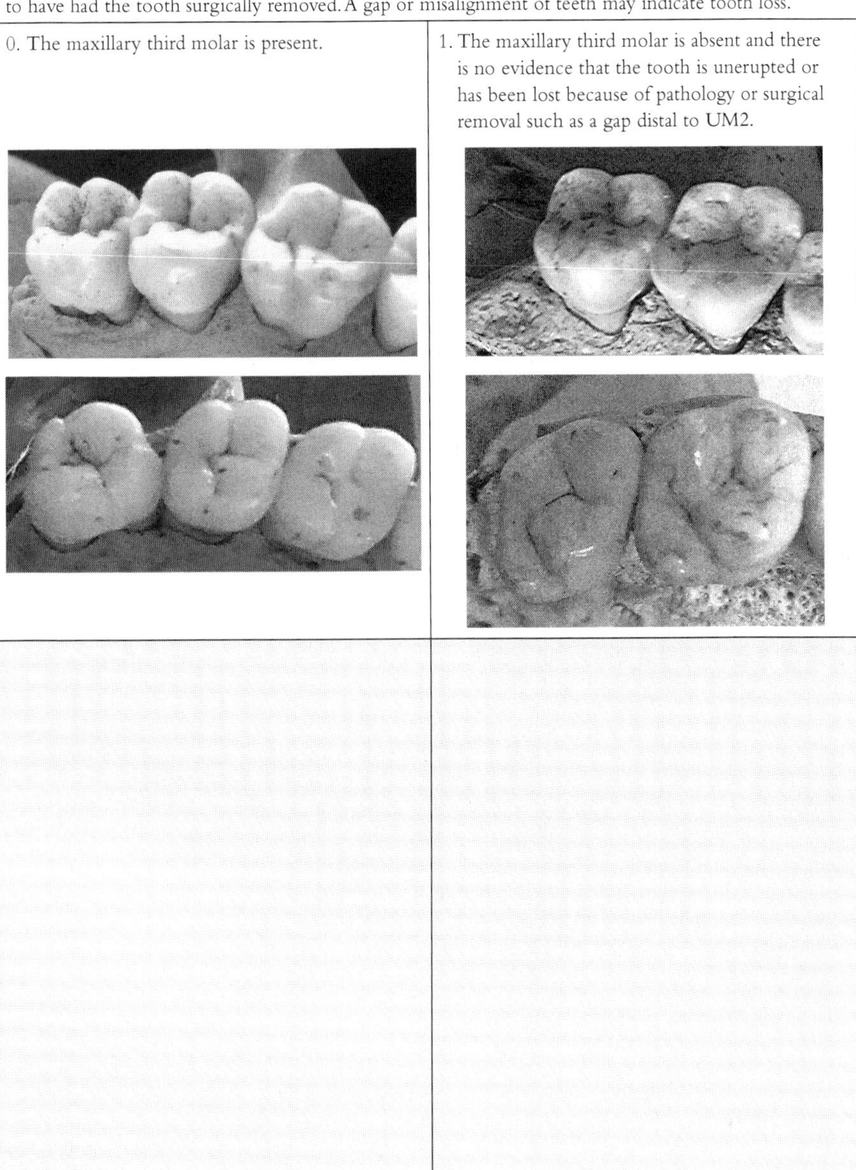

			ASUDAS Plaque: None
			Other Teeth Scored: UI2; LI1; LM3

Full Name of Trait (Abbrev.): Maxillary Incisor Reduction or Peg-shape—Second (UI2PEG)

Detailed Trait Description: The tooth is reduced in size compared to what might be expected given the size of the other teeth in the arch. It may or may not have normal morphology.

0. The maxillary lateral incisor is of the size expected given the size of the other teeth in the arch.	1. The tooth is reduced in size but has normal morphology for a maxillary lateral incisor.	2. The tooth is reduced in size and has simplified or peg-shaped morphology.
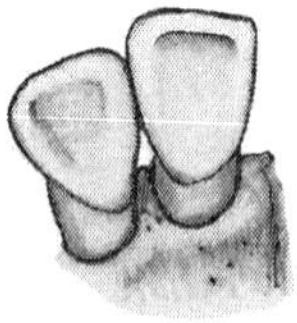	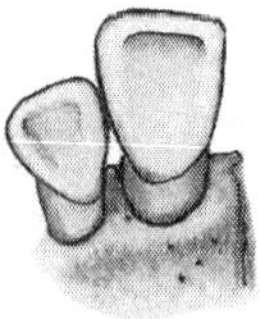	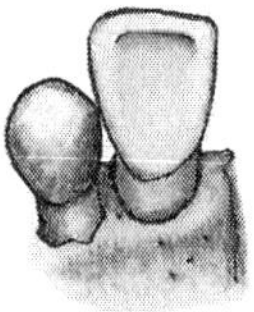 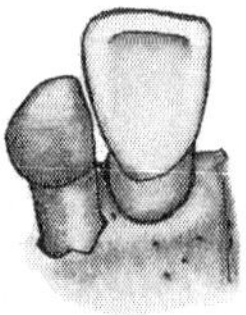
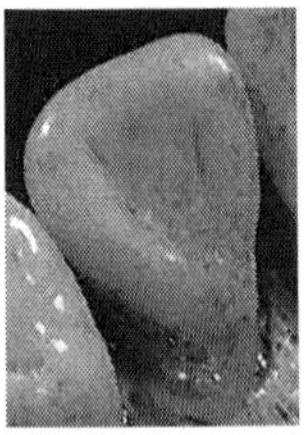	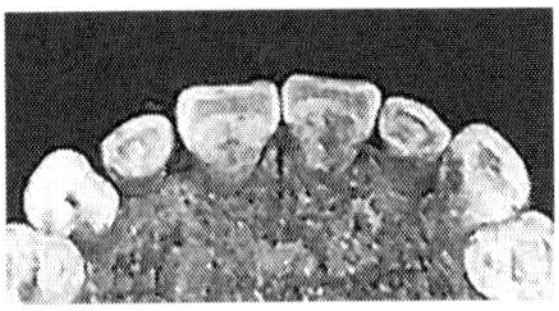	
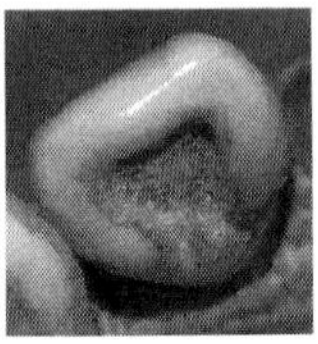		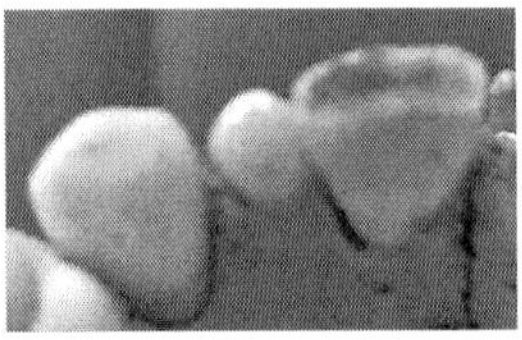

		ASUDAS Plaque: None
	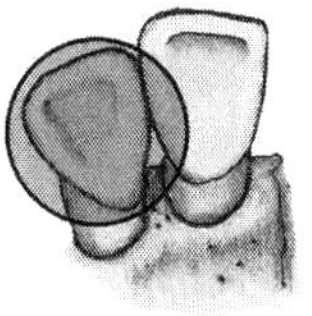	**Other Teeth Scored:** UM3

Full Name of Trait (Abbrev.): Maxillary Molar Peg or Reduction—Third (UM3PEG)		
Detailed Trait Description: The tooth is reduced in size compared to what might be expected given the size of the other teeth in the arch. It may or may not have normal morphology.		
0. The maxillary third molar is of the size expected given the size of the other teeth in the arch. 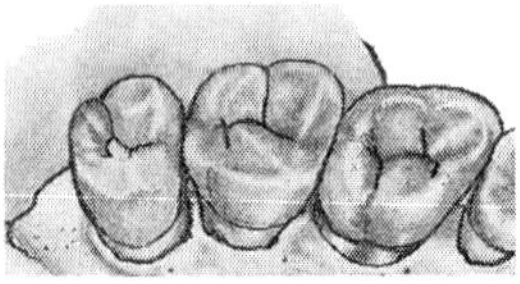 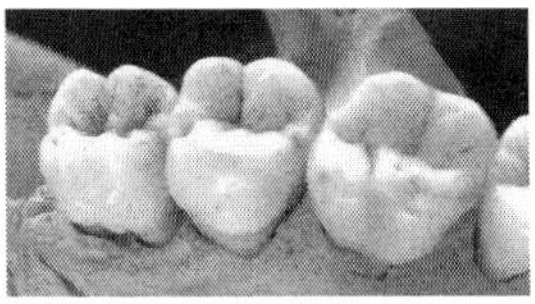 	1. The tooth is reduced in size, but has normal morphology for a maxillary third molar. 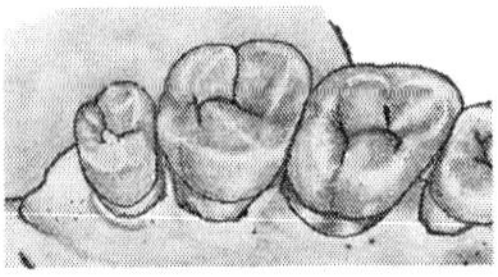  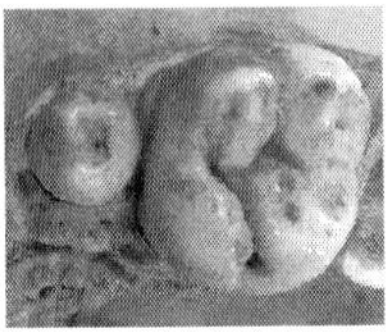	2. The tooth is reduced to less than 7 mm in diameter and has simplified or peg-shaped morphology. These teeth often have two rudimentary cusps. 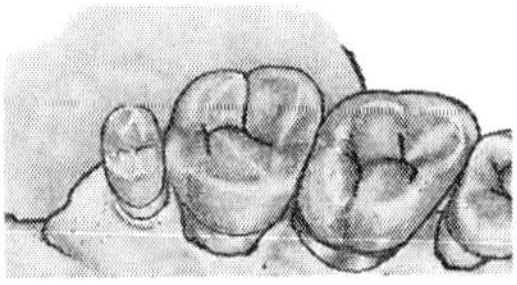 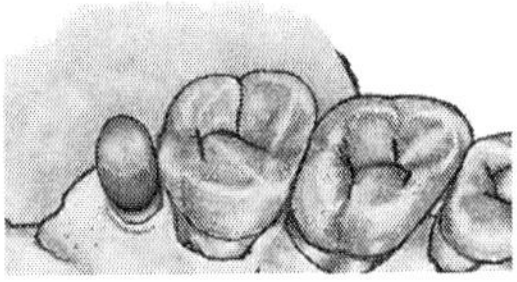 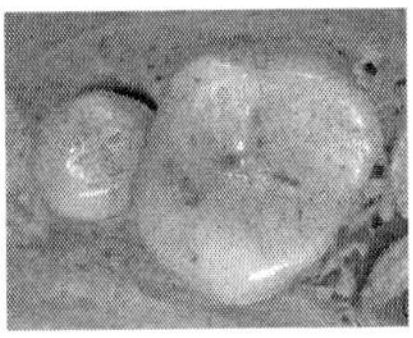

		ASUDAS Plaque: None
		Other Teeth Scored: UI2

Full Name of Trait (Abbrev.): Maxillary Incisor Interruption Groove—First (UI1IG)

Detailed Trait Description: The tooth has a groove that meets or crosses the cingulum and may continue onto the root. The expression of this trait is much rarer on the maxillary central incisor than on the maxillary lateral incisor.

0. There is no groove that crosses the cingulum.	1. There is a groove that meets or crosses the cingulum on the mesiolingual surface of the tooth.	2. There is a groove that meets or crosses the cingulum on the distolingual surface of the tooth.

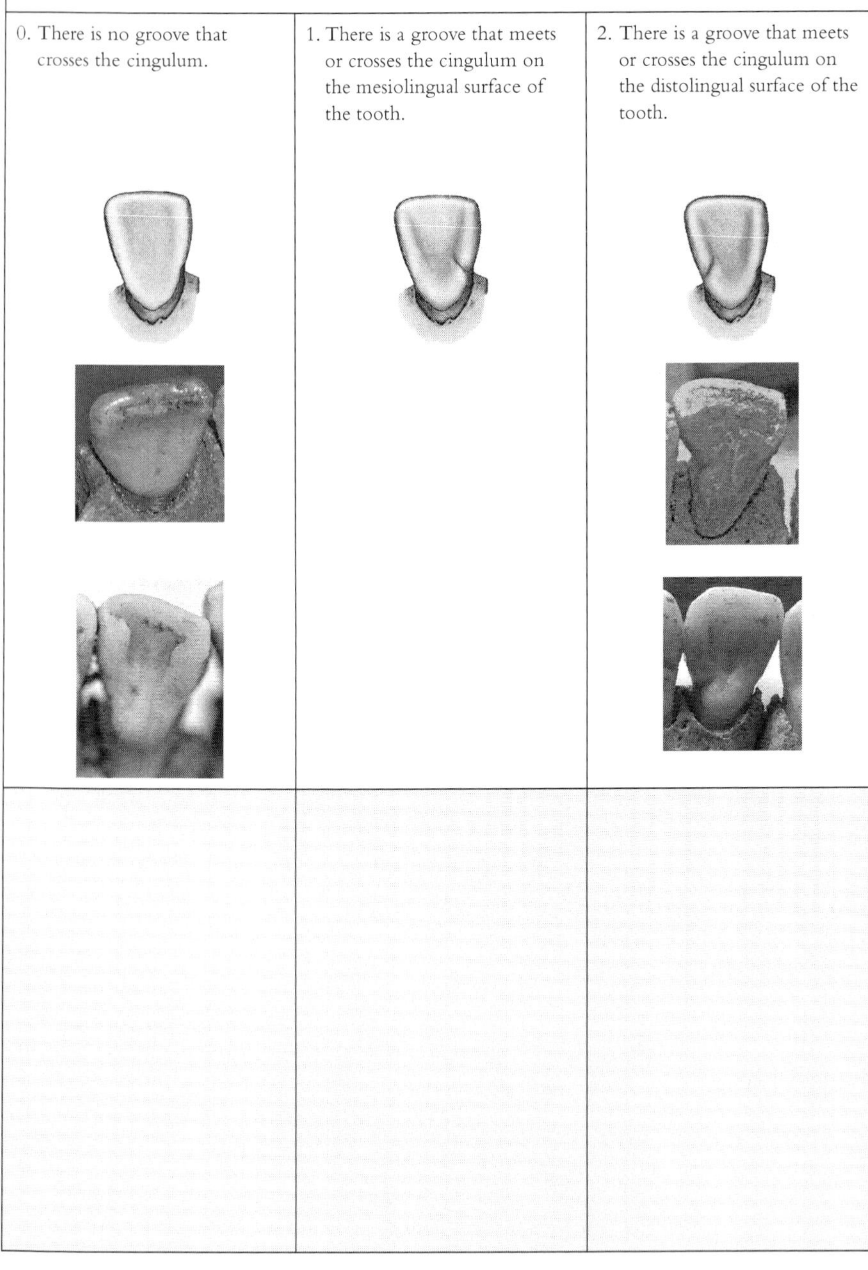

	ASUDAS Plaque: None
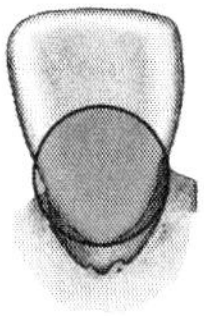	**Other Teeth Scored:** UI2
3. There are two grooves that meet or cross the cingulum of the tooth: one on the mesiolingual and one on the distolingual surface of the tooth. 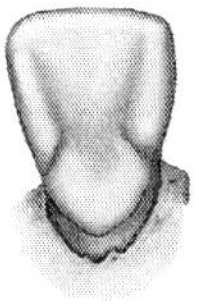	4. There are single or multiple grooves that meet or cross the cingulum in the middle of the lingual surface of the tooth. 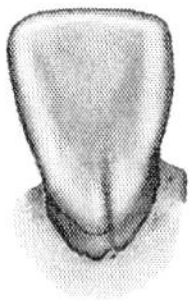 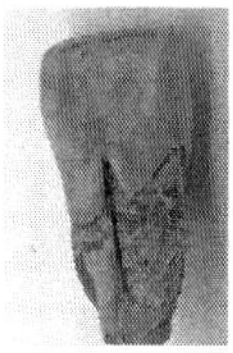 

Full Name of Trait (Abbrev.): Maxillary Incisor Interruption Groove—Second (UI2IG)

Detailed Trait Description: The tooth has a groove that meets or crosses the cingulum and may continue on to the root. The expression of this trait is much more common on the maxillary lateral incisor than on the maxillary central incisor.

0. There is no groove that crosses the cingulum. 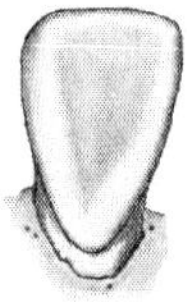  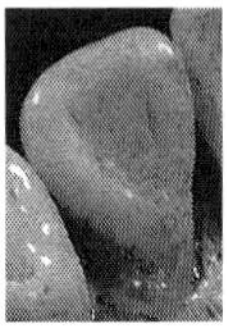	1. There is a groove that meets or crosses the cingulum on the mesiolingual surface of the tooth. 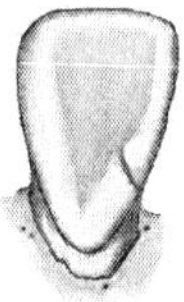 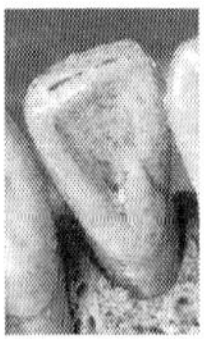 	2. There is a groove that meets or crosses the cingulum on the distolingual surface of the tooth. 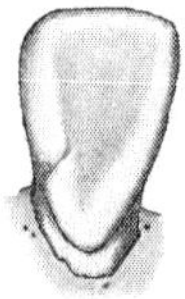 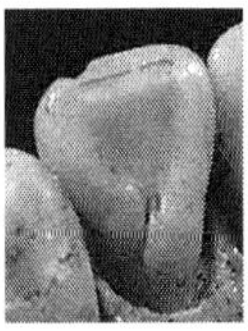 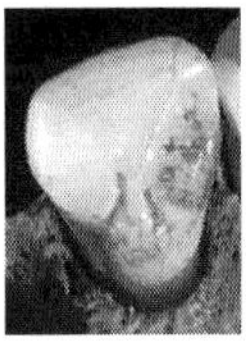

	ASUDAS Plaque: None
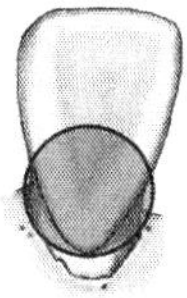	**Other Teeth Scored:** UI1
3. There are two grooves that meet or cross the cingulum of the tooth: one on the mesiolingual and one on the distolingual surface of the tooth. 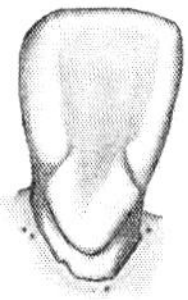 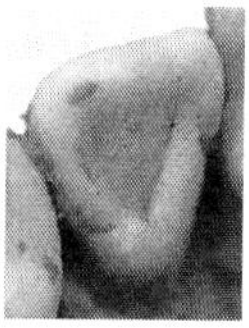 	4. There are single or multiple grooves that meet or cross the cingulum in the middle of the lingual surface of the tooth. 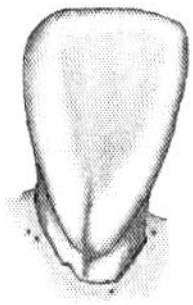  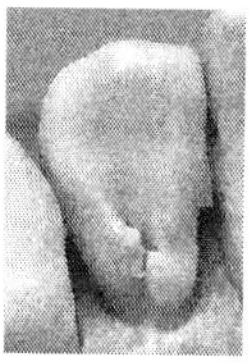

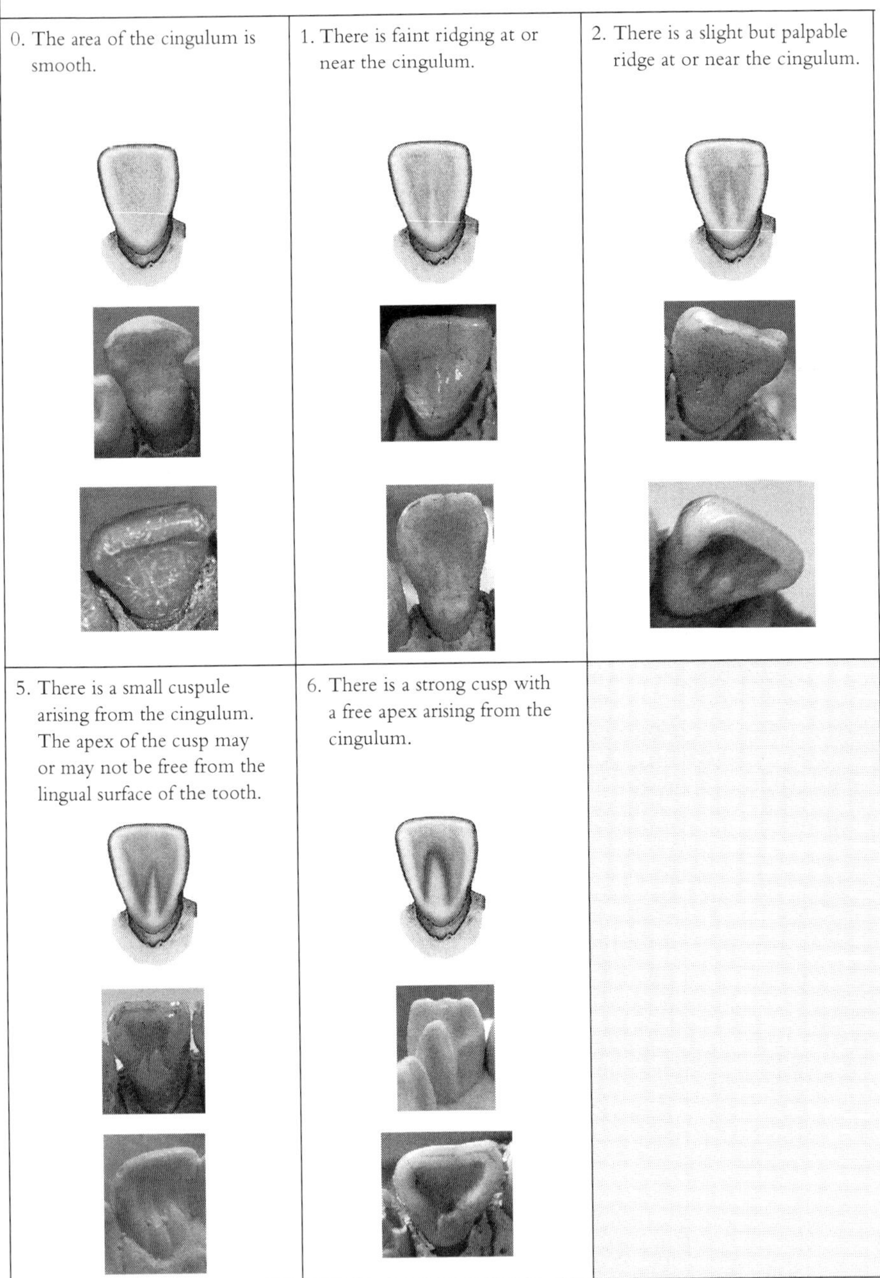

Full Name of Trait (Abbrev.): Maxillary Incisor Tuberculum Dentale—First (UI1TD)

Detailed Trait Description: The tuberculum dentale is a ridge, multiple ridges, or a tubercule that may be seen at or near the cingulum on the lingual tooth surface. Grades 5 and 6 are very rare on the first incisor.

0. The area of the cingulum is smooth.	1. There is faint ridging at or near the cingulum.	2. There is a slight but palpable ridge at or near the cingulum.
5. There is a small cuspule arising from the cingulum. The apex of the cusp may or may not be free from the lingual surface of the tooth.	6. There is a strong cusp with a free apex arising from the cingulum.	

	ASUDAS Plaque: TD UI1
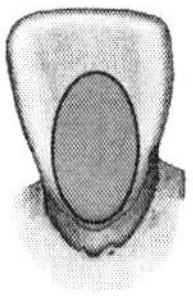	**Other Teeth Scored:** UI2, UC
3. There is a clearly discernable ridge at or near the cingulum. 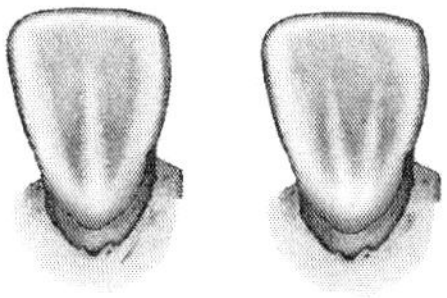  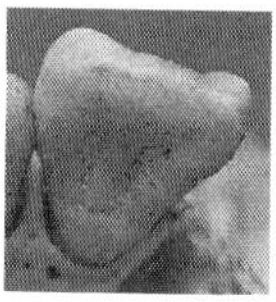	4. There is very strong ridging at or near the cingulum, which is thicker and longer than seen for lesser expressions. 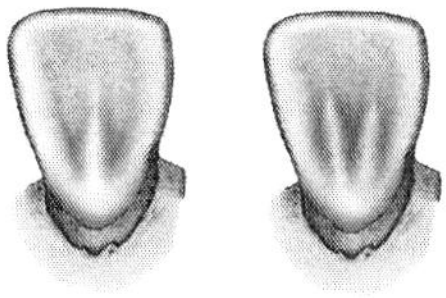  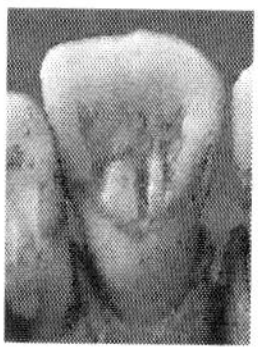

Full Name of Trait (Abbrev.): Maxillary Incisor Tuberculum Dentale—Second (UI2TD)

Detailed Trait Description: The tuberculum dentale is a ridge, multiple ridges, or a tubercule that may be seen at or near the cingulum on the lingual tooth surface.

0. The area of the cingulum is smooth. 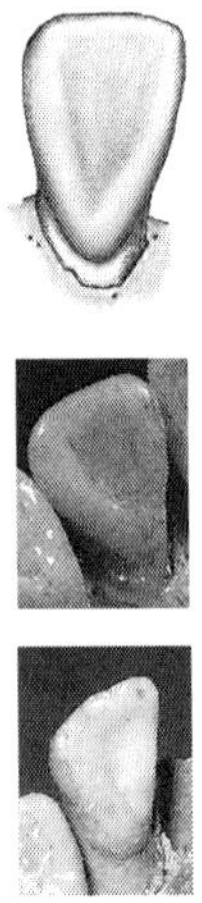	1. There is faint ridging at or near the cingulum. 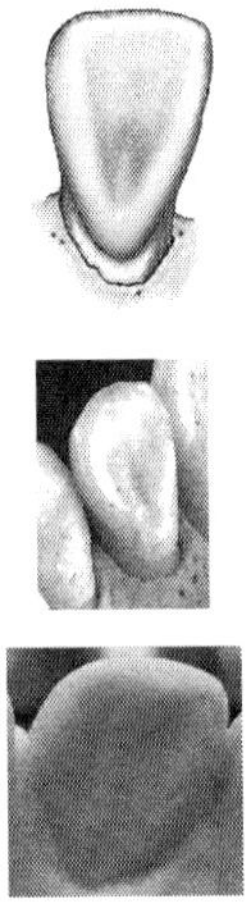	2. There is a slight but palpable ridge at or near the cingulum. 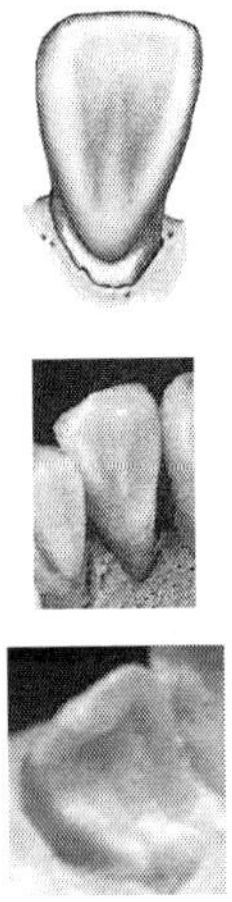
5. There is a small cuspule arising from the cingulum. The apex of the cusp may or may not be free from the lingual surface of the tooth. 	6. There is a strong cusp with a free apex arising from the cingulum. 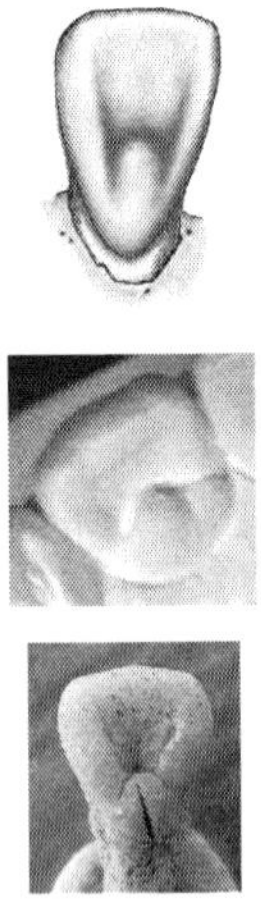	

	ASUDAS Plaque: TD UI1
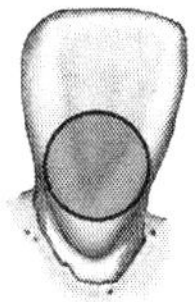	**Other Teeth Scored:** UI1; UC
3. There is a clearly discernable ridge at or near the cingulum. 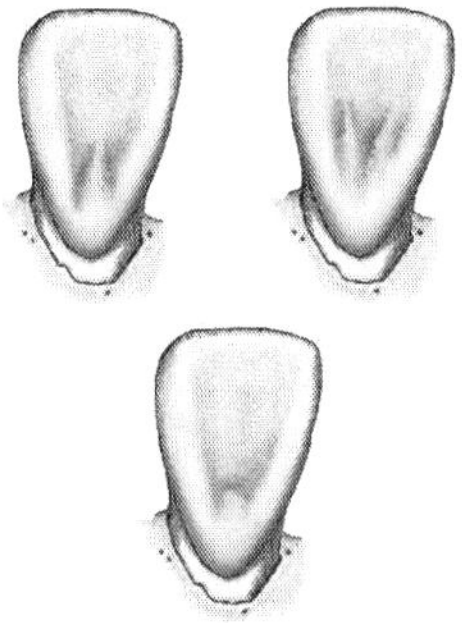 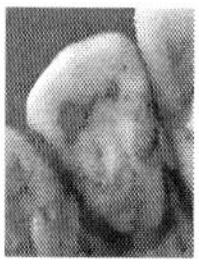 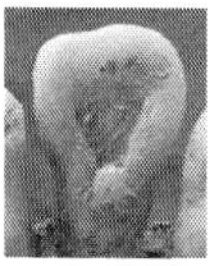	4. There is very strong ridging at or near the cingulum, which is thicker and longer than seen for lesser expressions. 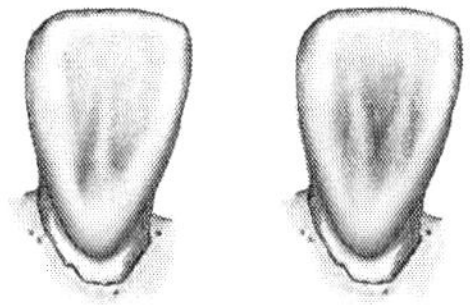 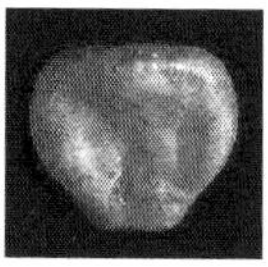 

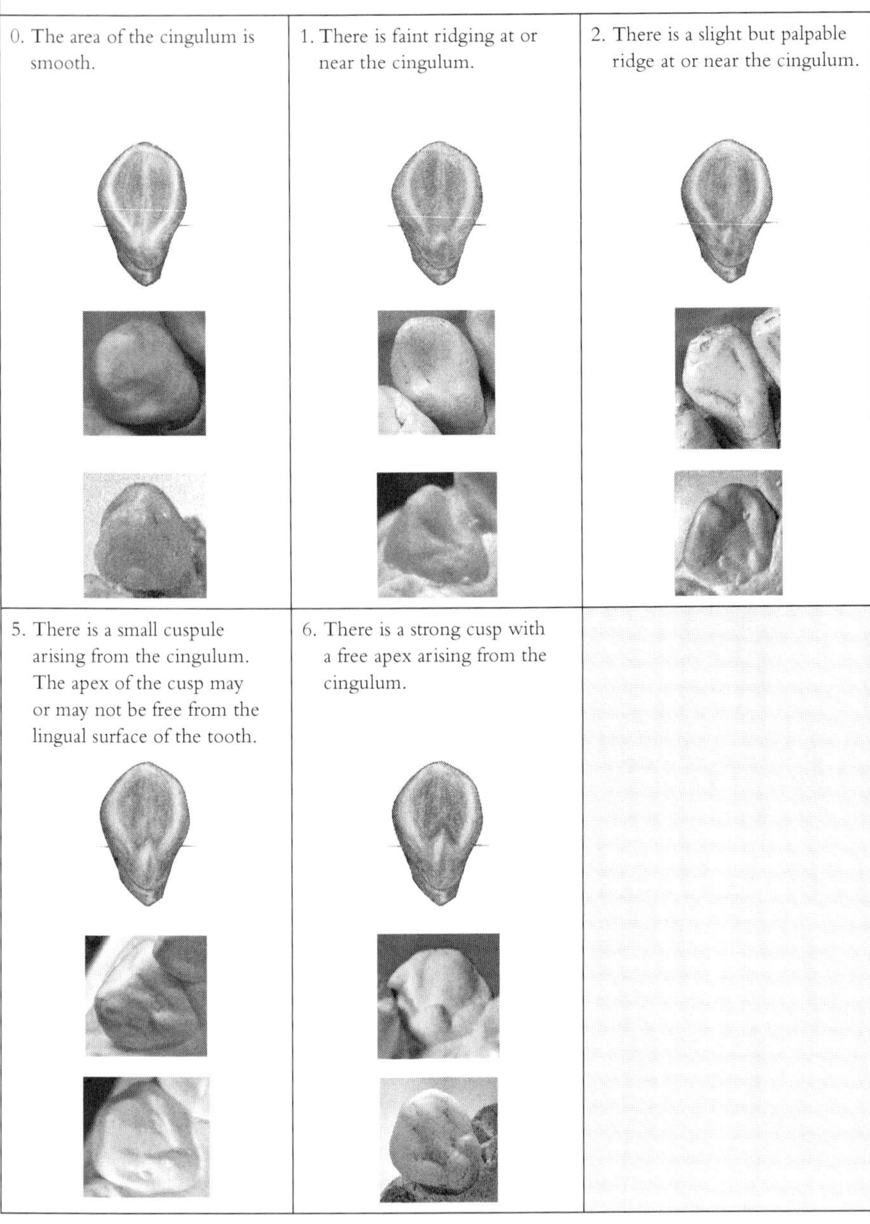

Full Name of Trait (Abbrev.): Maxillary Canine Tuberculum Dentale (UCTD)		
Detailed Trait Description: The tuberculum dentale is a ridge, multiple ridges, or a tubercule that may be seen at or near the cingulum on the lingual tooth surface.		
0. The area of the cingulum is smooth.	1. There is faint ridging at or near the cingulum.	2. There is a slight but palpable ridge at or near the cingulum.
5. There is a small cuspule arising from the cingulum. The apex of the cusp may or may not be free from the lingual surface of the tooth.	6. There is a strong cusp with a free apex arising from the cingulum.	

	ASUDAS Plaque: TD UI1
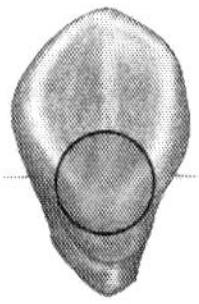	**Other Teeth Scored:** UI1; UI2
3. There is a clearly discernable ridge at or near the cingulum. 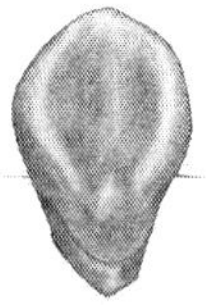  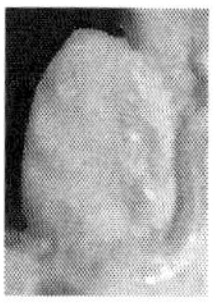	4. There is very strong ridging at or near the cingulum, which is thicker and longer than seen for lesser expressions. 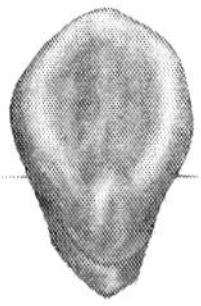  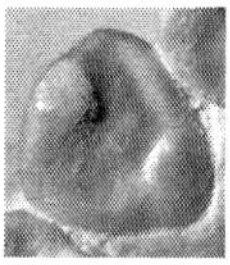

Full Name of Trait (Abbrev.): Maxillary Canine Mesial Ridge (UCMR)		
Detailed Trait Description: This observation consists of the relative size of the mesial and distal lingual margins, and the degree to which a tuberculum dentale is attached to the lingual margin		
0. The mesial and distal lingual marginal ridges are of equal size. Neither is attached to any present tuberculum dentale. 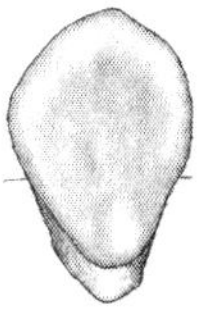 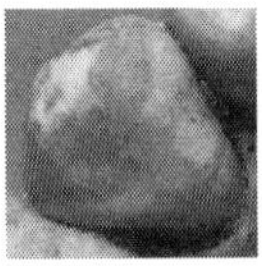 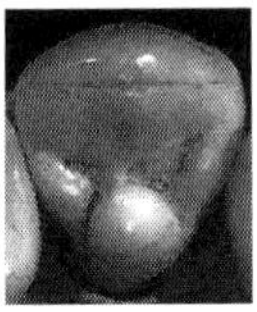	1. The mesiolingual margin is wider and/or more prominent than the distolingual margin. The separation between the mesiolingual margin and the tuberculum dentale may be blurred. 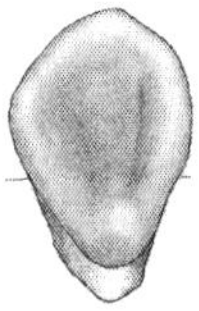 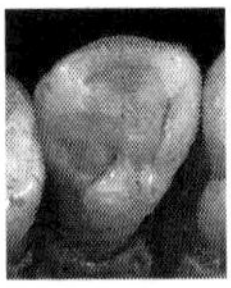 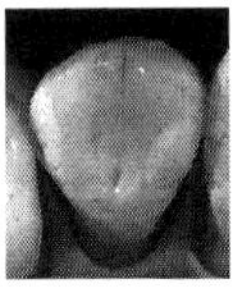	2. The mesiolingual margin is wider and/or more prominent than the distolingual margin. The mesiolingual margin and the tuberculum dentale are attached to each other, but it can still be seen that they are two separate morphological features. 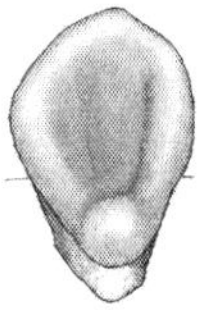 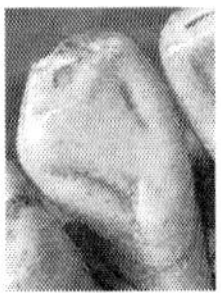 

	ASUDAS Plaque: BUSHMAN CANINE
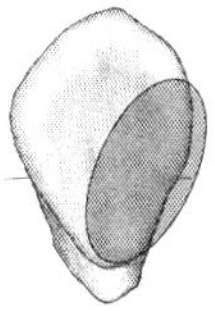	**Other Teeth Scored:** None
3. The mesiolingual margin is approximately half as wide and/or more prominent than the distolingual margin. The mesiolingual margin and the mesial side of the tuberculum dentale are incorporated in one continuous ridge. 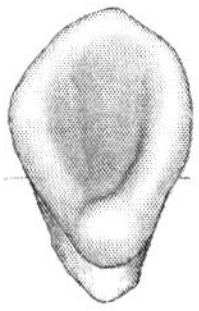  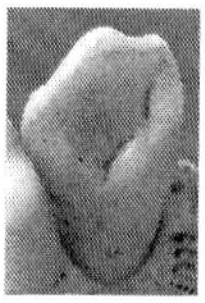	

Full Name of Trait (Abbrev.): Maxillary Canine Distal Accessory Ridge (UCDR)

Detailed Trait Description: The trait consists of a ridge that can exist on the distolingual surface of the tooth between the apex and distolingual marginal ridge. UC usually shows stronger expression of this trait than LC.

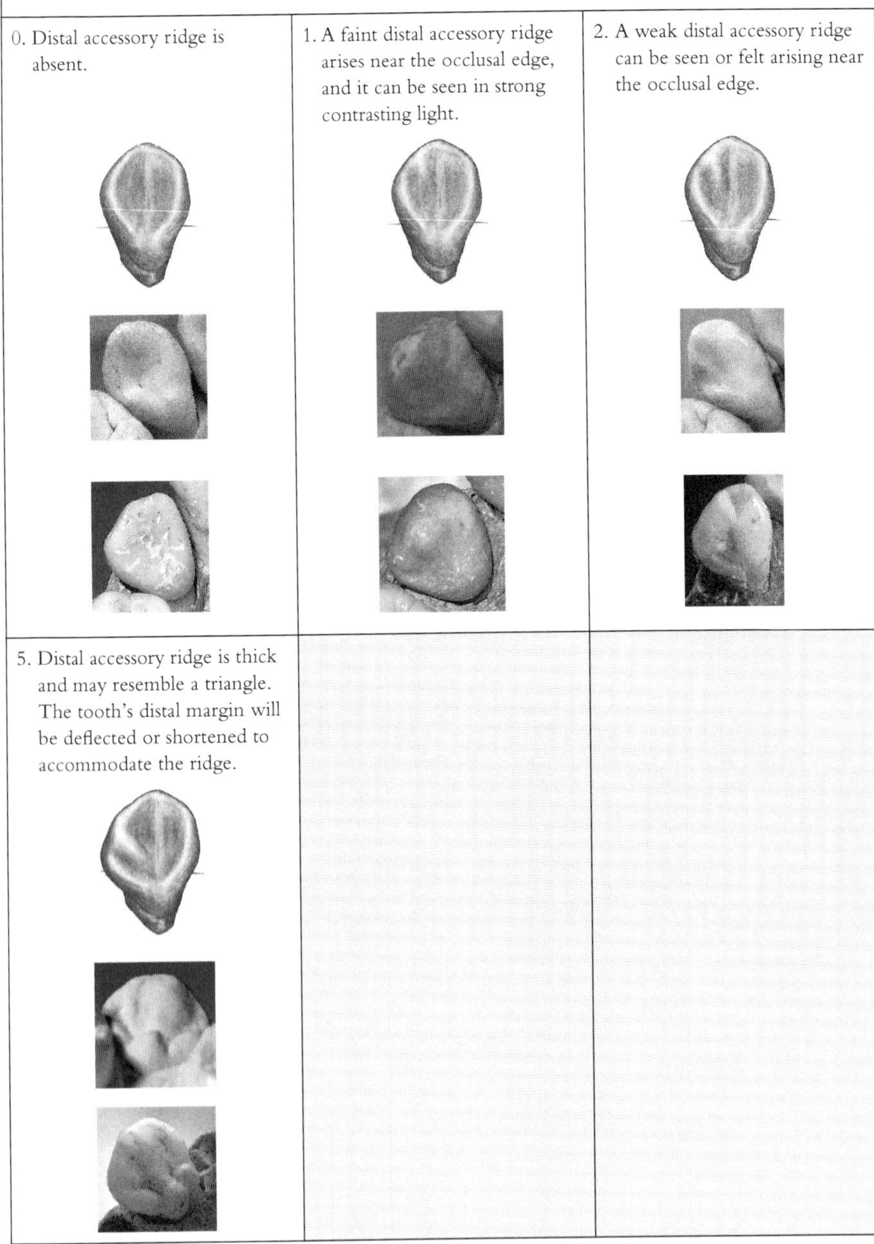

0. Distal accessory ridge is absent.	1. A faint distal accessory ridge arises near the occlusal edge, and it can be seen in strong contrasting light.	2. A weak distal accessory ridge can be seen or felt arising near the occlusal edge.
5. Distal accessory ridge is thick and may resemble a triangle. The tooth's distal margin will be deflected or shortened to accommodate the ridge.		

		ASUDAS Plaque: DAR UC
	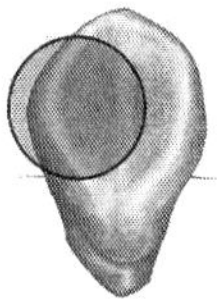	**Other Teeth Scored:** LC

3. A distal accessory ridge is thicker than seen in lower grades, but does not deflect the distal margin. 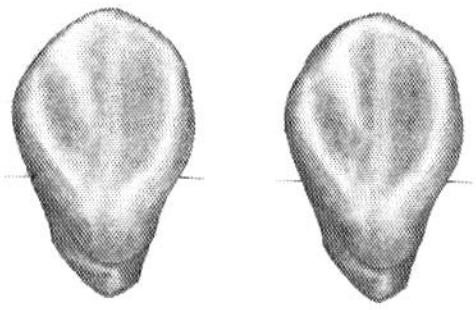 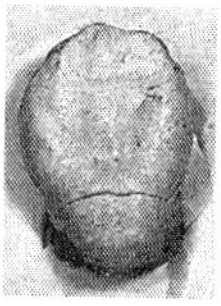 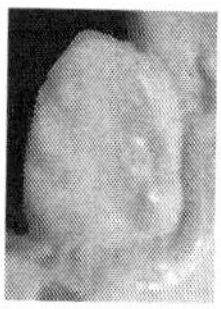	4. Distal accessory ridge is longer and thicker than seen in lower grades and may deflect or shorten the distal margin. 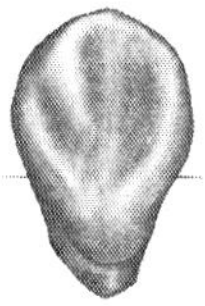 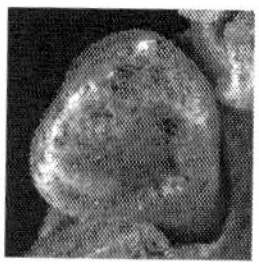 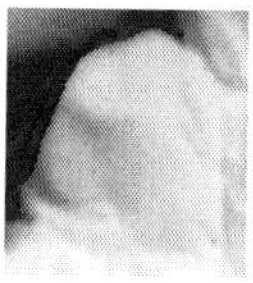

Full Name of Trait (Abbrev.): Maxillary Premolar Accessory Cusps—Third (UP3AC)		
Detailed Trait Description: This observation is of the presence of small cuspules on the mesial or distal margins of the occlusal surface of the premolar at the termination of the sagittal groove. These accessory cusps should be separated by grooves from both the mesial and buccal cusps. This trait should not be scored if there is tooth wear.		
0. There are no cuspules at the termination of the sagittal groove. The presence of only a very small ridge or bulge that is closely associated with either the buccal or the lingual cusp is considered grade 0. 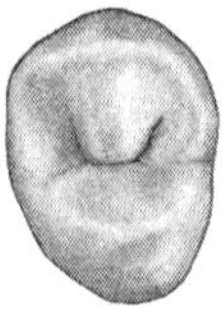 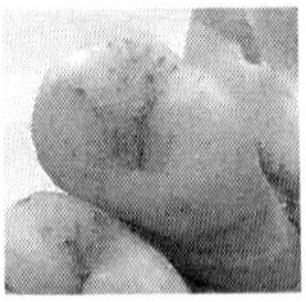 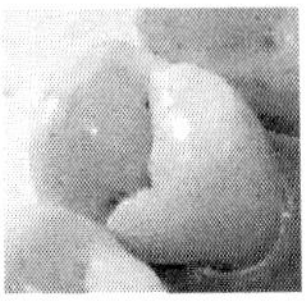	1. There is a cuspule on the mesial margin of the occlusal surface of the tooth at the termination of the sagittal groove. 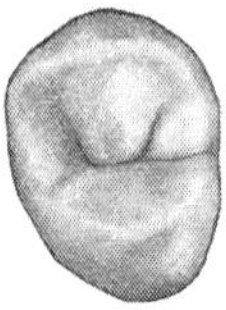 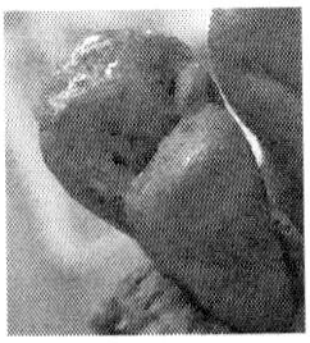 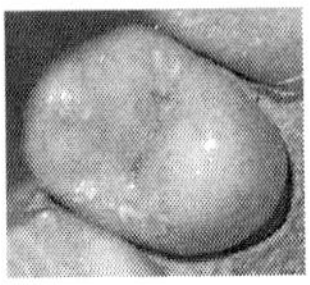	2. There is a cuspule on the distal margin of the occlusal surface of the tooth at the termination of the sagittal groove. 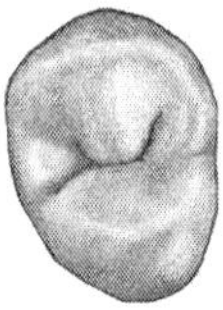 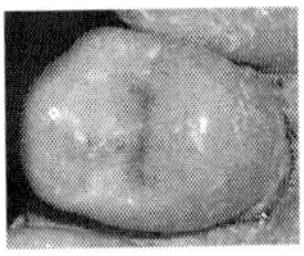 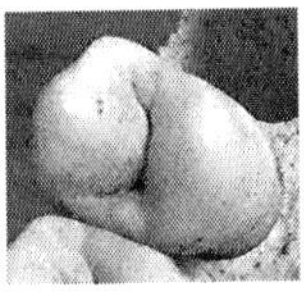

	ASUDAS Plaque: None
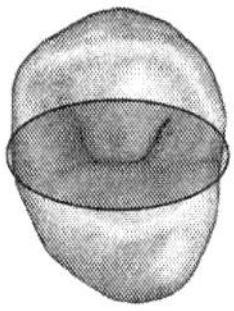	**Other Teeth Scored:** UP4
3. There are cuspules on the mesial and distal margins of the occlusal surface of the tooth at the termination of the sagittal groove. 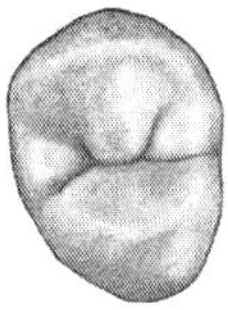  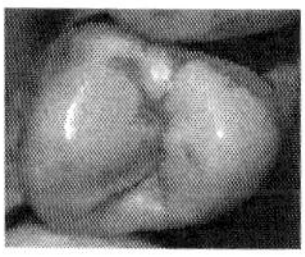	

Full Name of Trait (Abbrev.): Maxillary Premolar Accessory Cusps—Fourth (UP4AC)

Detailed Trait Description: This observation is of the presence of small cuspules on the mesial or distal margins of the occlusal surface of the premolar at the termination of the sagittal groove. These accessory cusps should be separated by grooves from both the mesial and buccal cusps. This trait should not be scored if there is tooth wear.

0. There are no cuspules at the termination of the sagittal groove. The presence of only a very small ridge or bulge that is closely associated with either the buccal or the lingual cusp is considered grade 0.	1. There is a cuspule on the mesial margin of the occlusal surface of the tooth at the termination of the sagittal groove.	2. There is a cuspule on the distal margin of the occlusal surface of the tooth at the termination of the sagittal groove.
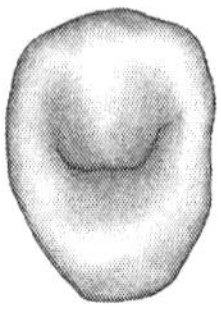	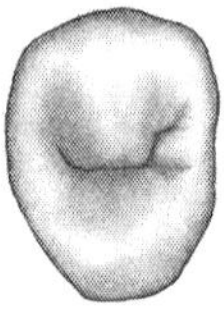	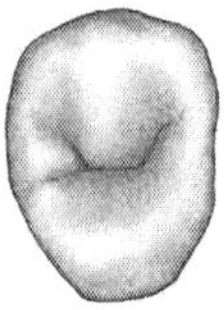
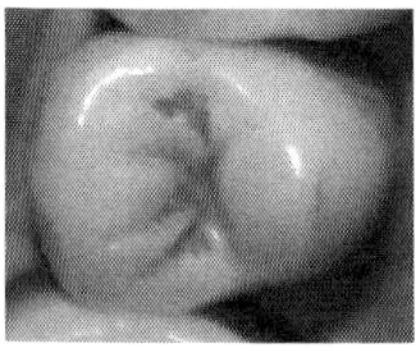	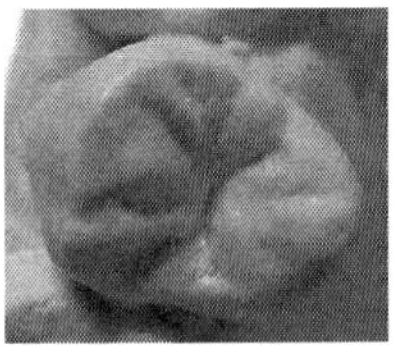	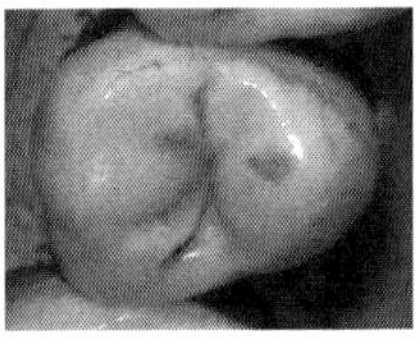
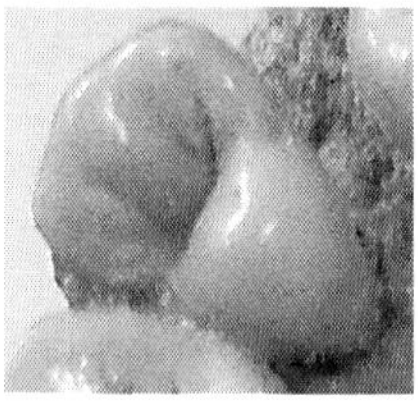	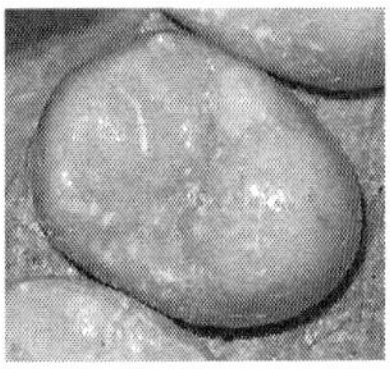	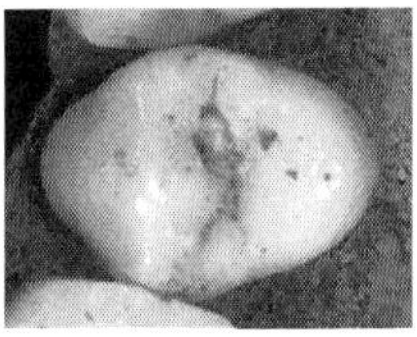

	ASUDAS Plaque: None
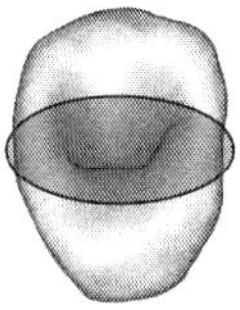	**Other Teeth Scored:** UP3
3. There are cuspules on the mesial and distal margins of the occlusal surface of the tooth at the termination of the sagittal groove. 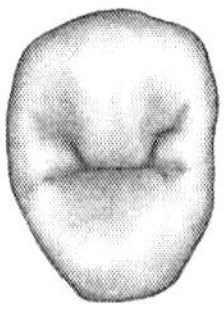 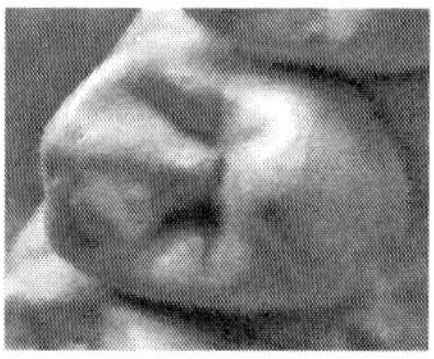 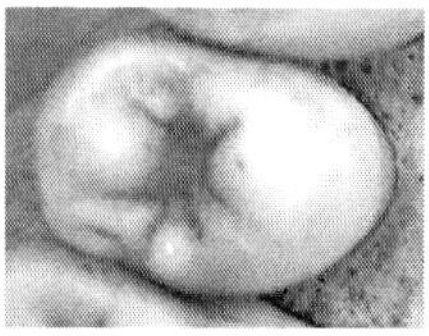	

Full Name of Trait (Abbrev.): Maxillary Premolar Distosagittal Ridge—Third (UP3DS)		
Detailed Trait Description: This observation is of the presence of a groove that runs from near or at the apex of the buccal cusp to the distal margin of the cusp. The presence of the groove results in a ridge oriented mesiodistally in an approximately sagittal (not mid-sagittal) plane. The buccal cusp is often enlarged and rotated so that the sagittal groove runs more buccolingually than usual.		
0. There is no sagittally oriented groove on the distal occlusal surface of the buccal cusp. 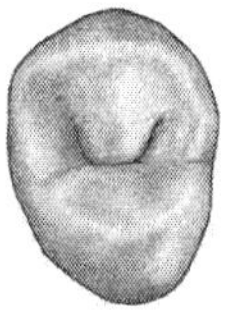 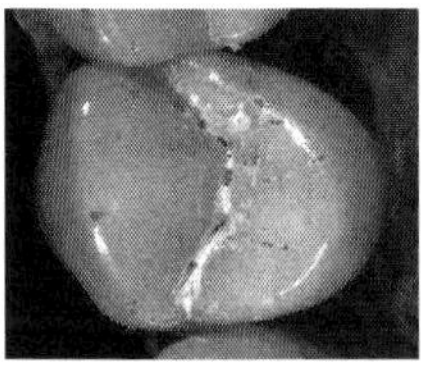 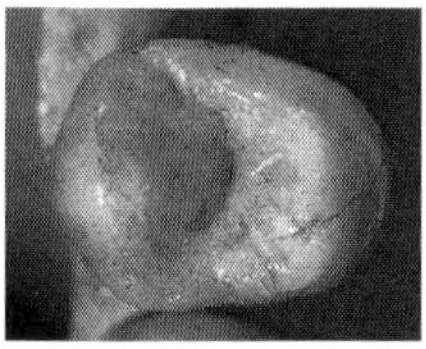	1. There is a sagittally oriented groove on the distal occlusal surface of the buccal cusp. This groove is associated with a ridge that runs distobuccaly from the apex of the buccal cusp.  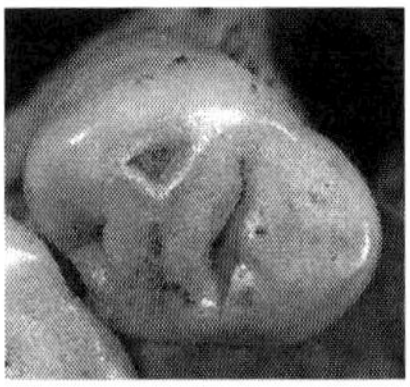 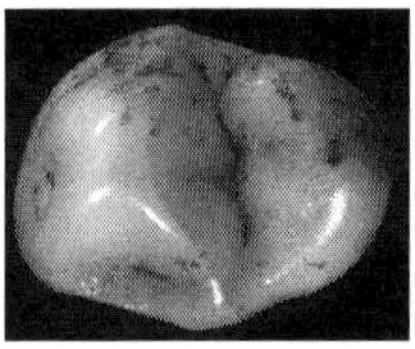	

		ASUDAS Plaque: UTO-AZTECAN PREMOLAR
		Other Teeth Scored: None

Full Name of Trait (Abbrev.): Maxillary Premolar Mesial Accessory Ridge—Third (UP3M MXPAR)		
Detailed Trait Description: Of interest here is an elevated crest mesial to the central ridge of the buccal cusp (the paracone). A crest distal to the central ridge is also scored. The original description (Burnett et al., 2010) includes an observation of whether the crest is truncated, meaning that it does not run the entire length of the cusp from the buccal margin to the medial groove. Whether a crest is truncated is not included in this description, as it is not used in statistical analyses.		
0. The area on the buccal cusp between the central ridge and the mesial margin is smooth, with no trace of a crest. 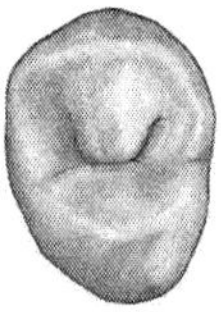 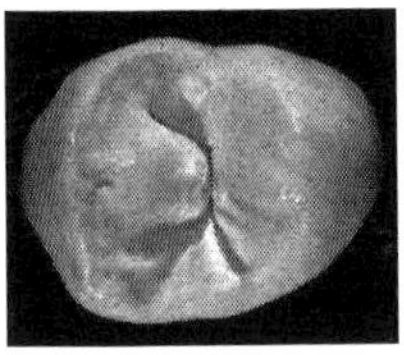 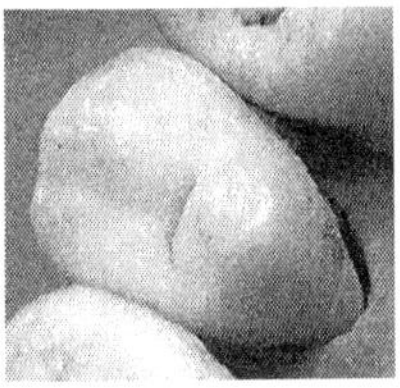	1. There is a slight crest that is observable in strong light in the area between the central ridge and the mesial margin of the buccal cusp. 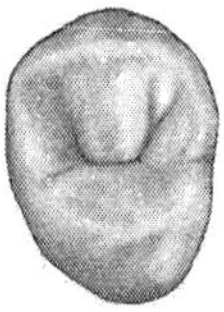 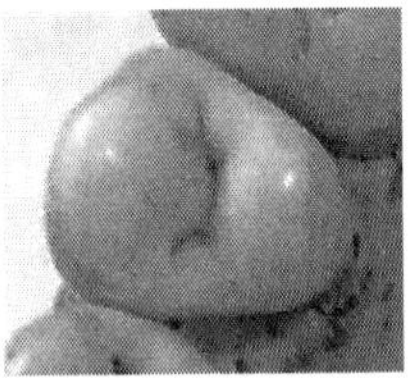 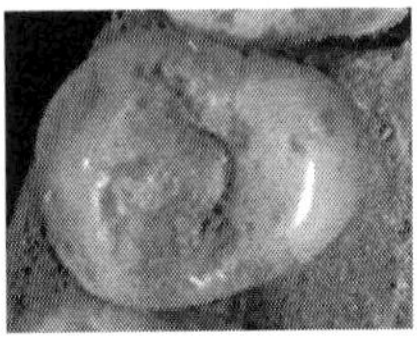	2. There is a thin crest in the area between the central ridge and the mesial margin of the buccal cusp. 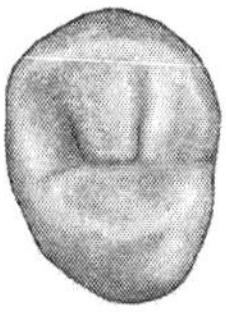 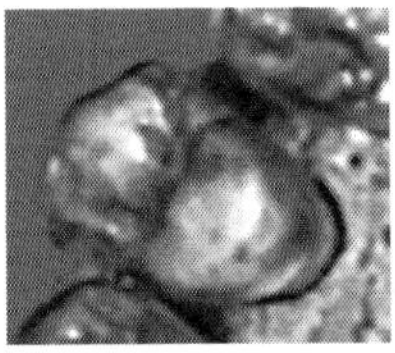 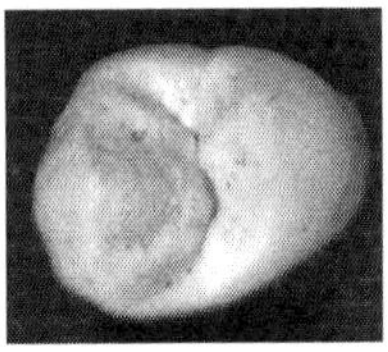

	ASUDAS Plaque: MXPAR UP1/UP2
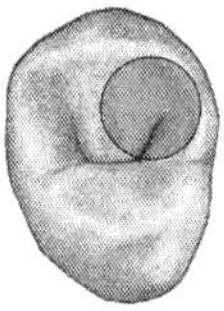	**Other Teeth Scored:** UP4
3. There is a crest in the area between the central ridge and the mesial margin of the buccal cusp. This crest is as readily observable as the central ridge, but thinner. 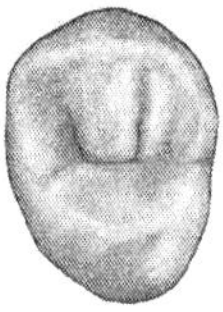 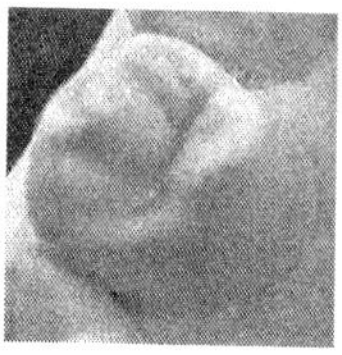	4. There is a crest in the area between the central ridge and the mesial margin of the buccal cusp. This crest is similar in size to the central ridge. 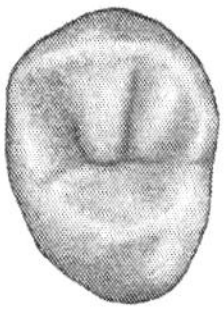 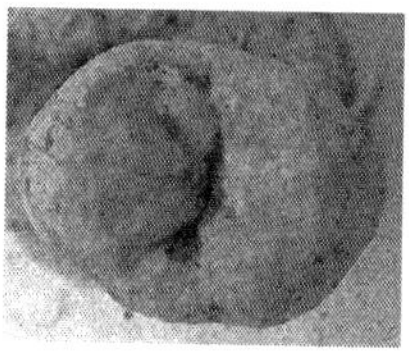 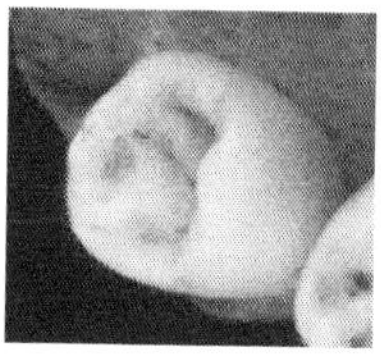

Full Name of Trait (Abbrev.): Maxillary Premolar Mesial Accessory Ridge—Fourth (UP4M MXPAR)

Detailed Trait Description: Of interest here is an elevated crest distal to the central ridge of the buccal cusp (the paracone). A crest mesial to the central ridge is also scored. The original description (Burnett et al., 2010) includes an observation of whether the crest is truncated, meaning that it does not run the entire length of the cusp from the buccal margin to the medial groove. Whether a crest is truncated is not included in this description, as it is not used in statistical analyses.

0. The area on the buccal cusp between the central ridge and the distal margin is smooth, with no trace of a crest. 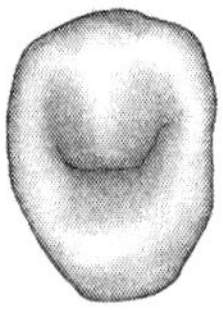 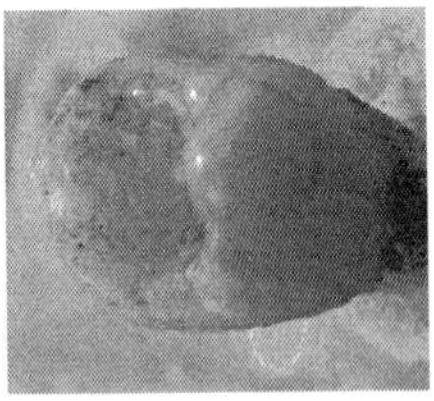 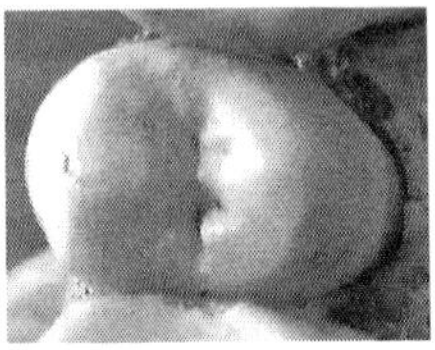	1. There is a slight crest that is observable in strong light in the area between the central ridge and the distal margin of the buccal cusp. 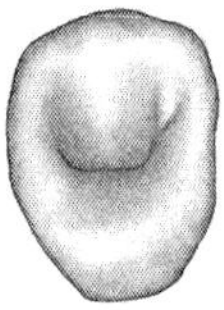	2. There is a thin crest in the area between the central ridge and the distal margin of the buccal cusp. 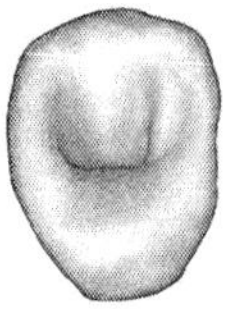 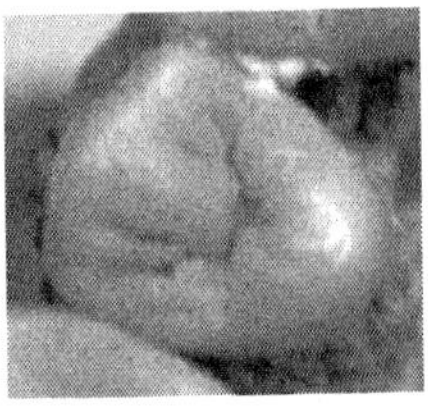 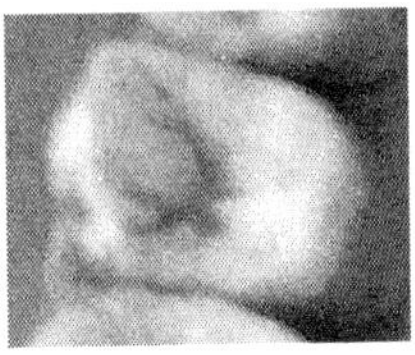

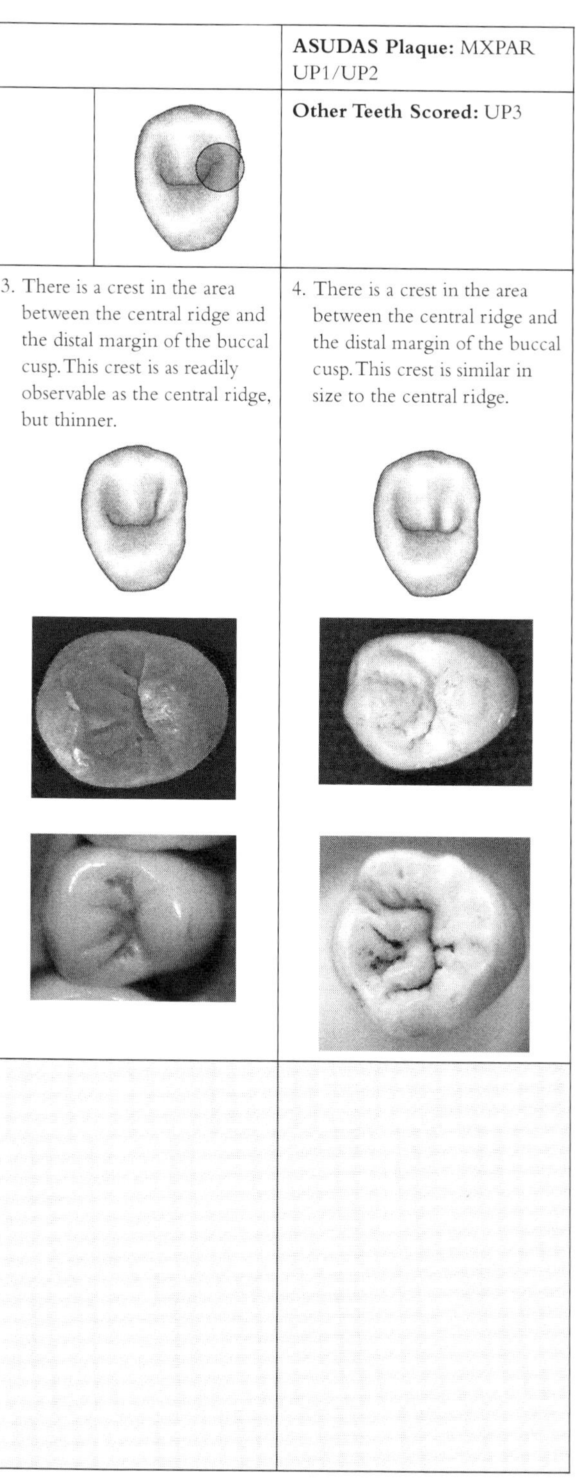

	ASUDAS Plaque: MXPAR UP1/UP2
	Other Teeth Scored: UP3
3. There is a crest in the area between the central ridge and the distal margin of the buccal cusp. This crest is as readily observable as the central ridge, but thinner.	4. There is a crest in the area between the central ridge and the distal margin of the buccal cusp. This crest is similar in size to the central ridge.

Full Name of Trait (Abbrev.): Maxillary Premolar Distal Accessory Ridge—Third (UP3D MXPAR)		
Detailed Trait Description: Of interest here is an elevated crest mesial to the central ridge of the buccal cusp (the paracone). A crest distal to the central ridge is also scored. The original description (Burnett et al., 2010) includes an observation of whether the crest is truncated, meaning that it does not run the entire length of the cusp from the buccal margin to the medial groove. Whether a crest is truncated is not included in this description, as it is not used in statistical analyses.		
0. The area on the buccal cusp between the central ridge and the mesial margin is smooth, with no trace of a crest. 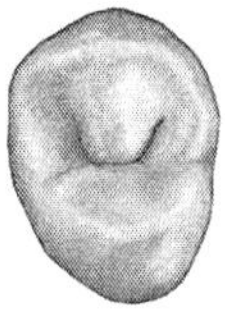 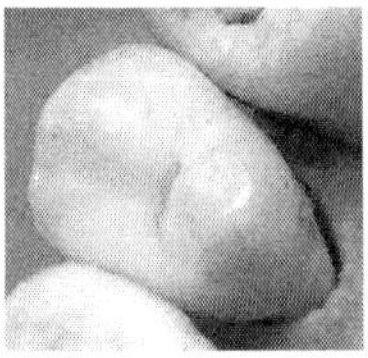 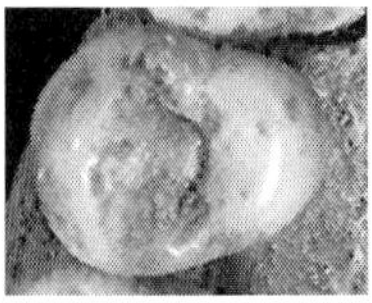	1. There is a slight crest that is observable in strong light in the area between the central ridge and the mesial margin of the buccal cusp. 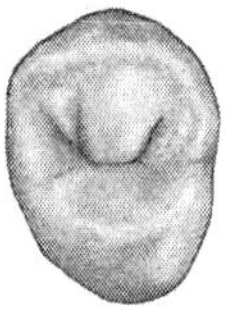 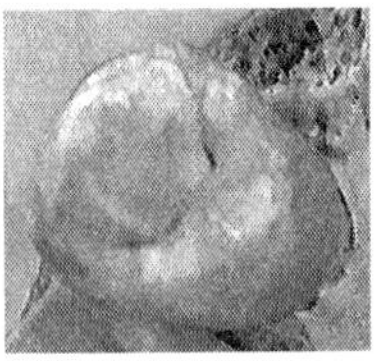 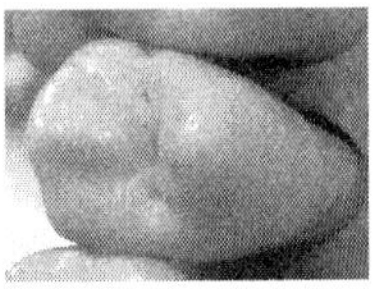	2. There is a thin crest in the area between the central ridge and the mesial margin of the buccal cusp. 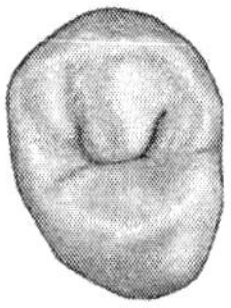 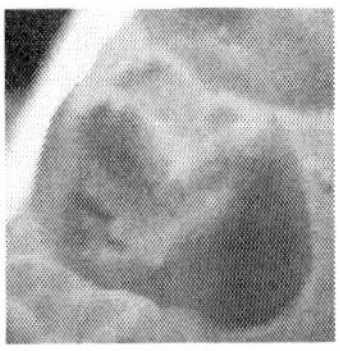 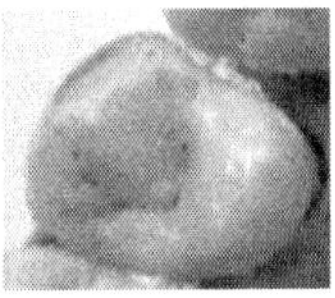

	ASUDAS Plaque: MXPAR UP1/UP2
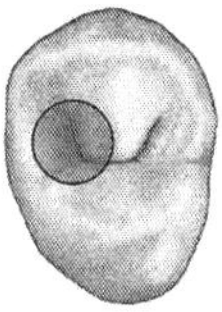	**Other Teeth Scored:** UP4
3. There is a crest in the area between the central ridge and the mesial margin of the buccal cusp. This crest is as readily observable as the central ridge, but thinner. 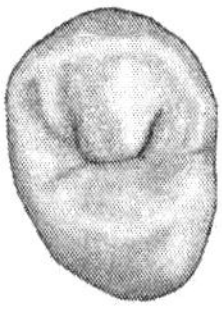 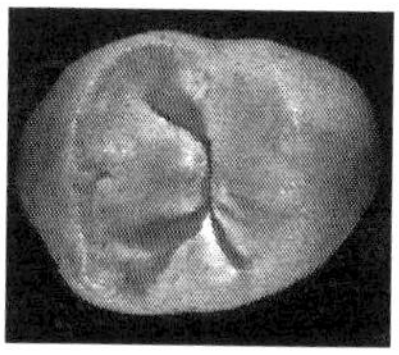 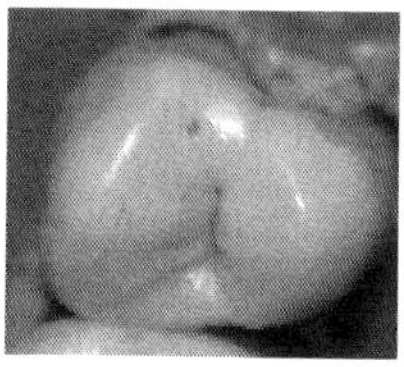	4. There is a crest in the area between the central ridge and the mesial margin of the buccal cusp. This crest is similar in size to the central ridge. 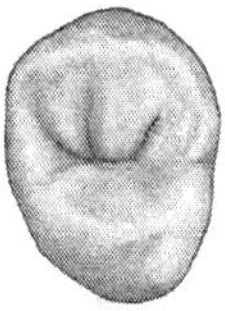 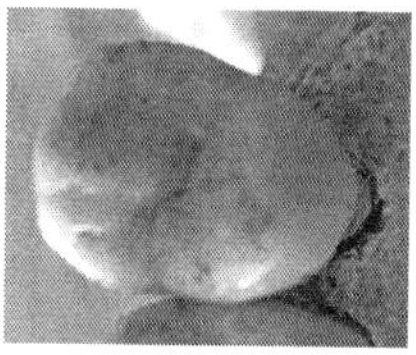 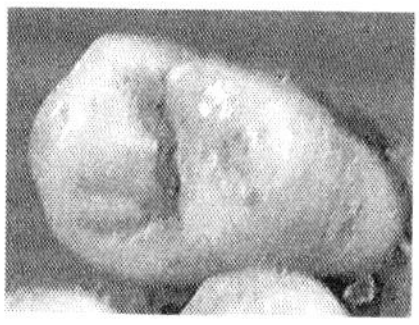

Full Name of Trait (Abbrev.): Maxillary Premolar Distal Accessory Ridge—Fourth (UP4D MXPAR)		
Detailed Trait Description: Of interest here is an elevated crest distal to the central ridge of the buccal cusp (the paracone). A crest mesial to the central ridge is also scored. The original description (Burnett et al., 2010) includes an observation of whether the crest is truncated, meaning that it does not run the entire length of the cusp from the buccal margin to the medial groove. Whether a crest is truncated is not included in this description, as it is not used in statistical analyses.		
0. The area on the buccal cusp between the central ridge and the distal margin is smooth, with no trace of a crest. 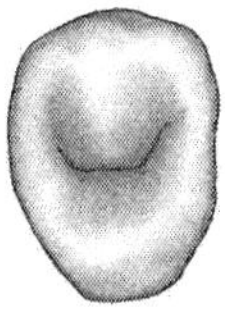 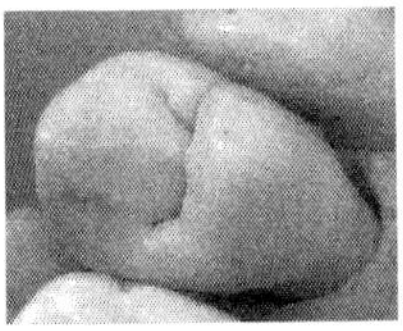 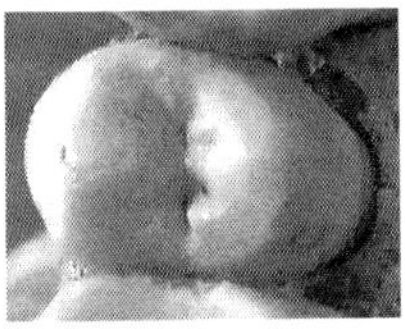	1. There is a slight crest that is observable in strong light in the area between the central ridge and the distal margin of the buccal cusp. 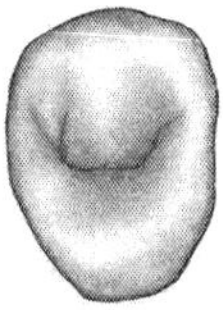 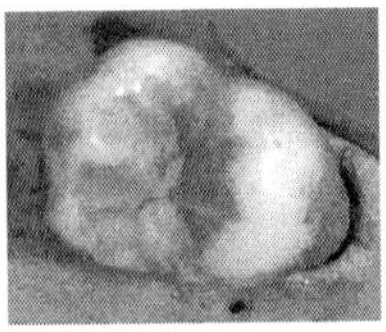 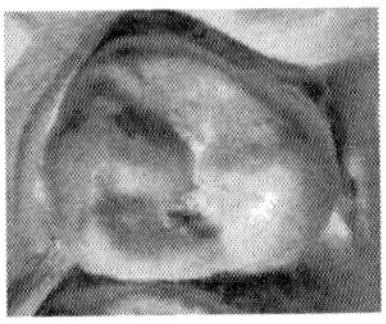	2. There is a thin crest in the area between the central ridge and the distal margin of the buccal cusp. 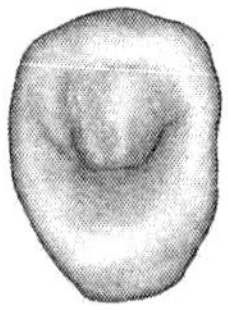 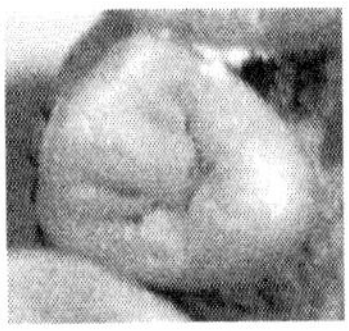

	ASUDAS Plaque: MXPAR UP1/UP2
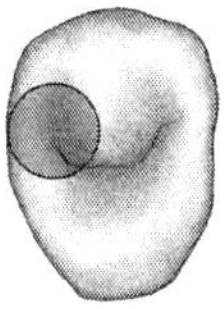	**Other Teeth Scored:** UP3
3. There is a crest in the area between the central ridge and the distal margin of the buccal cusp. This crest is as readily observable as the central ridge, but thinner. 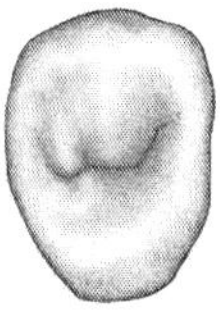 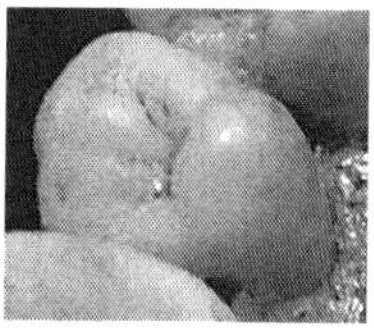 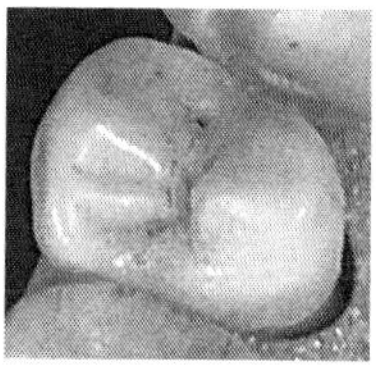	4. There is a crest in the area between the central ridge and the distal margin of the buccal cusp. This crest is similar in size to the central ridge. 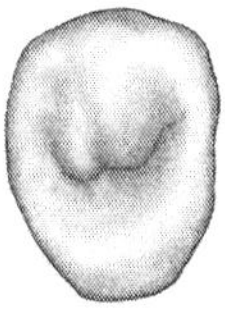 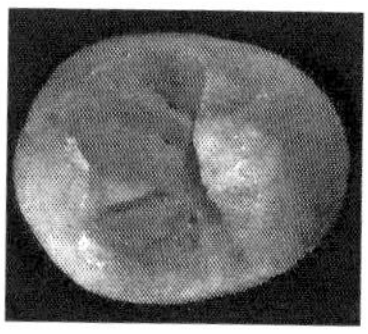

<table>
<tr><td colspan="3">Full Name of Trait (Abbrev.): Maxillary Molar Metacone—First (UM1MC)</td></tr>
<tr><td colspan="3">Detailed Trait Description: This observation concerns the size of cusp 3: the distobuccal cusp of the tooth. In general, the more square the tooth appears, the higher the grade of the trait. For ease of statistical analysis, Turner et al.'s (1991) scores 3, 3.5, 4, and 5 are listed here as 3, 4, 5, and 6.</td></tr>
<tr><td>0. No third cusp is present. The area is smooth.
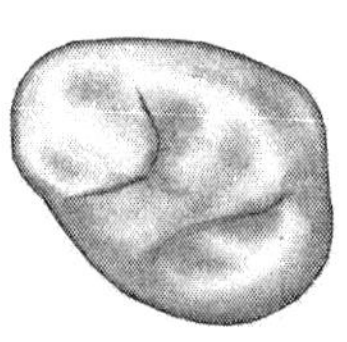
</td><td>1. There is a ridge without a free apex at the site of the metacone.
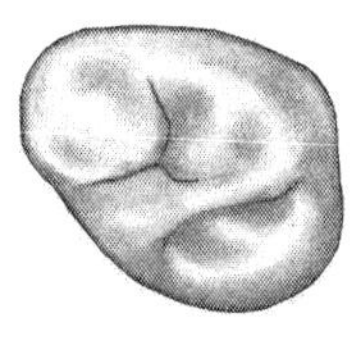
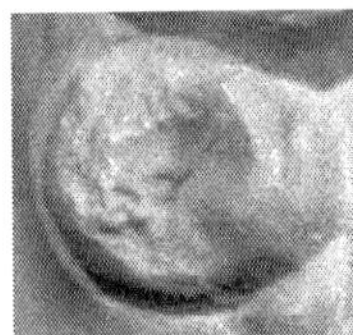</td><td>2. A faint cuspule with a free apex is present.
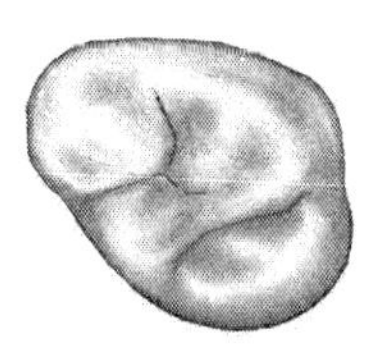
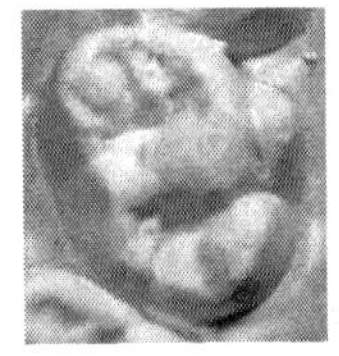
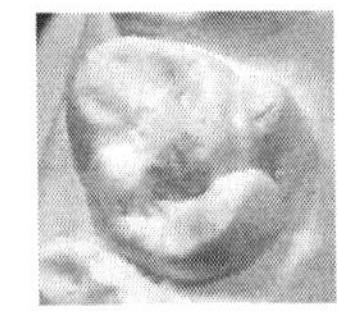</td></tr>
<tr><td>5. A large cusp is present. The cusp will be approximately the same size as the mesiobuccal cusp (cusp 1).
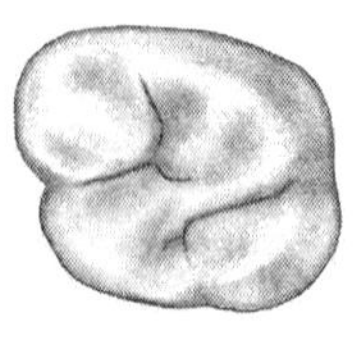

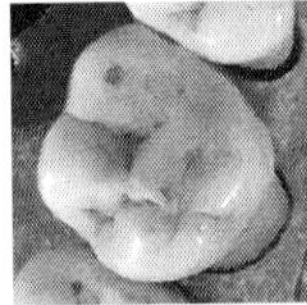</td><td>6. A very large cusp is present. The cusp will be larger than the mesiobuccal cusp (cusp 1).
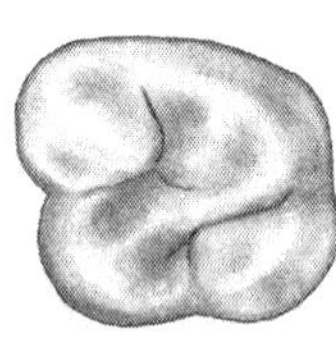
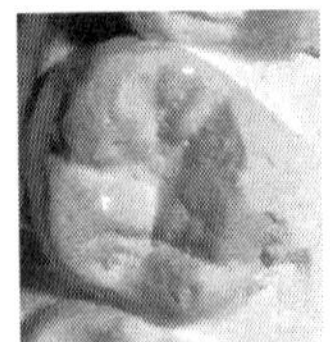</td><td></td></tr>
</table>

	ASUDAS Plaque: METACONE CUSP 3
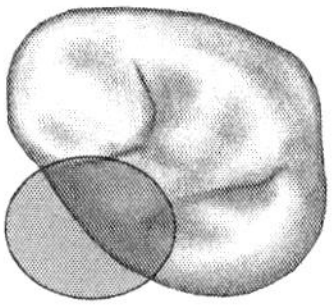	**Other Teeth Scored:** UM2; UM3
3. A small cusp, about one-third the size of the mesiobuccal cusp (cusp 1), is present. 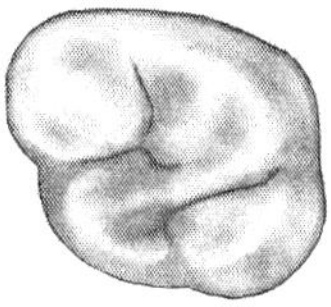 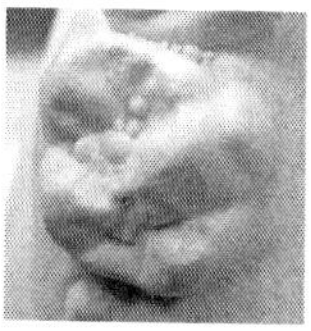 	4. A moderate cusp, half to two-thirds the size of the mesiobuccal cusp (cusp 1), is present. 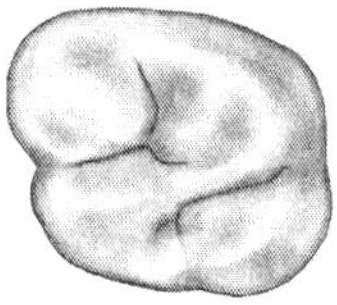 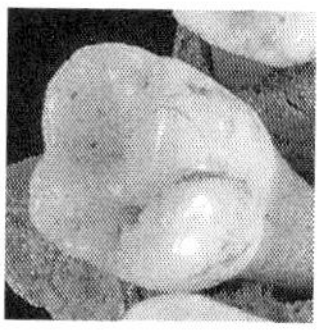 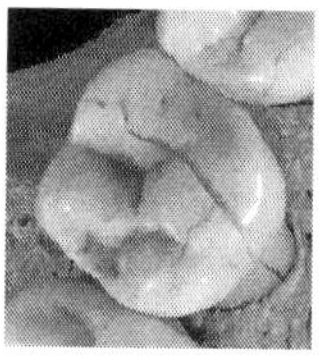

Full Name of Trait (Abbrev.): Maxillary Molar Metacone—Second (UM2MC)

Detailed Trait Description: This observation concerns the size of cusp 3, the distobuccal cusp of the tooth. In general, the more square the tooth appears, the higher the grade of the trait. For ease of statistical analysis, Turner et al.'s (1991) scores 3, 3.5, 4, and 5, are listed here as 3, 4, 5, and 6.

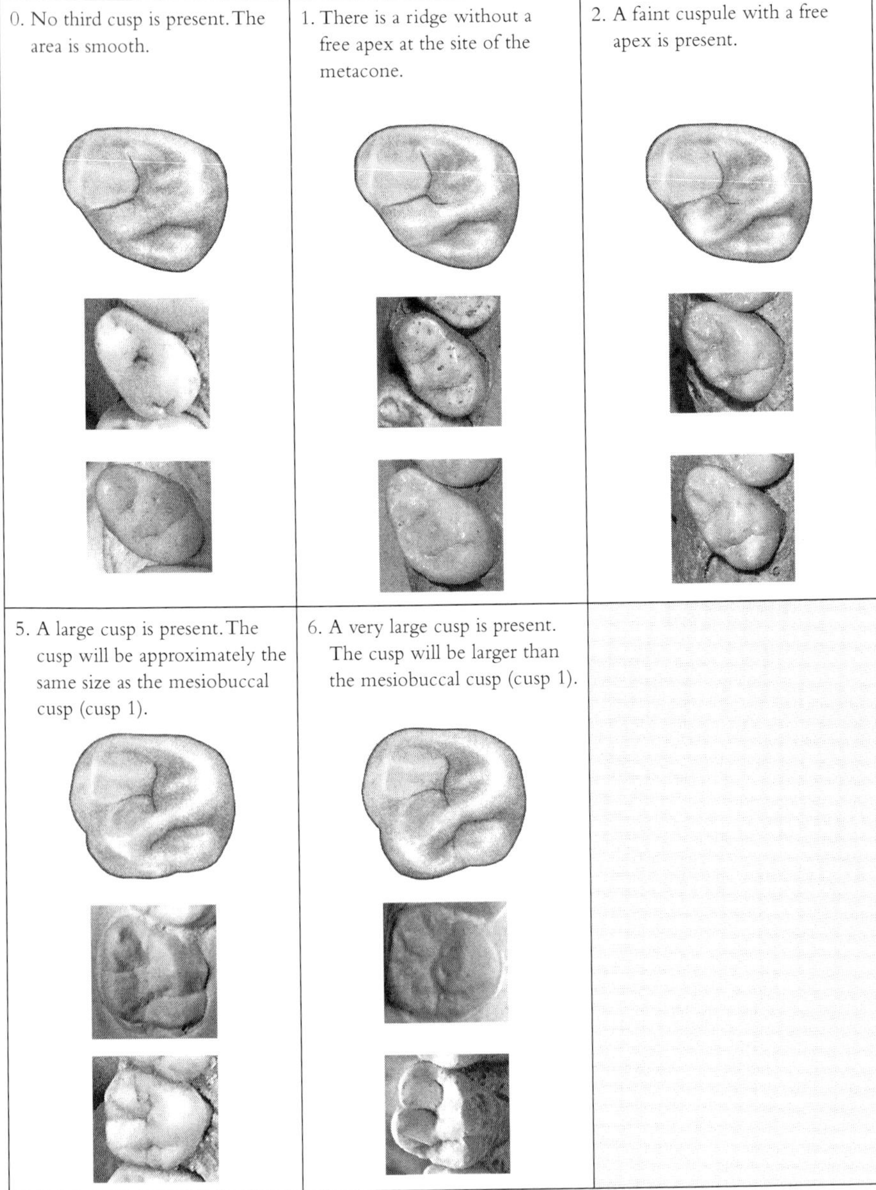

0. No third cusp is present. The area is smooth.	1. There is a ridge without a free apex at the site of the metacone.	2. A faint cuspule with a free apex is present.
5. A large cusp is present. The cusp will be approximately the same size as the mesiobuccal cusp (cusp 1).	6. A very large cusp is present. The cusp will be larger than the mesiobuccal cusp (cusp 1).	

	ASUDAS Plaque: METACONE CUSP 3
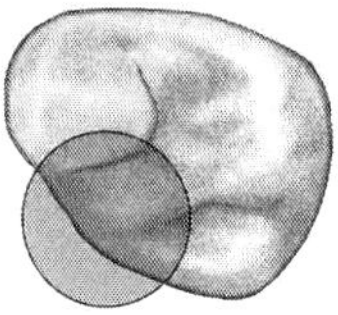	**Other Teeth Scored:** UM1; UM3
3. A small cusp, about one-third the size of the mesiobuccal cusp (cusp 1), is present. 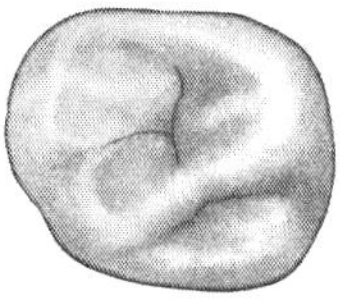 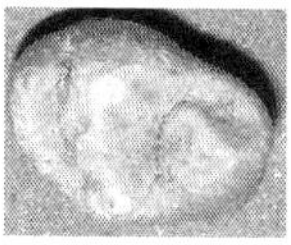 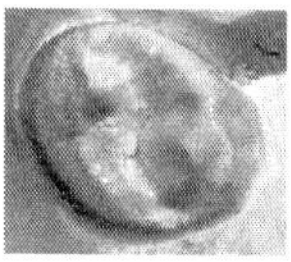	4. A moderate cusp, half to two-thirds the size of the mesiobuccal cusp (cusp 1), is present. 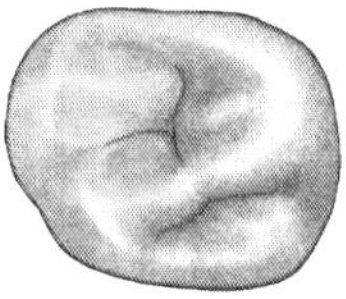  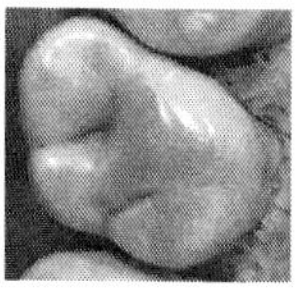

Full Name of Trait (Abbrev.): Maxillary Molar Hypocone—First (UM1HC)

Detailed Trait Description: This observation concerns the size of cusp 4, the distolingual cusp of the tooth. In general, more triangular teeth are associated with lower grades, while more square teeth are associated with higher grades for this trait. For ease of statistical analysis, Turner et al.'s (1991) scores 3, 3.5, 4, and 5, are listed here as 3, 4, 5, and 6.

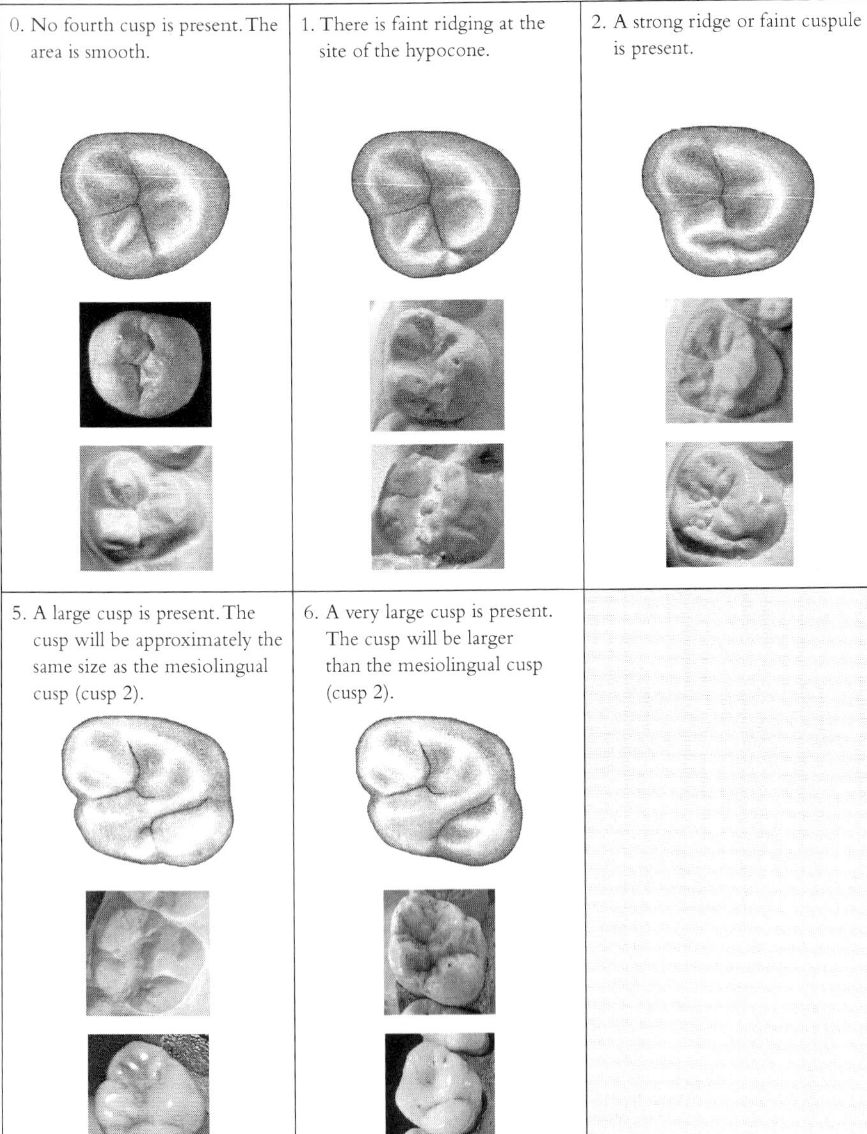

	ASUDAS Plaque: HYPOCONE CUSP 4
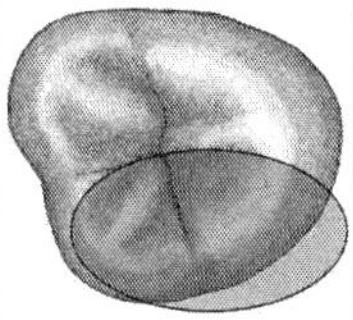	**Other Teeth Scored:** UM2; UM3
3. A small cusp is present and is one-third to two-thirds the size of the mesiolingual cusp (cusp 2). 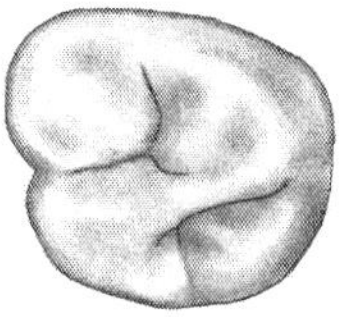  	4. A moderate cusp is present and is almost as large as the mesiolingual cusp (cusp 2). 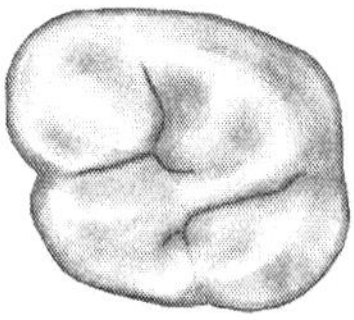  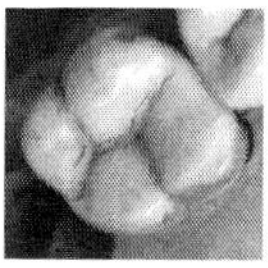

Full Name of Trait (Abbrev.): Maxillary Molar Hypocone—Second (UM2HC)

Detailed Trait Description: This observation concerns the size of cusp 4, the distolingual cusp of the tooth. In general, more triangular teeth are associated with lower grades, while more square teeth are associated with higher grades for this trait. For ease of statistical analysis, Turner et al.'s (1991) scores 3, 3.5, 4, and 5, are listed here as 3, 4, 5, and 6.

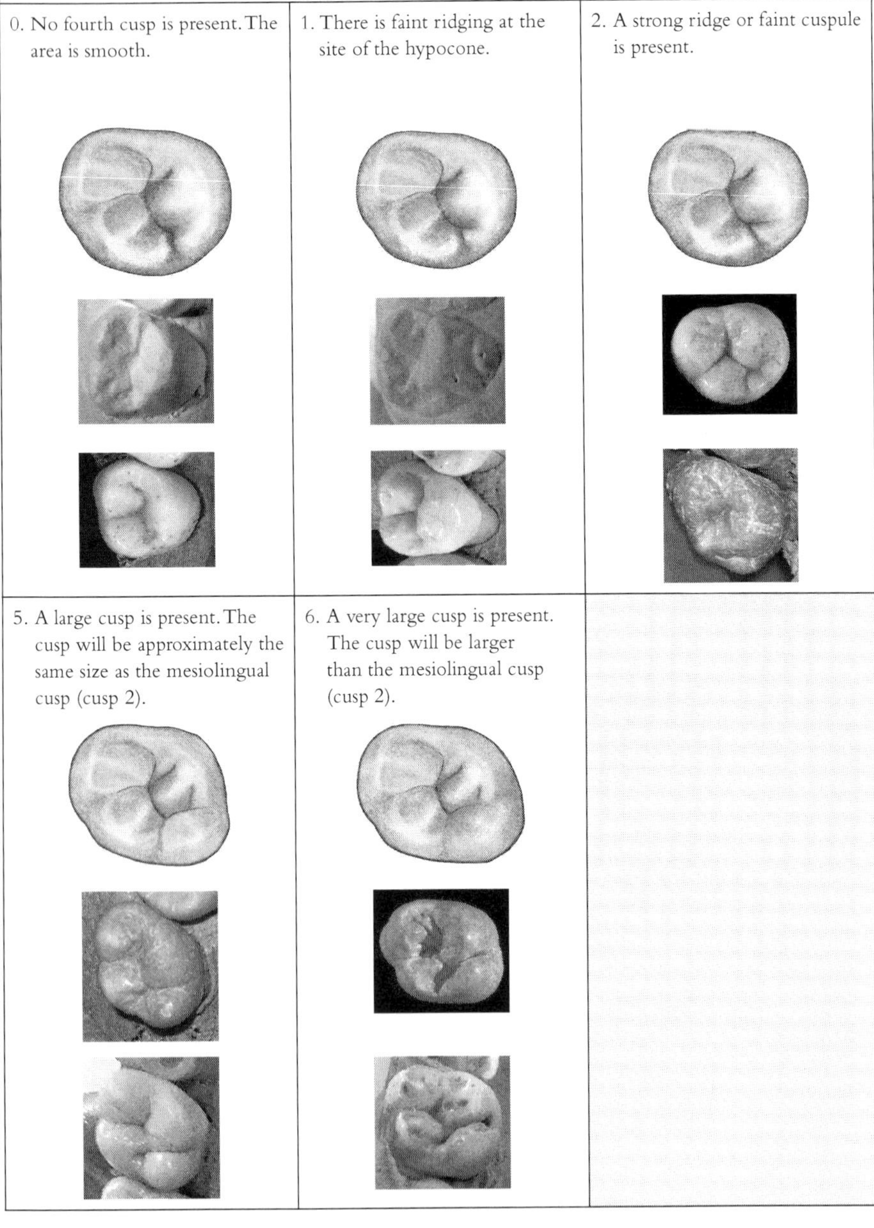

0. No fourth cusp is present. The area is smooth.

1. There is faint ridging at the site of the hypocone.

2. A strong ridge or faint cuspule is present.

5. A large cusp is present. The cusp will be approximately the same size as the mesiolingual cusp (cusp 2).

6. A very large cusp is present. The cusp will be larger than the mesiolingual cusp (cusp 2).

	ASUDAS Plaque: HYPOCONE CUSP 4
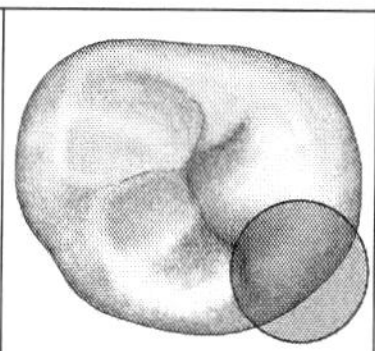	**Other Teeth Scored:** UM1; UM3
3. A small cusp is present and is one-third to two-thirds the size of the mesiolingual cusp (cusp 2). 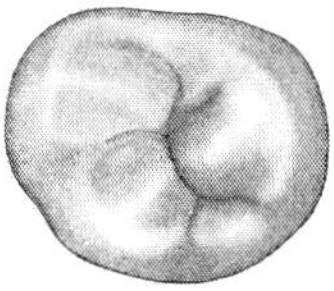 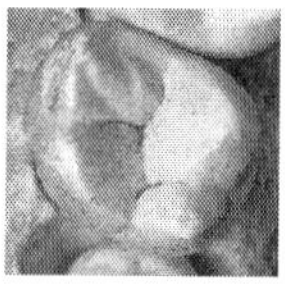 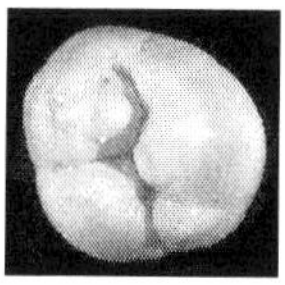	4. A moderate cusp is present and is almost as large as the mesiolingual cusp (cusp 2). 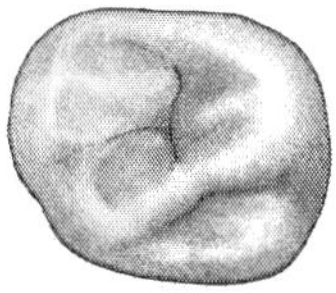 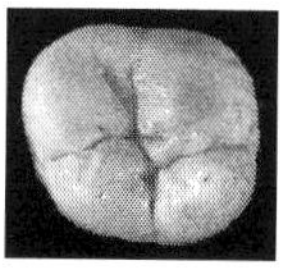 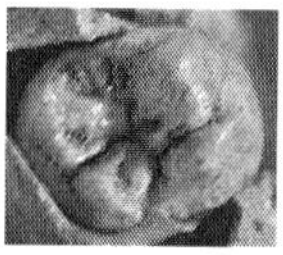

Full Name of Trait (Abbrev.): Maxillary Molar Metaconule—First (UM1C5)		
Detailed Trait Description: There can be a fifth cusp, or metaconule, along the distal margin of the occlusal surface of the tooth between the metacone (cusp 3) and the hypocone (cusp 4). Metaconule expression is usually higher on M1 than on M2.		
0. The site of the metaconule is a groove separating the distobuccal and distolingual cusps (cusps 3 and 4).	1. The groove separating the distobuccal and distolingual cusps (cusps 3 and 4) is absent. Instead, there is a flat area or a very small cuspule.	2. A low cuspule about one-quarter the size of the distobuccal cusp (cusp 3) is present.
5. A large cusp is present, and is one-half or more the size of the distobuccal cusp (cusp 3), causing a bulge in the distal margin of the tooth.		

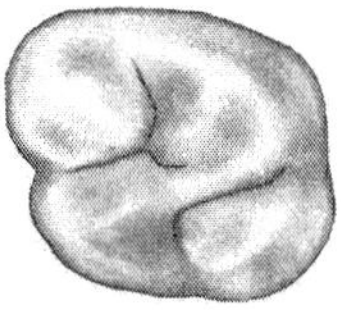

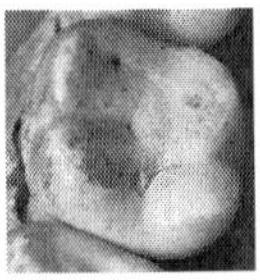

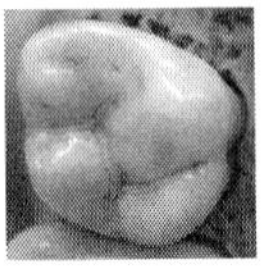

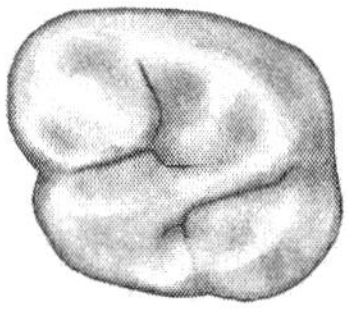

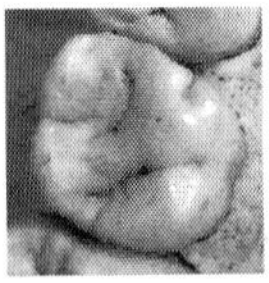

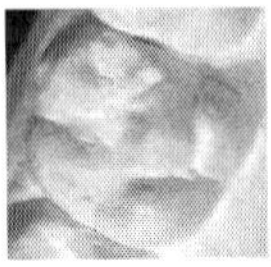

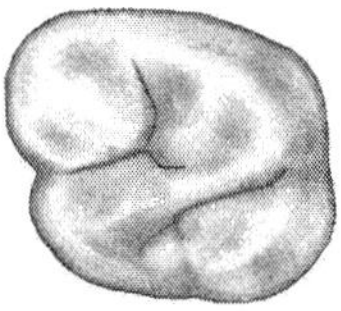

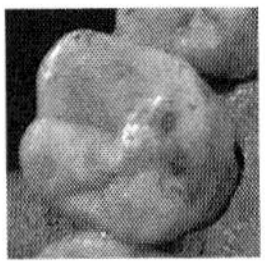

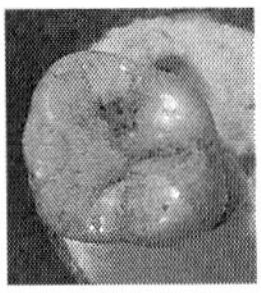

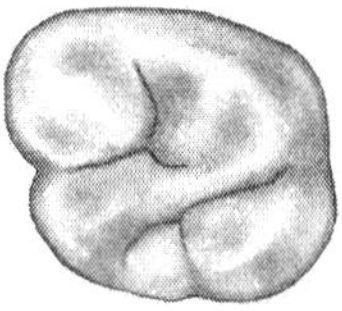

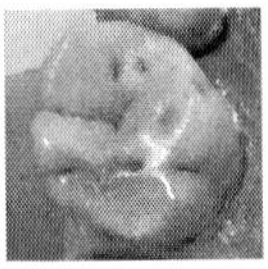

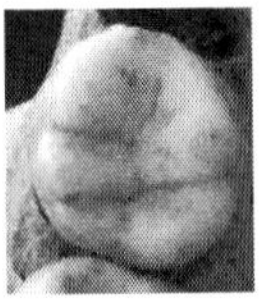

	ASUDAS Plaque: UM CUSP 5
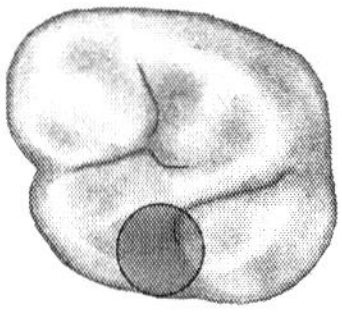	**Other Teeth Scored:** UM2; UM3
3. A small cusp is present. The cusp is more prominent than in lower grades and approximately one-quarter to one-third the size of the distobuccal cusp (cusp 3). 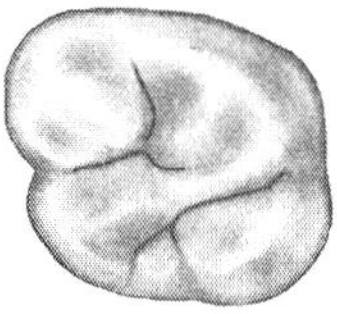 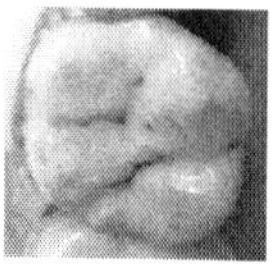 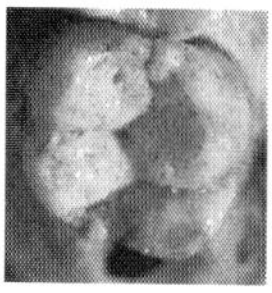	4. A medium cusp is present. The cusp is between one-third and one-half the size of the distobuccal cusp (cusp 3). 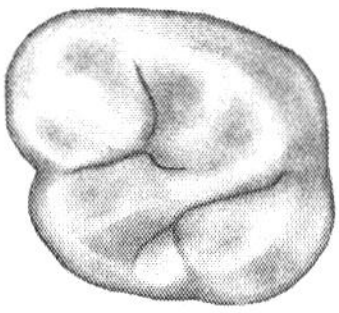 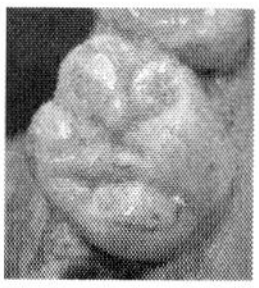 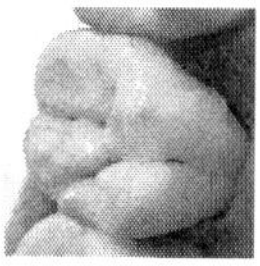

Full Name of Trait (Abbrev.): Maxillary Molar Metaconule—Second (UM2C5)

Detailed Trait Description: There can be a fifth cusp, or metaconule, along the distal margin of the occlusal surface of the tooth, between cusps 3 and 4. Metaconule expression is usually weaker on M2 than on M1.

0. The site of the metaconule is a groove separating the distobuccal and distolingual cusps (cusps 3 and 4).	1. The groove separating the distobuccal and distolingual cusps (cusps 3 and 4) is absent. Instead, there is a flat area or a very small cuspule.	2. A low cuspule about one-quarter the size of the distobuccal cusp (cusp 3) is present.
5. A large cusp is present, and is one-half or more the size of the distobuccal cusp (cusp 3), causing a bulge in the distal margin of the tooth.		

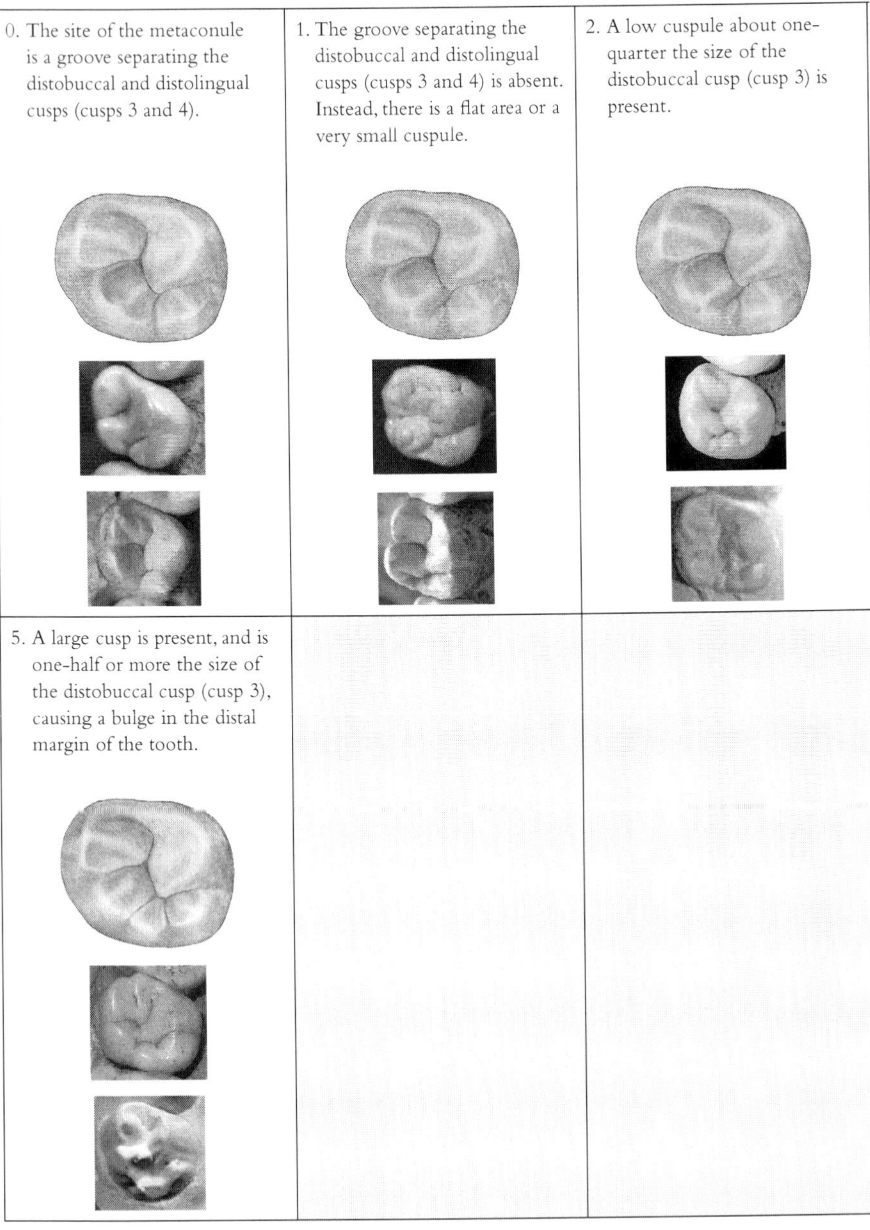

	ASUDAS Plaque: UM CUSP 5
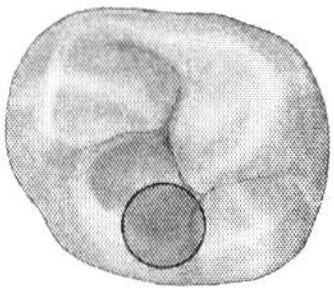	**Other Teeth Scored:** UM1; UM3
3. A small cusp is present. The cusp is more prominent than in lower grades and approximately one-quarter to one-third the size of the distobuccal cusp (cusp 3). 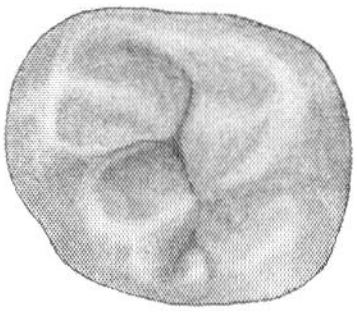 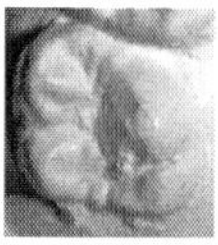 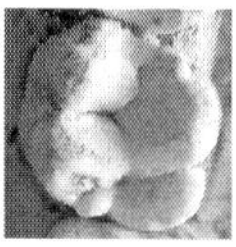	4. A medium cusp is present. The cusp is between one-third and one-half the size of the distobuccal cusp (cusp 3). 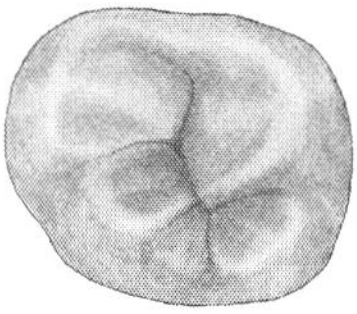  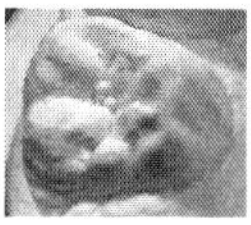

Full Name of Trait (Abbrev.): Maxillary Molar Carabelli's Trait—First (UM1CB)

Detailed Trait Description: This trait is found on the lingual surface of the mesiolingual cusp (cusp 1). It varies from a groove to a pit, complex groove, or accessory cusp. Expression is generally much stronger and more common on UM1 than on UM2.

<table>
<tr>
<td>0. The lingual surface of the mesiolingual cusp (cusp 1) is smooth.
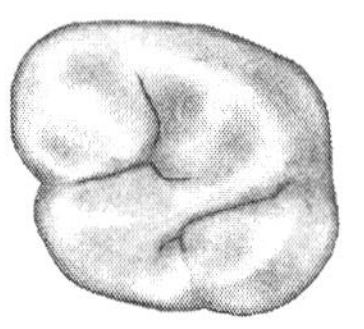
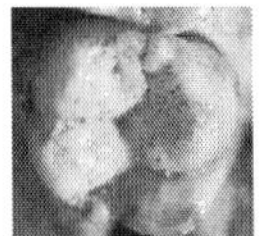
</td>
<td>1. A shallow groove runs in an occlusal-apical direction on the mesiolingual cusp.
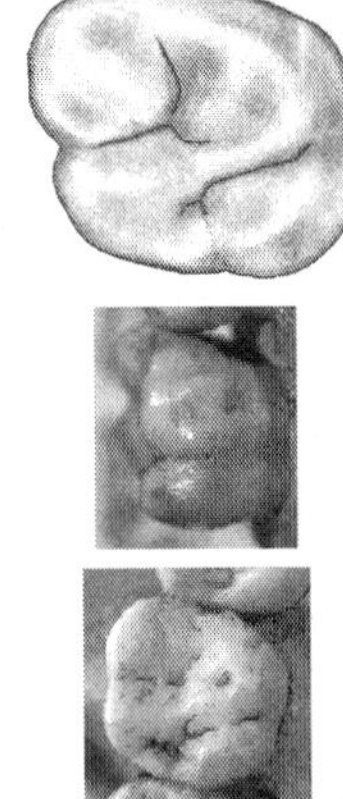</td>
<td>2. There is a pit on the lingual surface of the mesiolingual cusp.
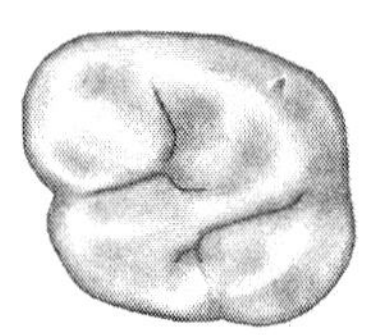
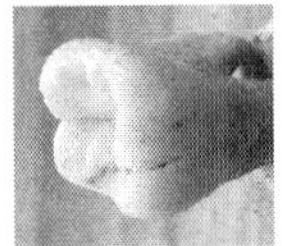
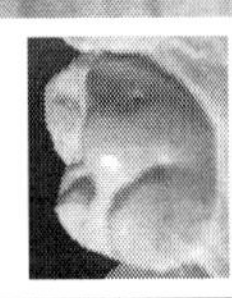</td>
</tr>
<tr>
<td>5. There is a bulge that forms a small cusp without a free apex. The distal margin of this bulge does not contact the groove that separates the lingual surfaces of the mesiolingual and distolingual cusps.
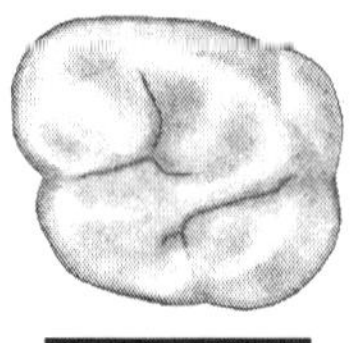

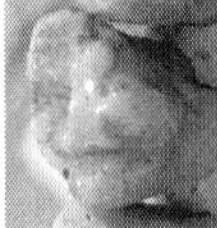</td>
<td>6. There is a distinct cusp without a free apex on the lingual surface. The margin of this cusp is in contact with the groove that separates the lingual surfaces of the mesiolingual and distolingual cusps.
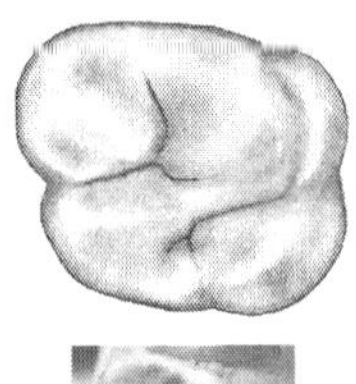
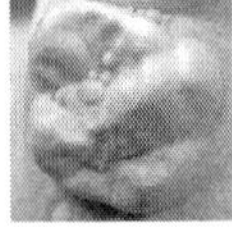
</td>
<td>7. The cusp on the lingual surface of the mesiolingual cusp is large and has a free apex.
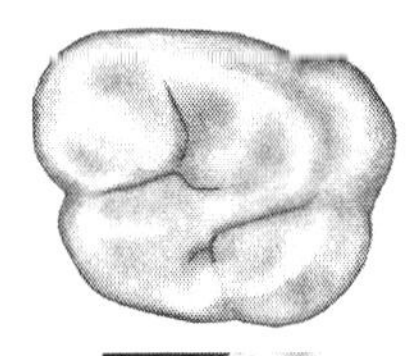
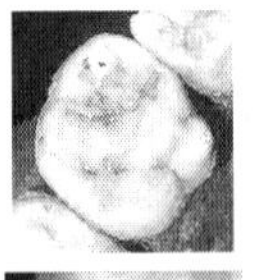
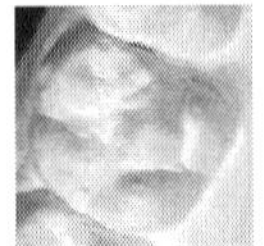</td>
</tr>
</table>

	ASUDAS Plaque: CARABELLIS CUSP
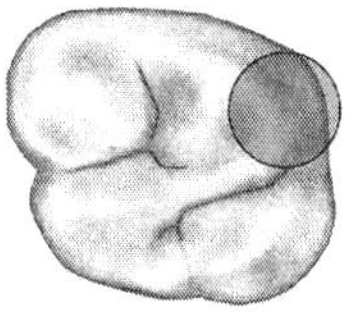	**Other Teeth Scored:** UM2; UM3
3. There is a small, shallow Y-shaped groove on the lingual surface of the mesiolingual cusp. 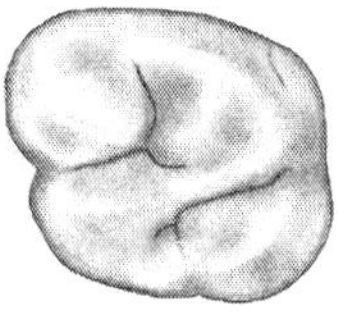  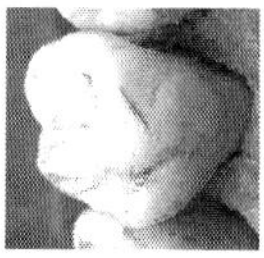	4. There is a distinct Y-shaped groove on the lingual surface of the mesiolingual cusp. 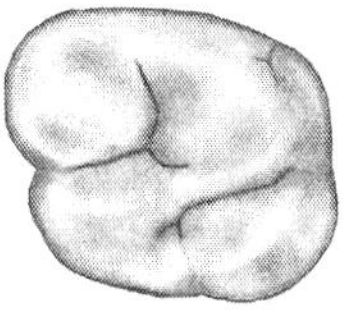 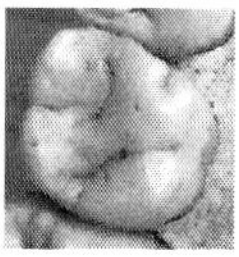 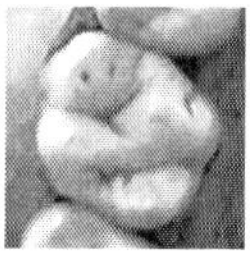

Full Name of Trait (Abbrev.): Maxillary Molar Carabelli's Trait—Second (UM2CB)

Detailed Trait Description: This trait is found on the lingual surface of the mesiolingual cusp (cusp 1). It varies from a groove to a pit, complex groove, or accessory cusp. Expression is generally much stronger and more common on UM1 than on UM2.

0. The lingual surface of the mesiolingual cusp (cusp 1) is smooth.

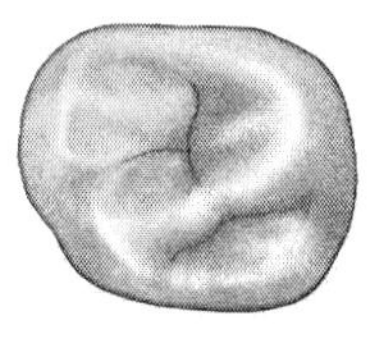
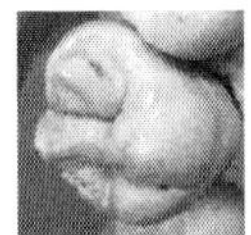
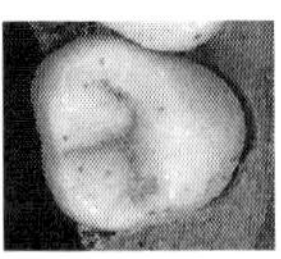

1. A shallow groove runs in an occlusal-apical direction on the mesiolingual cusp.

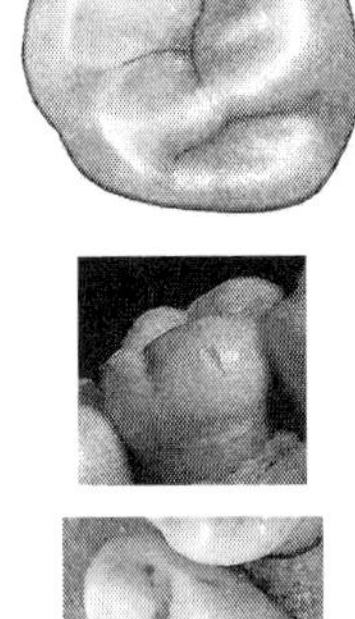

2. There is a pit on the lingual surface of the mesiolingual cusp.

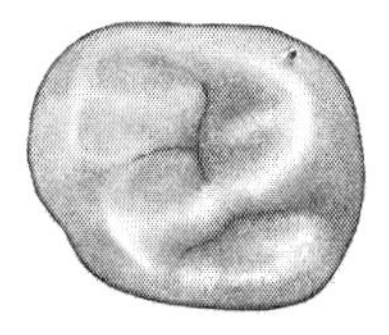

5. There is a bulge that forms a small cusp without a free apex. The distal margin of this bulge does not contact the groove that separates the lingual surfaces of the mesiolingual and distolingual cusps.

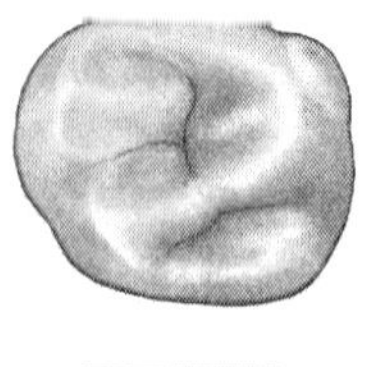
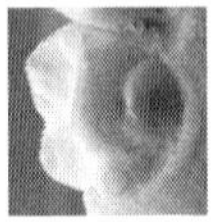
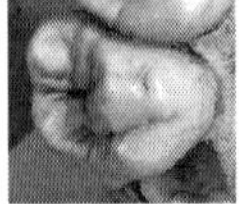

6. There is a distinct cusp without a free apex on the lingual surface. The margin of this cusp is in contact with the groove that separates the lingual surfaces of the mesiolingual and distolingual cusps.

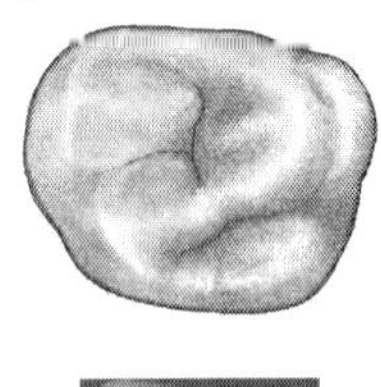
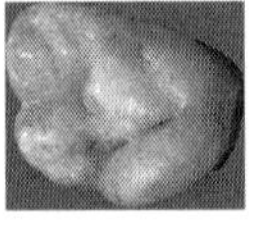

7. The cusp on the lingual surface of the mesiolingual cusp is large and has a free apex.

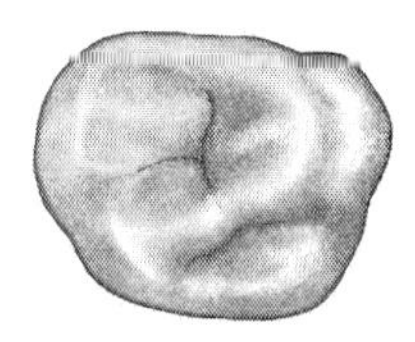
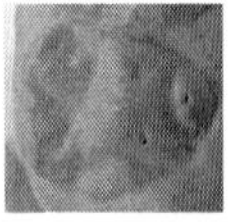
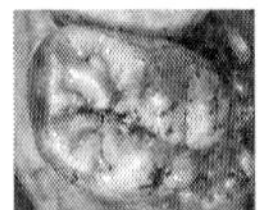

	ASUDAS Plaque: CARABELLIS CUSP
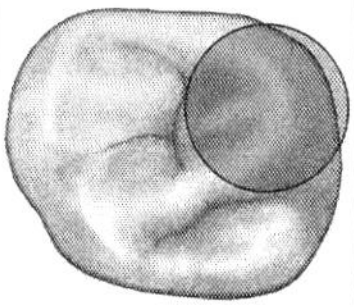	**Other Teeth Scored:** UM2; UM3
3. There is a small, shallow Y-shaped groove on the lingual surface of the mesiolingual cusp. 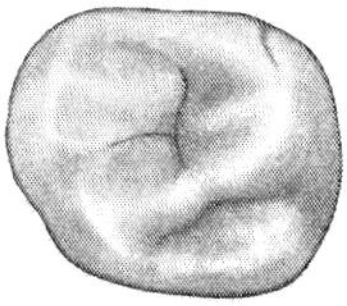  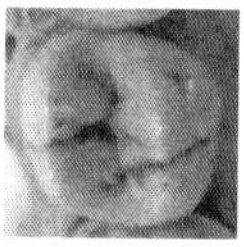	4. There is a distinct Y-shaped groove on the lingual surface of the mesiolingual cusp. 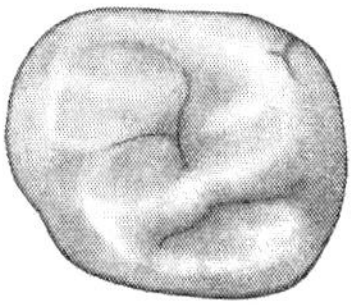 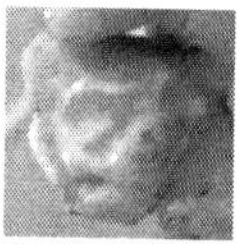 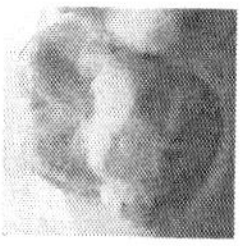

Full Name of Trait (Abbrev.): Maxillary Molar Parastyle—First (UM1PS)
Detailed Trait Description: This trait is found on the buccal surface of the mesiobuccal cusp (cusp 2). On a rare occasion, it may be found on the buccal surface of the distobuccal cusp (cusp 3). It ranges from a pit to a large cusp. It is most often found on the third molar and is often expressed only on one antimere.

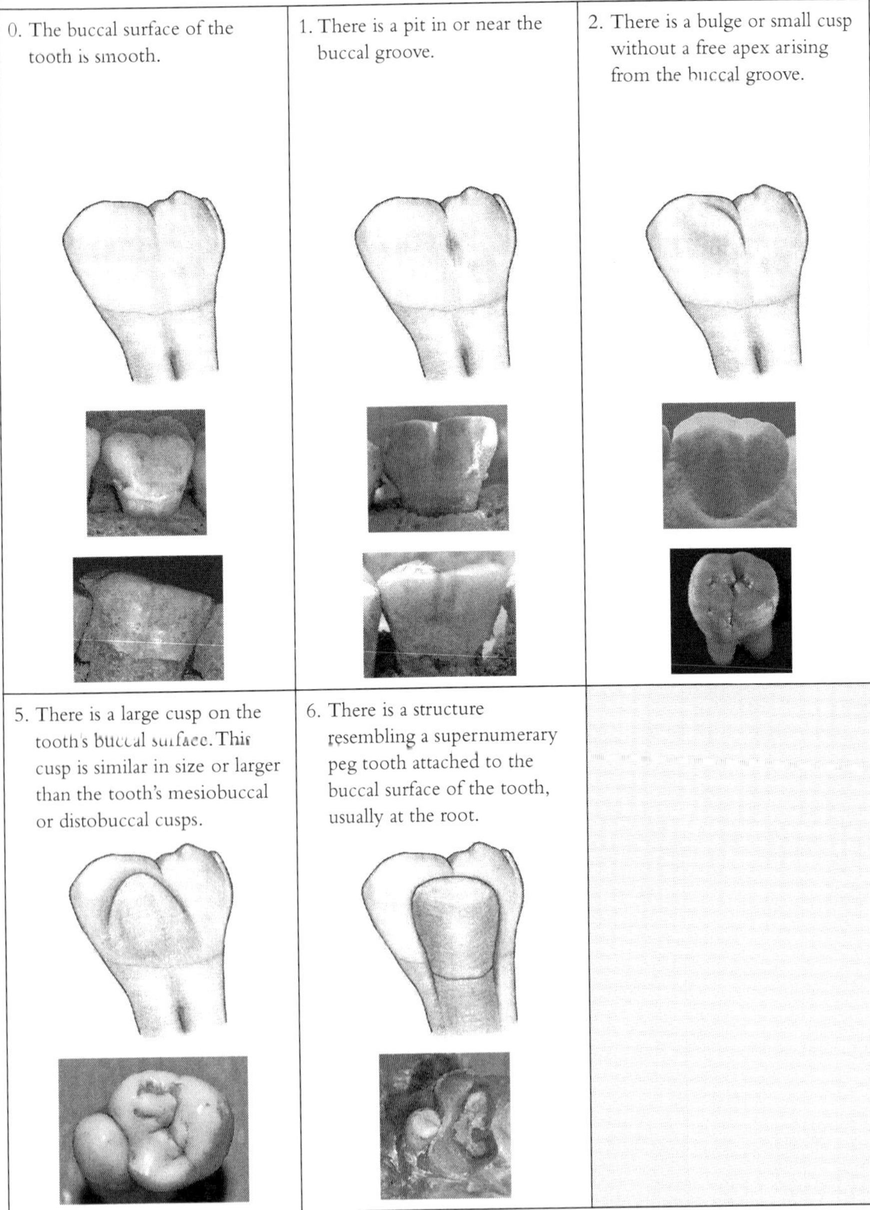

0. The buccal surface of the tooth is smooth.	1. There is a pit in or near the buccal groove.	2. There is a bulge or small cusp without a free apex arising from the buccal groove.
5. There is a large cusp on the tooth's buccal surface. This cusp is similar in size or larger than the tooth's mesiobuccal or distobuccal cusps.	6. There is a structure resembling a supernumerary peg tooth attached to the buccal surface of the tooth, usually at the root.	

	ASUDAS Plaque: PARASTYLE
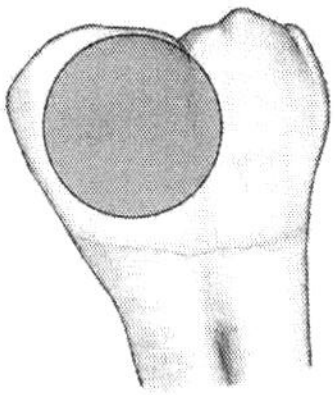	**Other Teeth Scored:** UM2; UM3
3. There is a small- to medium-sized cusp with a free apex on the buccal surface. This cusp is one-quarter to one-half the size of the mesiobuccal cusp (cusp 2). 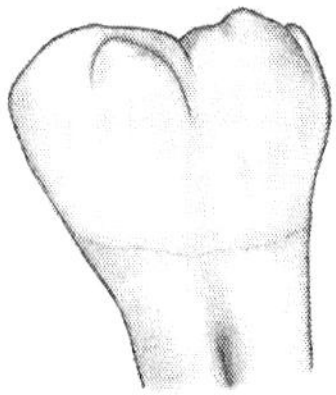 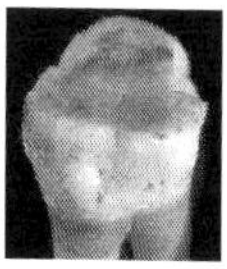	4. There is a medium to large cusp on the tooth's buccal surface. This cusp is distinct, but still smaller than the tooth's mesiobuccal or distobuccal cusps. 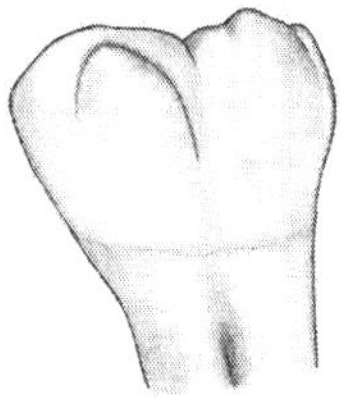 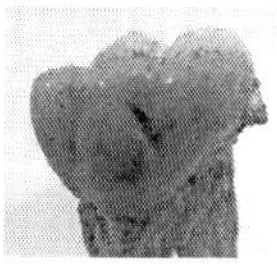

Full Name of Trait (Abbrev.): Maxillary Molar Parastyle—Second (UM2PS)

Detailed Trait Description: This trait is found on the buccal surface of the mesiobuccal cusp (cusp 2). On a rare occasion, it may be found on the buccal surface of the distobuccal cusp (cusp 3). It ranges from a pit to a large cusp. It is most often found on the third molar and is often expressed only on one antimere.

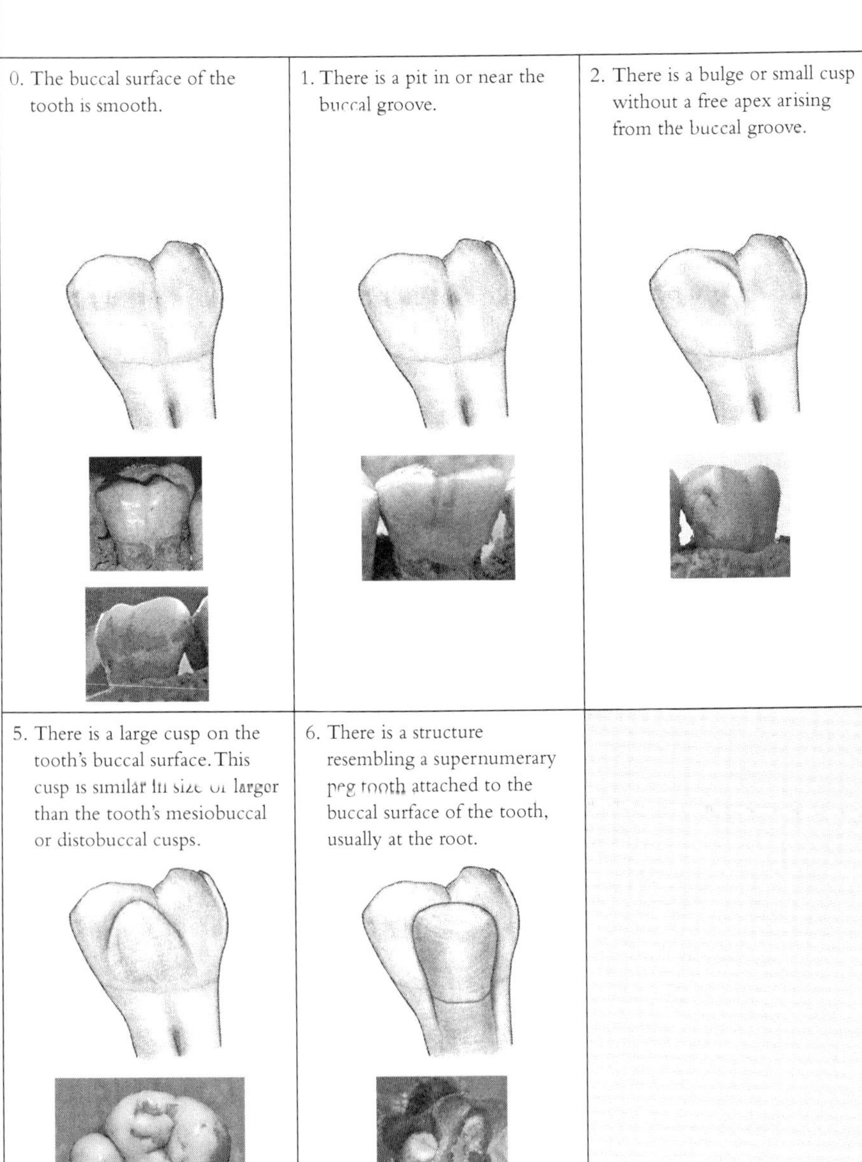

0. The buccal surface of the tooth is smooth.

1. There is a pit in or near the buccal groove.

2. There is a bulge or small cusp without a free apex arising from the buccal groove.

5. There is a large cusp on the tooth's buccal surface. This cusp is similar in size or larger than the tooth's mesiobuccal or distobuccal cusps.

6. There is a structure resembling a supernumerary peg tooth attached to the buccal surface of the tooth, usually at the root.

	ASUDAS Plaque: PARASTYLE
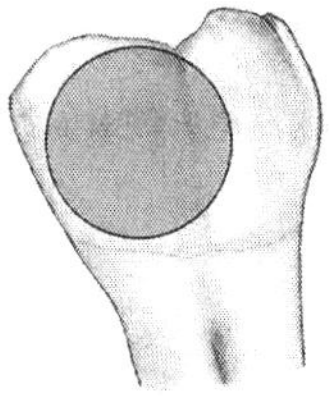	**Other Teeth Scored:** UM1; UM3
3. There is a small- to medium-sized cusp with a free apex on the buccal surface. This cusp is one-quarter to one-half the size of the mesiobuccal cusp (cusp 2). 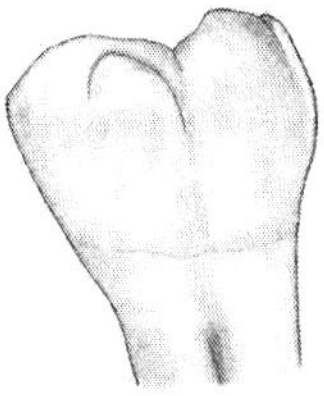  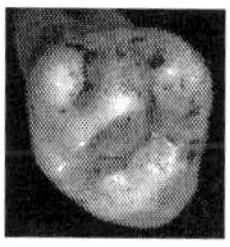	4. There is a medium to large cusp on the tooth's buccal surface. This cusp is distinct, but still smaller than the tooth's mesiobuccal or distobuccal cusps. 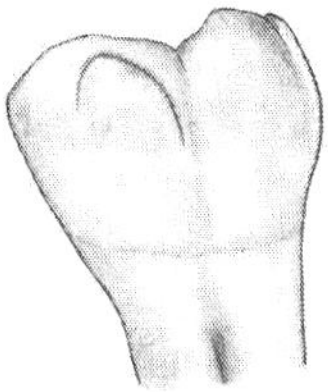  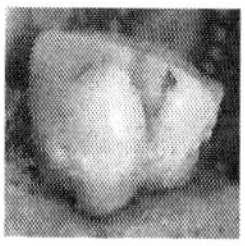

Full Name of Trait (Abbrev.): Maxillary Molar Enamel Extension (UMEE)

Detailed Trait Description: This trait is an apical extension of the enamel from a straight line that is the usual cemeto-enamel junction on the buccal surface, usually in line with the buccal groove. It is more common on maxillary than mandibular molars. Enamel in the buccal groove but not attached to the tooth crown is not considered an enamel extension, but may be an enamel pearl.

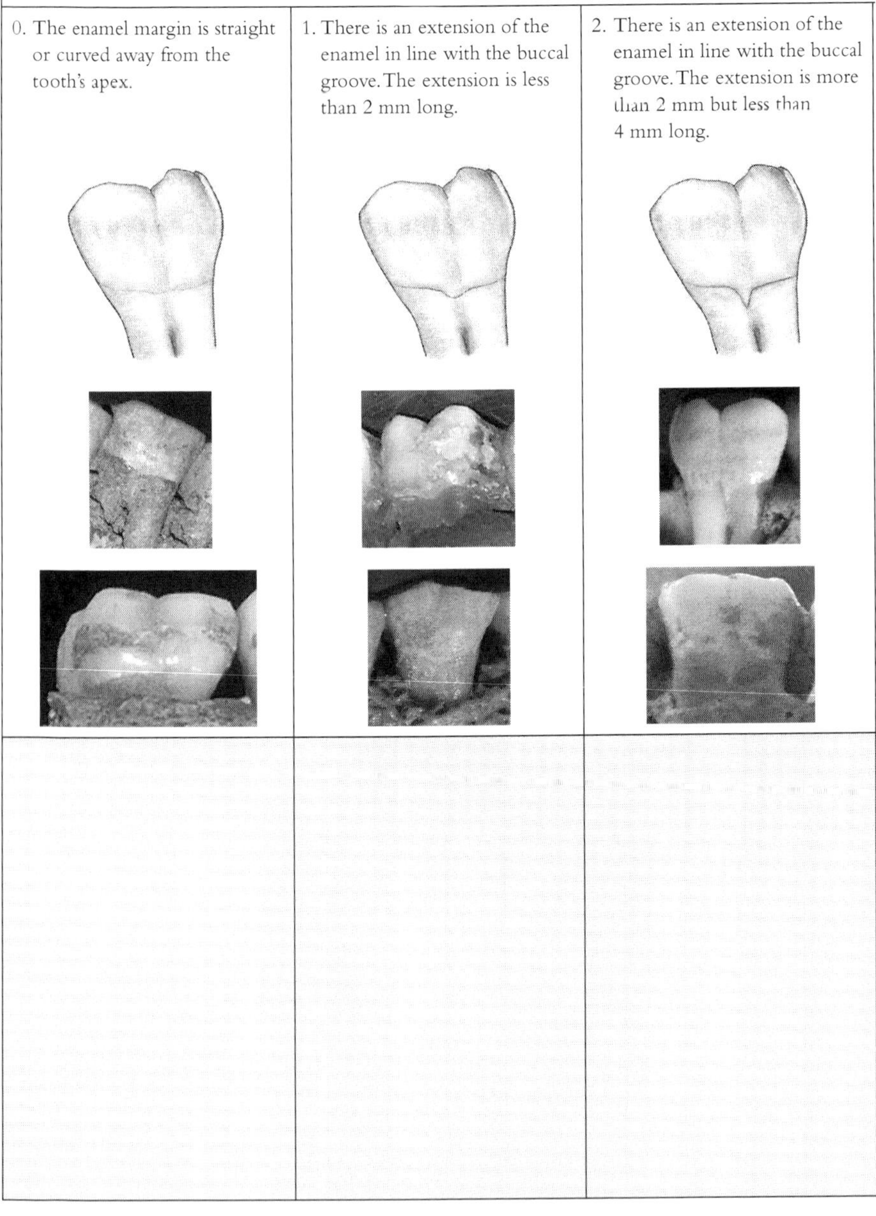

	ASUDAS Plaque: None
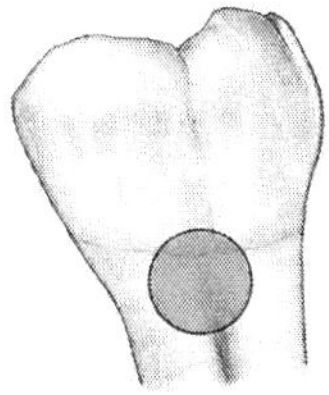	**Other Teeth Scored:** Lower molars
3. There is an extension of the enamel in line with the buccal groove. The extension is more than 4 mm long. 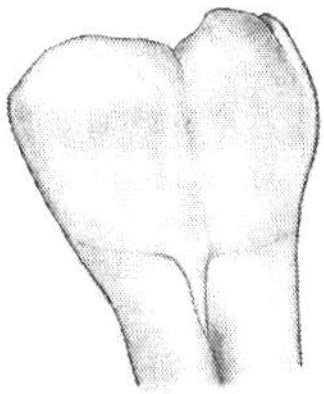 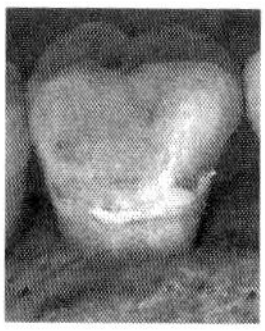 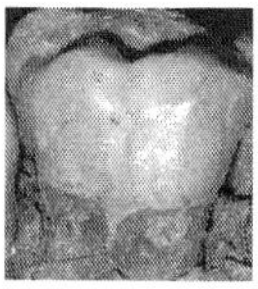	

Full Name of Trait (Abbrev.): Mandibular Incisor Shovel Shape—First (LI1SS)

Detailed Trait Description: Of interest are the marginal ridges on the lingual side of the tooth. LI1 usually shows less shoveling than LI2.

0. Lingual surface is basically flat with no marginal ridges.	1. There are very slight elevations along the mesial and distal margins that can be seen and felt.	2. Lingual marginal ridges can be easily seen, but they are still slight and do not run the length of the margin.

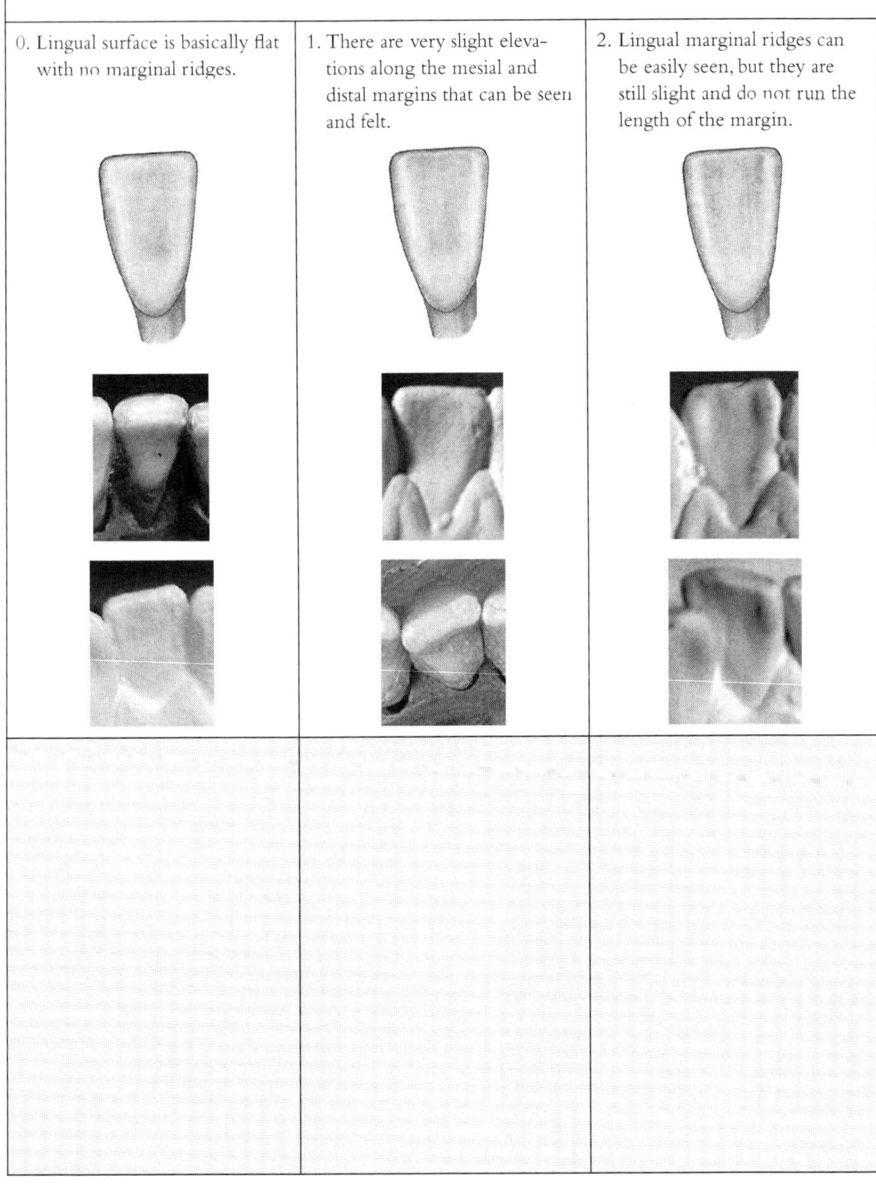

	ASUDAS Plaque: LOWER I SHOVEL
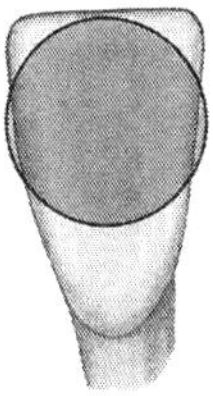	**Other Teeth Scored:** UI1; UI2; UC; LI2
3. There is stronger lingual marginal ridging present. The ridges may converge toward the cingulum. 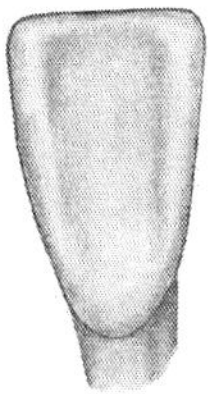  	

Full Name of Trait (Abbrev.): Mandibular Incisor Shovel Shape—Second (LI2SS)

Detailed Trait Description: Of interest are the marginal ridges on the lingual side of the tooth. LI2 usually shows more shoveling than LI1.

0. Lingual surface is basically flat with no marginal ridges.	1. There are very slight elevations along the mesial and distal margins that can be seen and felt.	2. Lingual marginal ridges can be easily seen, but they are still slight and do not run the length of the margin.
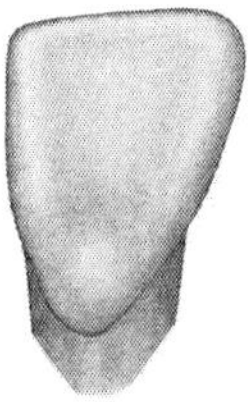	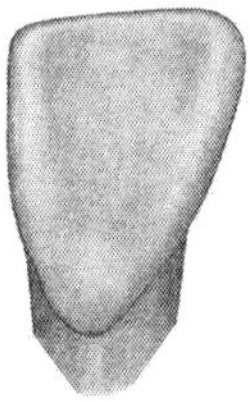	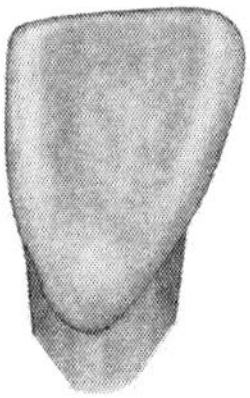
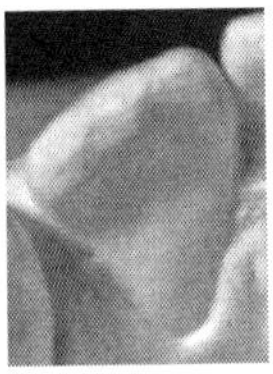		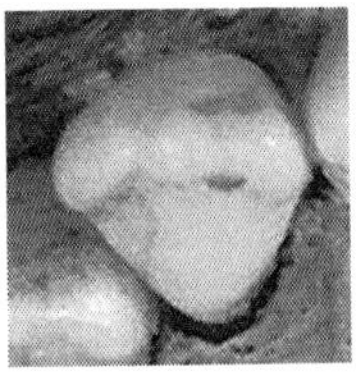
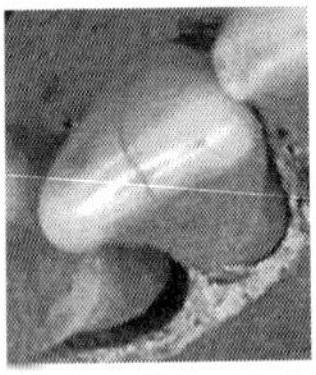	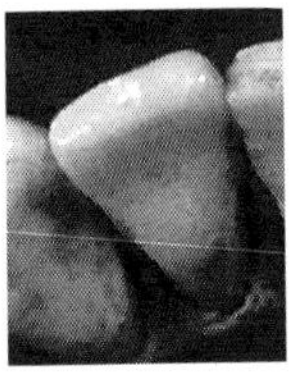	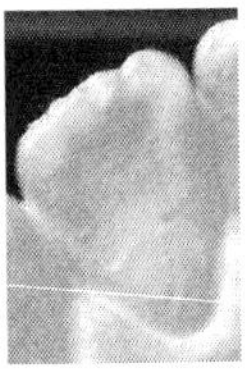

	ASUDAS Plaque: LOWER I SHOVEL
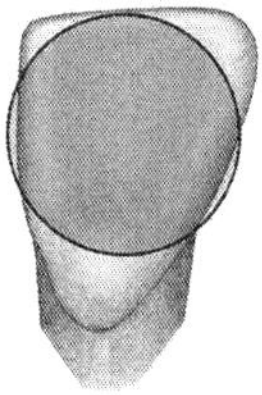	**Other Teeth Scored:** UI1; UI2; UC; LI1
3. There is stronger lingual marginal ridging present. The ridges may converge toward the cingulum. 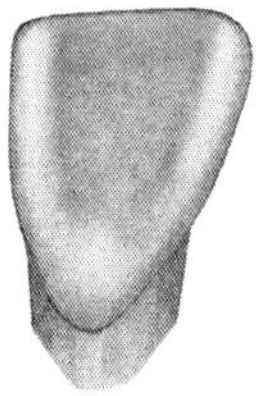 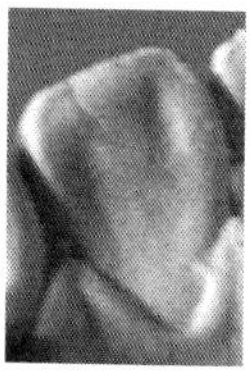 	

Full Name of Trait (Abbrev.): Mandibular Incisor Congenital Absence—First (LI1CA)	
Detailed Trait Description: There is no evidence of a mandibular central incisor mesial to the lateral incisor. Optimally, this trait is scored using radiographic images. However, it can be scored without them, if care is taken not to include individuals who may have lost the tooth because of wear or caries, or in contemporary western populations where an individual is likely to have had the tooth surgically removed. A gap or misalignment may indicate tooth loss.	
0. The mandibular central incisor is present.	1. The mandibular central incisor is absent, and there is no evidence that the tooth is unerupted or has been lost because of pathology, such as a gap between LI1 and LC.

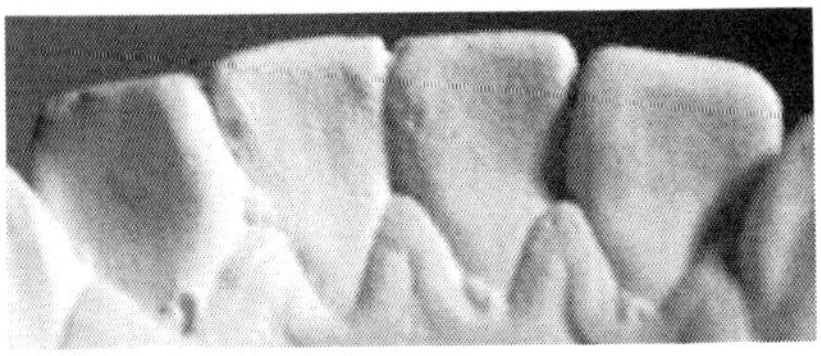

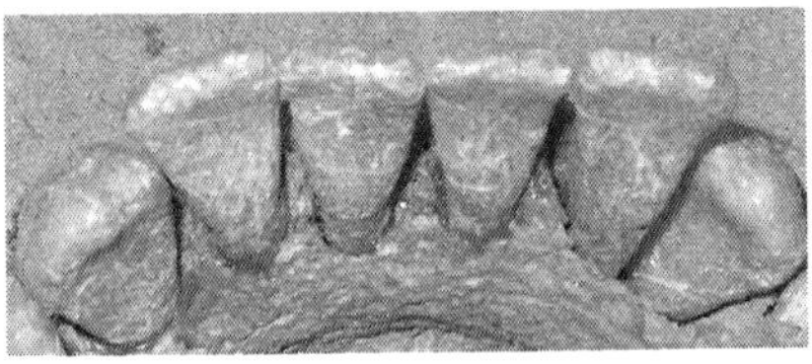

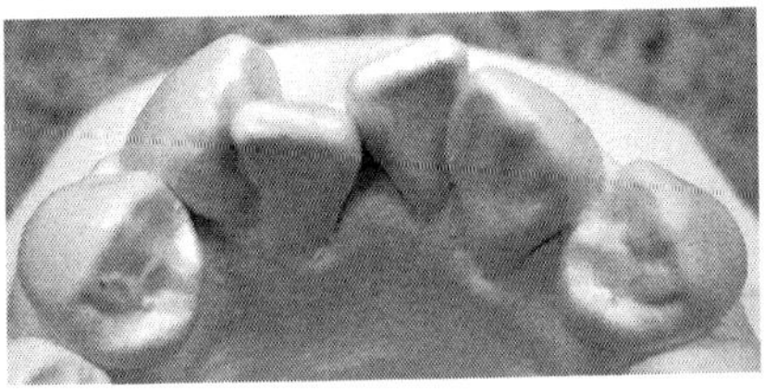

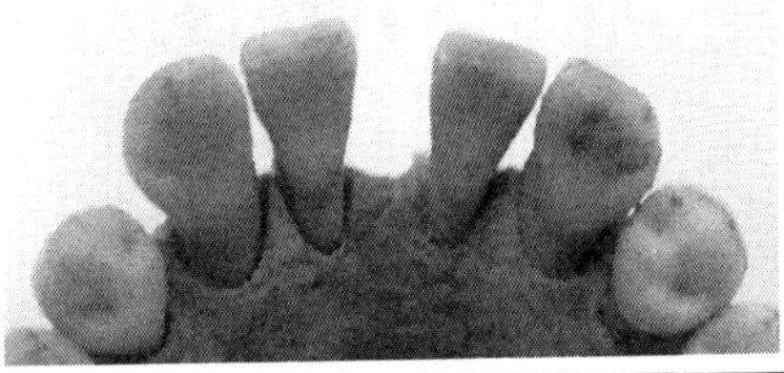

			ASUDAS Plaque: None
			Other Teeth Scored: UI2; UM3; LM3

Full Name of Trait (Abbrev.): Mandibular Molar Congenital Absence—Third (LM3CA)	
Detailed Trait Description: There is no evidence of a mandibular third molar distal to the second molar. Optimally, this trait is scored using radiographic images. However, it can be scored without them, if care is taken not to include individuals who may have lost the tooth because of wear or caries, or in contemporary western populations where an individual is likely to have had the tooth surgically removed. A gap or misalignment may indicate tooth loss.	
0. The mandibular third molar is present.  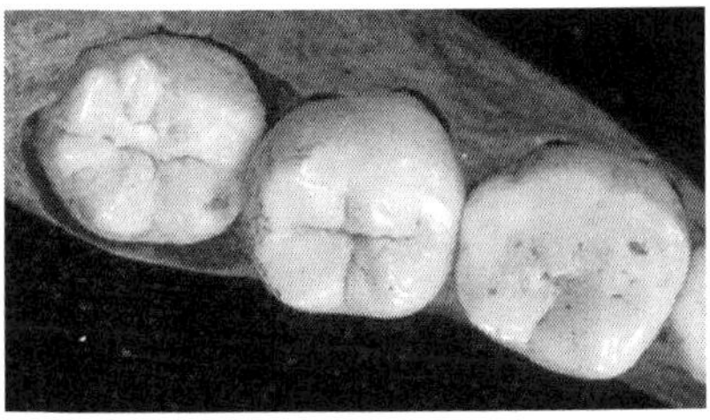	1. The mandibular third molar is absent and is unlikely to be unerupted or have been lost because of pathology or surgical removal, such as a gap sital to LM2.  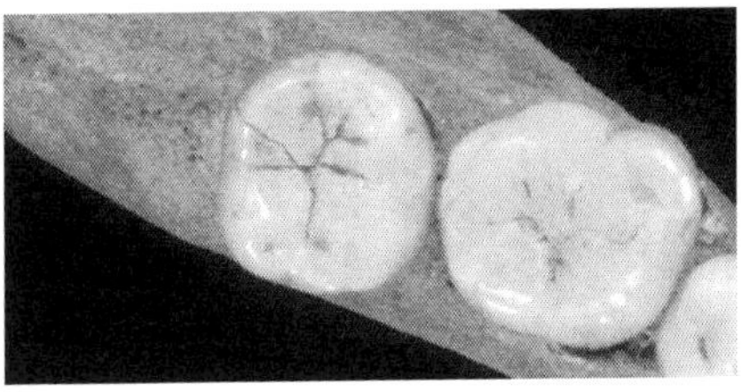

			ASUDAS Plaque: None
			Other Teeth Scored: UI2; UM3; LI1

Full Name of Trait (Abbrev.): Mandibular Canine Distal Accessory Ridge (LCDR)

Detailed Trait Description: The trait consists of a ridge that can exist on the distolingual surface of the tooth between the apex and distolingual marginal ridge. LC usually shows weaker expression of this trait than UC.

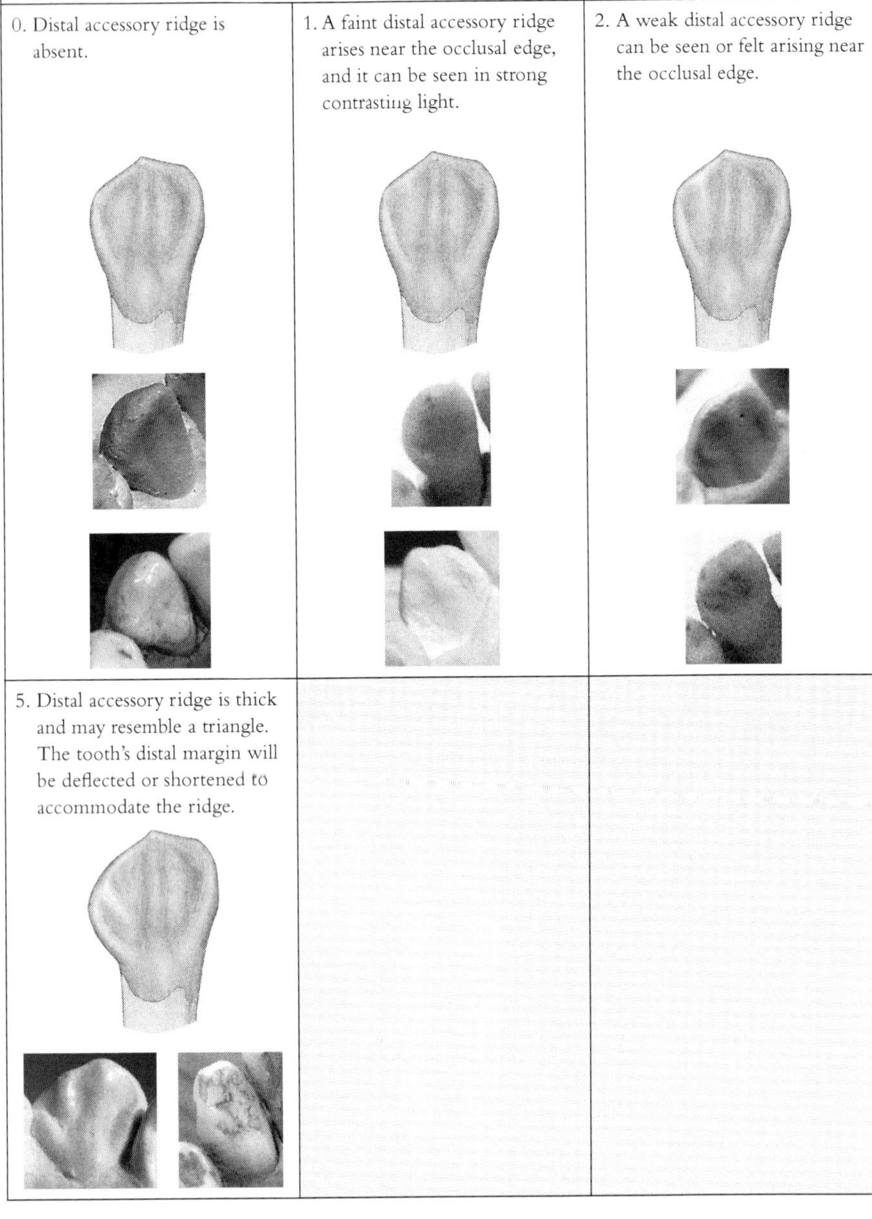

0. Distal accessory ridge is absent.	1. A faint distal accessory ridge arises near the occlusal edge, and it can be seen in strong contrasting light.	2. A weak distal accessory ridge can be seen or felt arising near the occlusal edge.
5. Distal accessory ridge is thick and may resemble a triangle. The tooth's distal margin will be deflected or shortened to accommodate the ridge.		

	ASUDAS Plaque: DAR LC
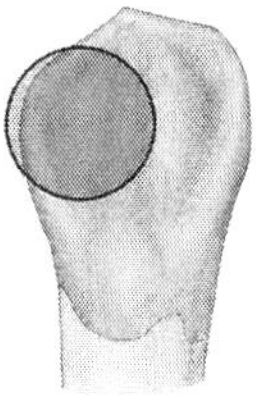	**Other Teeth Scored:** UC
3. A distal accessory ridge is thicker than seen in lower grades, but does not deflect the distal margin. 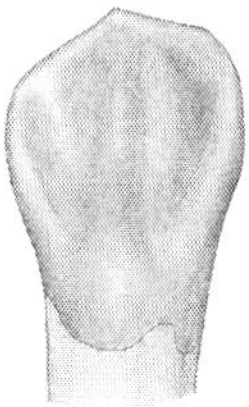 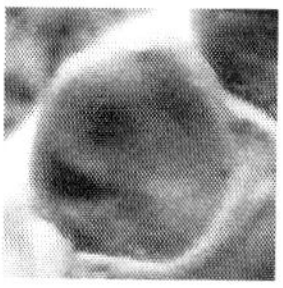 	4. Distal accessory ridge is longer and thicker than seen in lower grades and may deflect or shorten the distal margin. 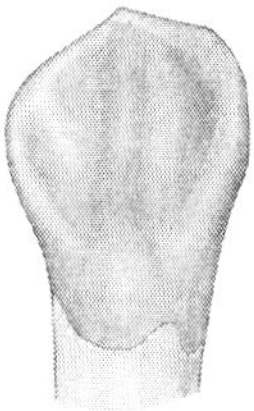  

Full Name of Trait (Abbrev.): Mandibular Premolar Lingual Cusp Complexity—Third (LP3LC)

Detailed Trait Description: This observation concerns the number and form of the lingual cusps of the tooth. Because of differences in tooth morphology, expressions are quite different in the two teeth for which it is scored. Counting the cusps is the easiest way to begin scoring this trait. It is often harder to score on P3 than P4, perhaps because there can be less differentiation between lingual cusps on LP3.

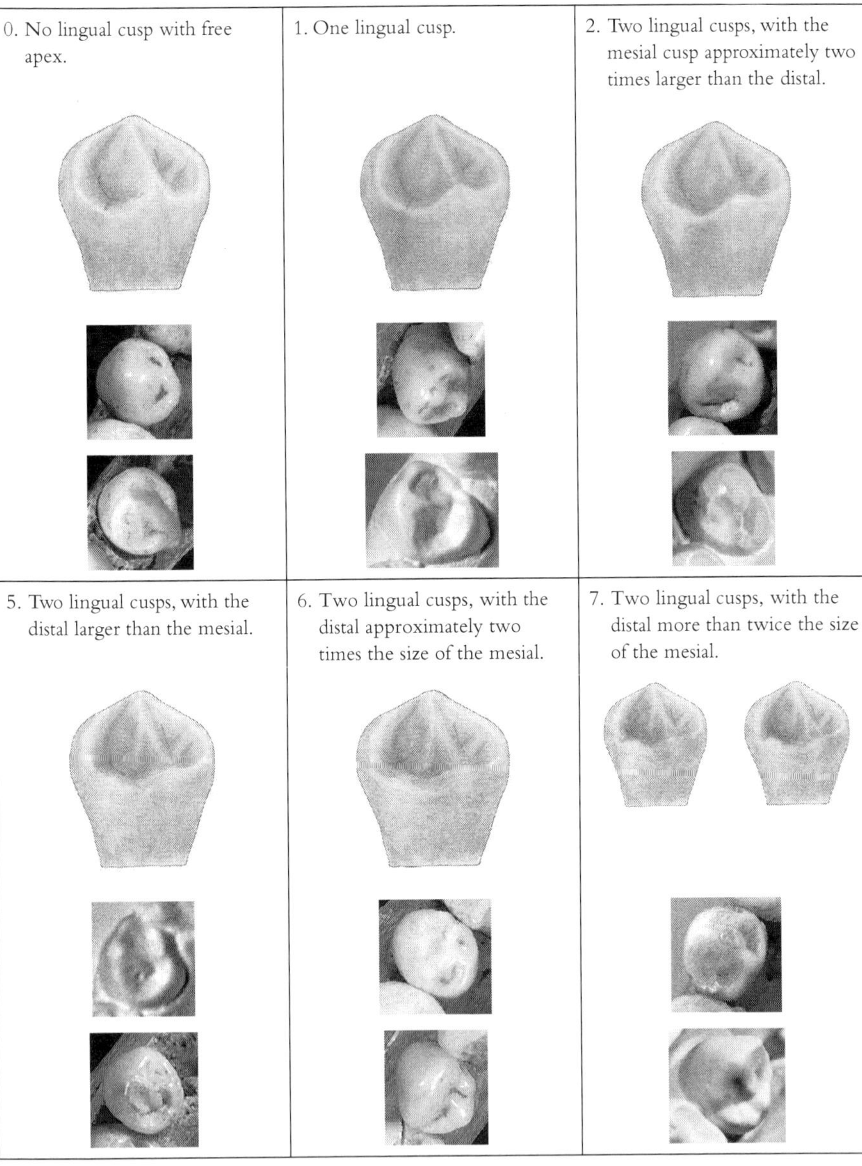

0. No lingual cusp with free apex.	1. One lingual cusp.	2. Two lingual cusps, with the mesial cusp approximately two times larger than the distal.
5. Two lingual cusps, with the distal larger than the mesial.	6. Two lingual cusps, with the distal approximately two times the size of the mesial.	7. Two lingual cusps, with the distal more than twice the size of the mesial.

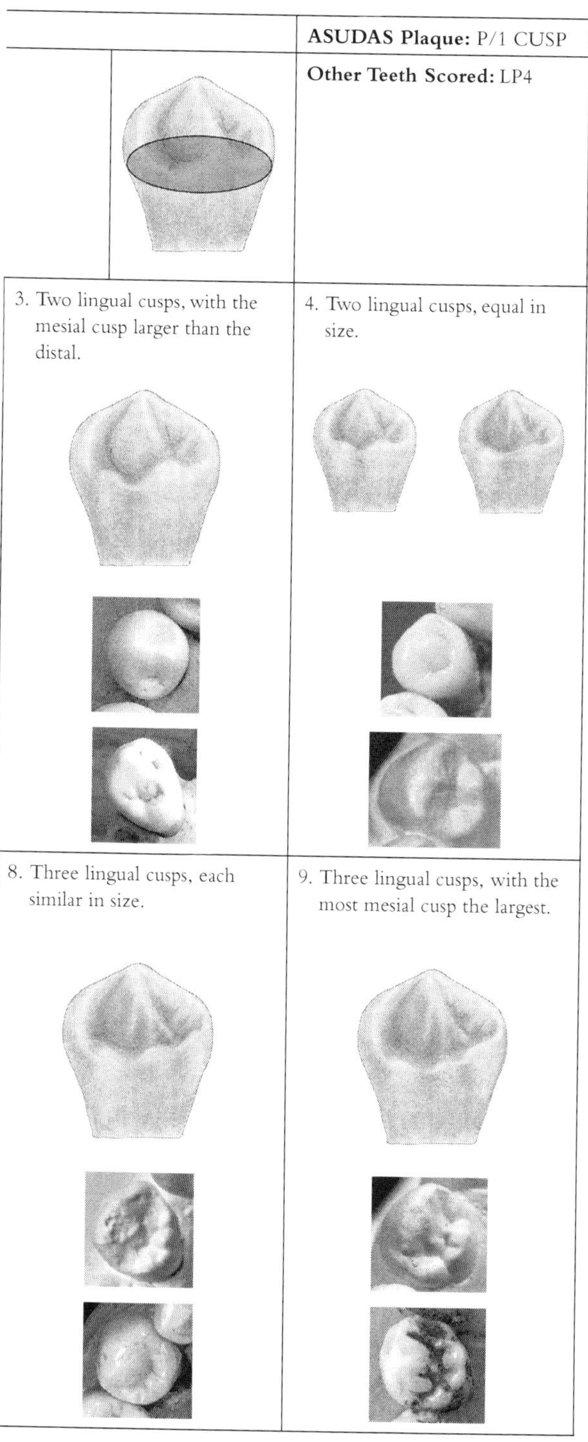

	ASUDAS Plaque: P/1 CUSP
	Other Teeth Scored: LP4
3. Two lingual cusps, with the mesial cusp larger than the distal.	4. Two lingual cusps, equal in size.
8. Three lingual cusps, each similar in size.	9. Three lingual cusps, with the most mesial cusp the largest.

Full Name of Trait (Abbrev.): Mandibular Premolar Lingual Cusp Complexity—Fourth (LP4LC)

Detailed Trait Description: This observation concerns the number and form of the lingual cusps of the tooth. Because of differences in tooth morphology, expressions are quite different in the two teeth for which it is scored. Counting the cusps is the easiest way to begin scoring this trait. It is often easier to score on P4 than on P3, perhaps because lingal cusps are more differentiated on LP4 than LP3.

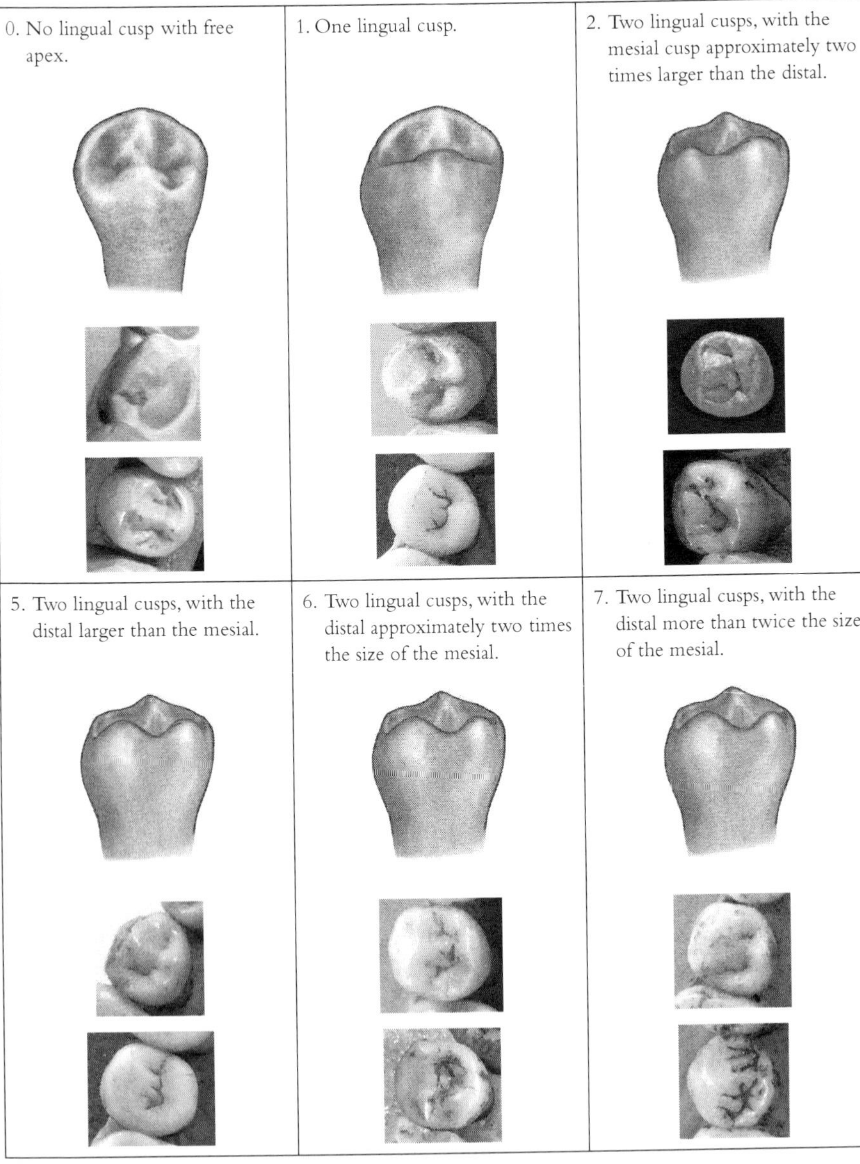

	ASUDAS Plaque: P/2 CUSP
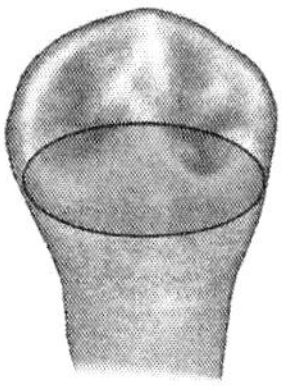	**Other Teeth Scored:** LP3
3. Two lingual cusps, with the mesial cusp larger than the distal. 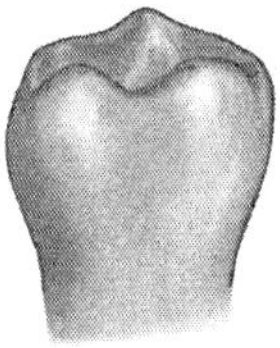 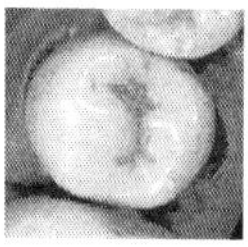 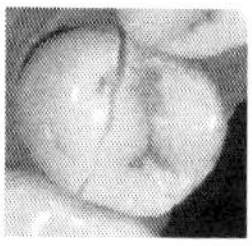	4. Two lingual cusps, equal in size. 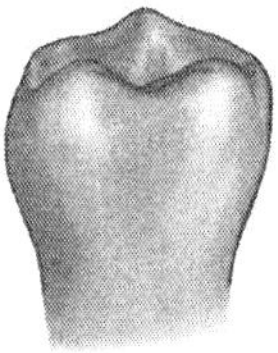 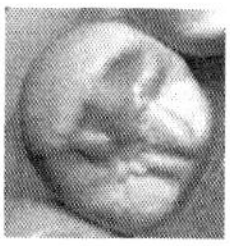 
8. Three lingual cusps, each similar in size. 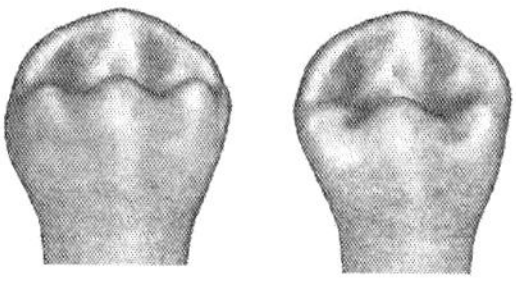  	9. Three lingual cusps, with the most mesial cusp the largest. 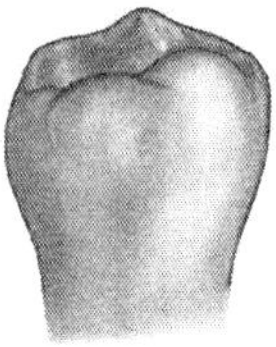 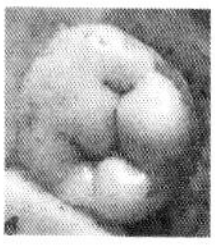 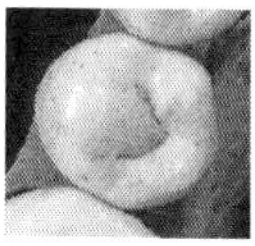

Full Name of Trait (Abbrev.): Mandibular Premolar Elongated Form—Third (LP3EF)		
Detailed Trait Description: This observation considers whether the overall tooth shape is more rectangular, with the long axis in the mesiodistal plane, or more square or round.		
0. The overall tooth shape is square or round, with the buccolingual breadth appearing approximately the same as the mesiodistal length. 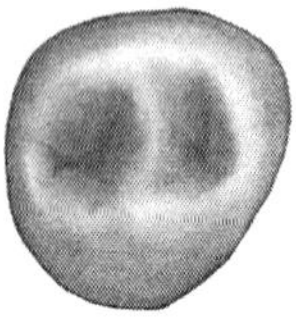 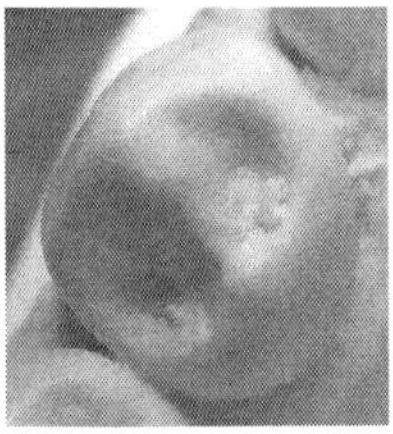 	1. The overall tooth shape is more rectangular, with the mesiodistal length appearing longer than the buccolingual breadth. 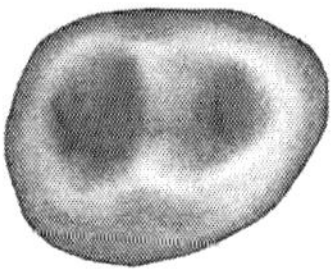 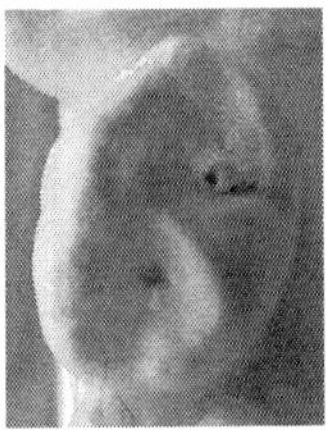 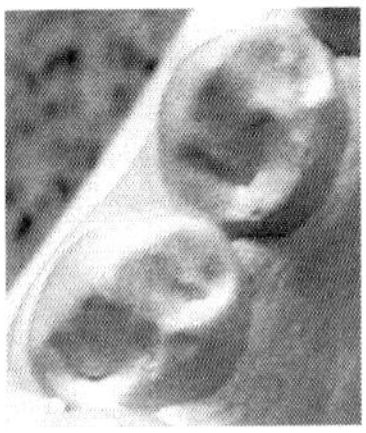	

		ASUDAS Plaque: None
		Other Teeth Scored: LP4

Full Name of Trait (Abbrev.): Mandibular Premolar Elongated Form—Fourth (LP4EF)		
Detailed Trait Description: This observation considers whether the overall tooth shape is more rectangular, with the long axis in the mesiodistal plane, or more square or round.		
0. The overall tooth shape is square or round, with the buccolingual breadth appearing approximately the same as the mesiodistal length. 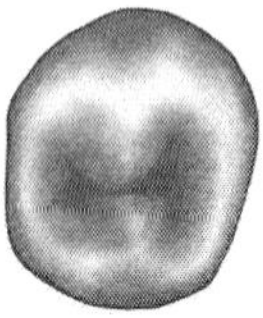 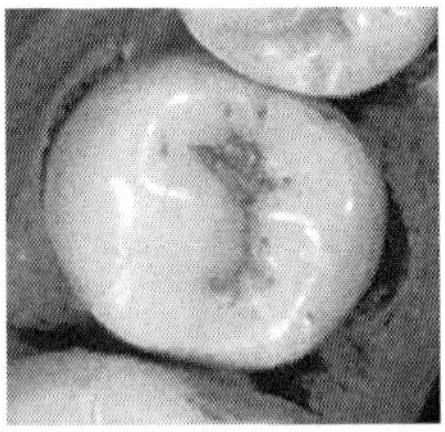 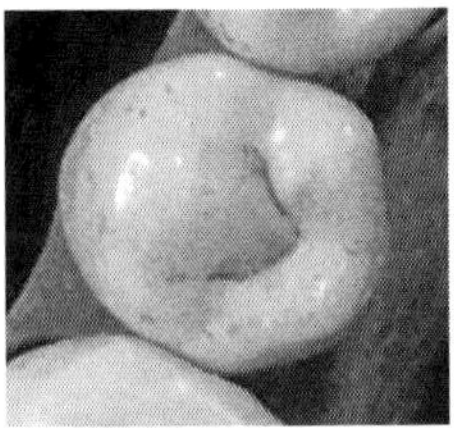	1. The overall tooth shape is more rectangular, with the mesiodistal length appearing longer than the buccolingual breadth. 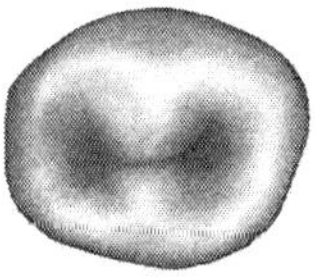  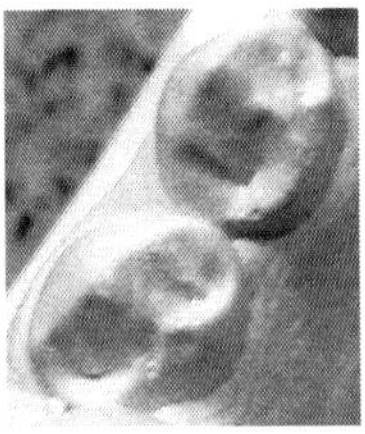	

		ASUDAS Plaque: None
		Other Teeth Scored: LP3

Full Name of Trait (Abbrev.): Mandibular Molar Anterior Fovea—First (LM1AF)		
Detailed Trait Description: This trait is an occlusal groove mesial to the mesial cusps of the tooth that may be formed by a ridge that may connect the apices of the mesiobuccal and mesiolingual cusps.		
0. No anterior fovea. The sulcus that runs mesiodistally between the mesiobuccal and mesiolingual cusps (1 and 2) continues with no interruption to the mesial border of the occlusal surface. 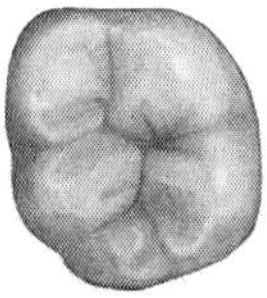 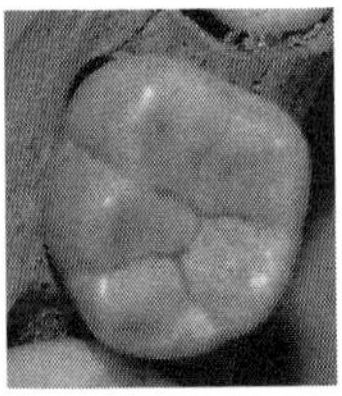 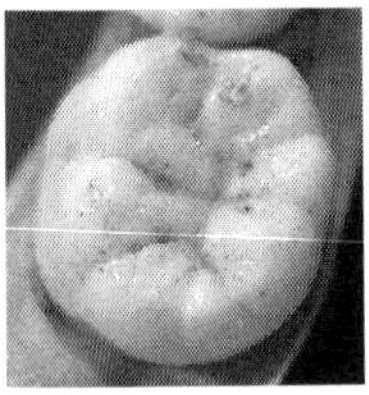	1. There is a faint or short groove between the mesio-buccal and mesiolingual cusps, which may be produced by a ridge connecting the mesial aspects of the cusps. 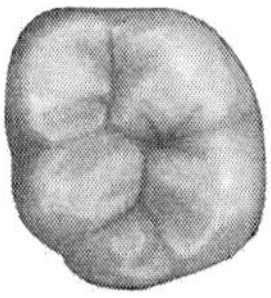 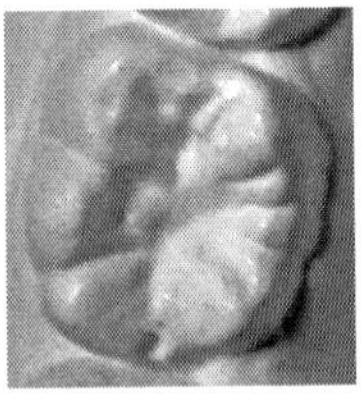 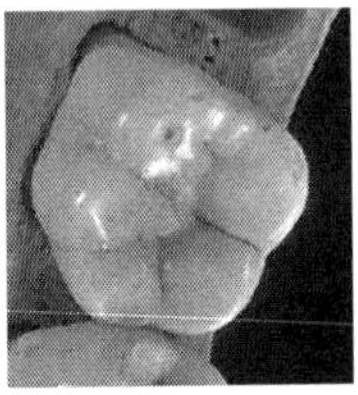	2. The groove stretches approximately one-third across the occlusal surface of the tooth. 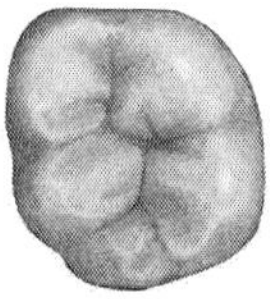  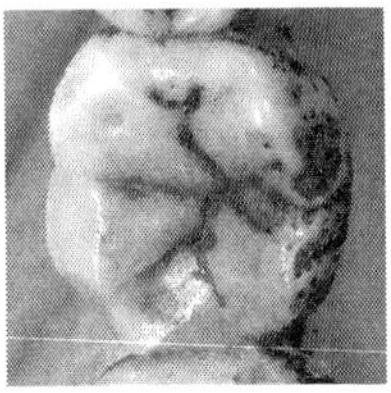

	ASUDAS Plaque: ANTERIOR FOVEA LM1
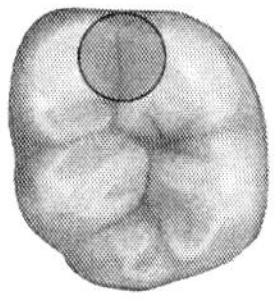	**Other Teeth Scored:** None
3. The groove stretches approximately half way across the occlusal surface of the tooth. 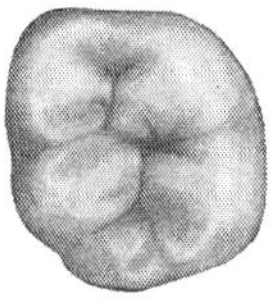 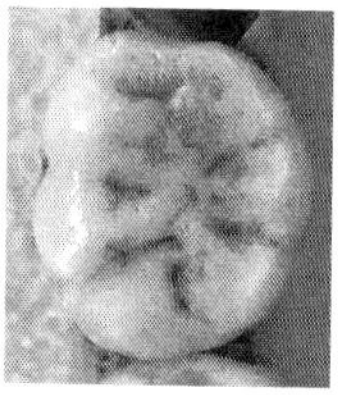 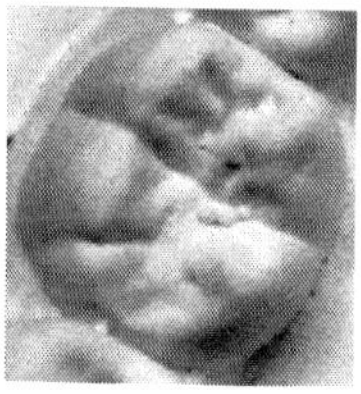	4. The groove stretches to or almost to the distal and mesial margins of the tooth. 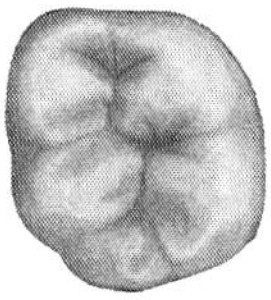 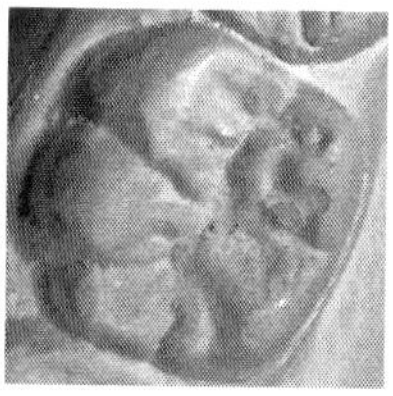 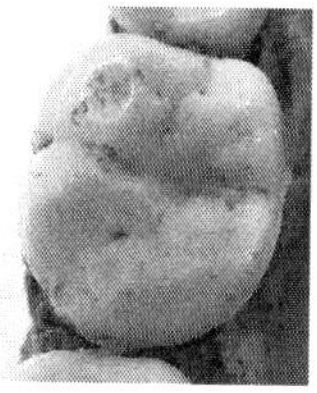

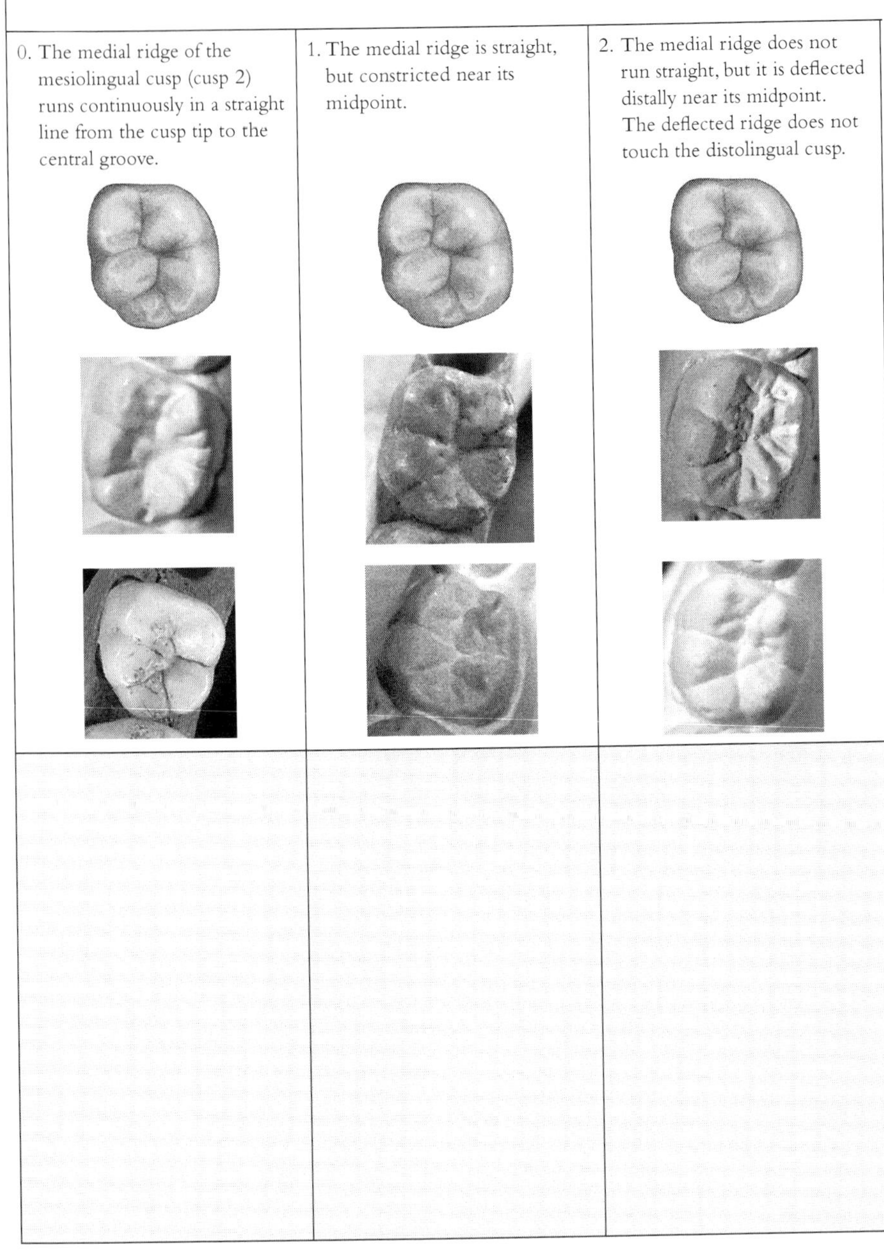

Full Name of Trait (Abbrev.): Mandibular Molar Deflecting Wrinkle—First (LM1DW)

Detailed Trait Description: The observation makes note of the form of the medial ridge on the mesiolingual cusp (cusp 2), as it descends from the cusp tip to the mesiodistally-oriented groove. The observation is often lost to wear or restoration.

0. The medial ridge of the mesiolingual cusp (cusp 2) runs continuously in a straight line from the cusp tip to the central groove.	1. The medial ridge is straight, but constricted near its midpoint.	2. The medial ridge does not run straight, but it is deflected distally near its midpoint. The deflected ridge does not touch the distolingual cusp.

	ASUDAS Plaque: DEFLECTING WRINKLE
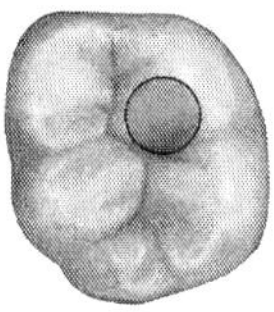	**Other Teeth Scored:** None
3. The medial ridge is deflected distally so that it is L-shaped and contacts the distolingual cusp. 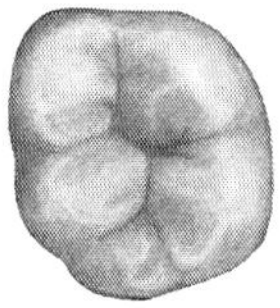  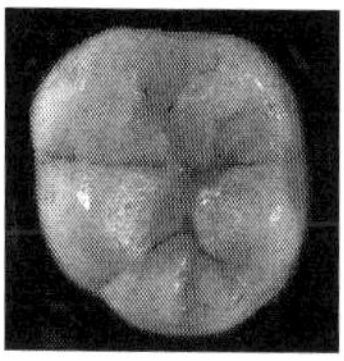	

<table>
<tr><td colspan="3">Full Name of Trait (Abbrev.): Mandibular Molar Groove Pattern—First (LM1GP)</td></tr>
<tr><td colspan="3">Detailed Trait Description: Of interest is the relationship between the four main tooth cusps as indicated by the grooves that separate them. Despite Y-form being scored as zero, when the trait is dichotomized, Y has usually been considered present, and + and X have usually been considered absent.</td></tr>
<tr>
<td>0. Y-groove. The mesiolingual cusp (cusp 2) and distobuccal cusp (cusp 3) meet at a groove, and the mesiobuccal cusp (cusp 1) and the distolingual cusp (cusp 4) do not appear to meet. This form is by far the most common on LM1.
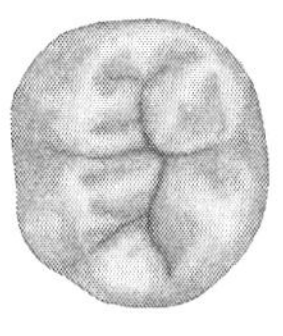
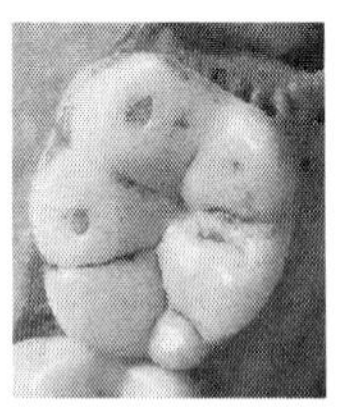
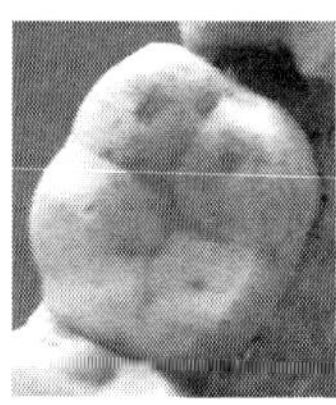</td>
<td>1. +-groove. All four main cusps appear to touch at the center of the tooth so that the primary grooves form a plus sign.
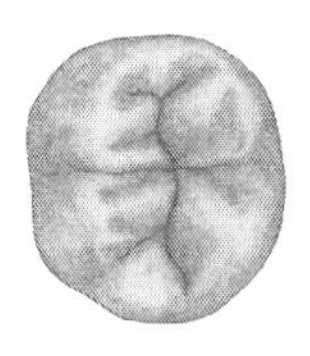
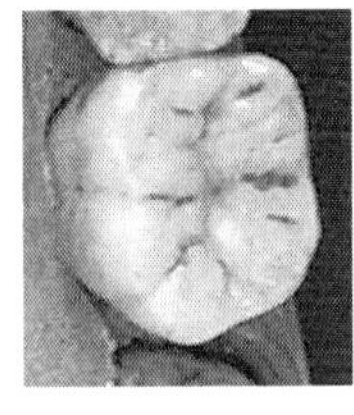
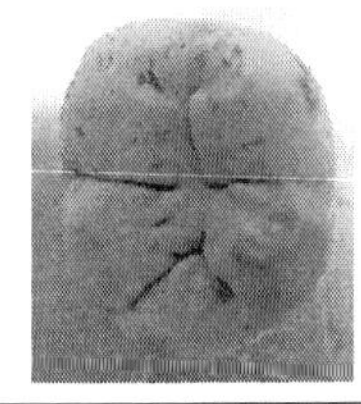</td>
<td>2. X-groove. The mesiobuccal cusp (cusp 1) and the distolingual cusp (cusp 4) meet at a groove and appear to touch, and the mesiolingual cusp (cusp 2) and distobuccal cusp (cusp 3) do not appear to meet.
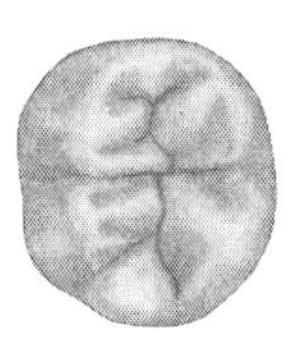
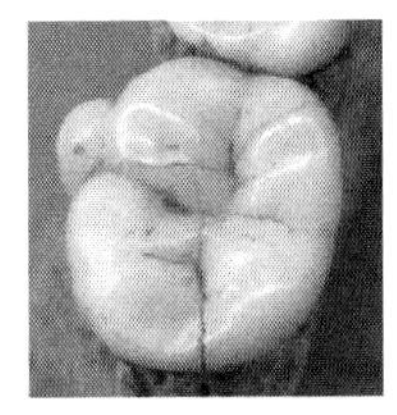
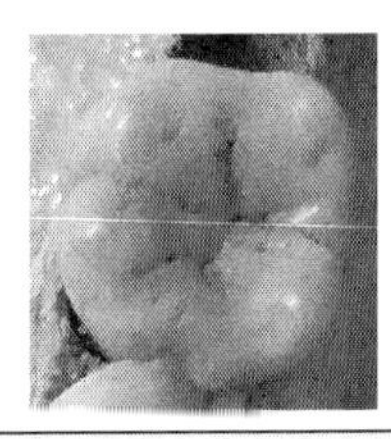</td>
</tr>
<tr><td></td><td></td><td></td></tr>
</table>

		ASUDAS Plaque: None
	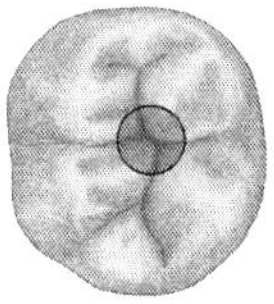	**Other Teeth Scored:** LM2; LM3

Full Name of Trait (Abbrev.): Mandibular Molar Groove Pattern—Second (LM2GP)

Detailed Trait Description: Of interest is the relationship between the four main tooth cusps as indicated by the grooves that separate them. Despite Y-form being scored as zero, when the trait is dichotomized, Y has been considered present, and + and X have been considered absent.

0. Y-groove. The mesiolingual cusp (cusp 2) and distobuccal cusp (cusp 3) meet at a groove, and the mesiobuccal cusp (cusp 1) and the distolingual cusp (cusp 4) do not appear to meet.	1. +-groove. All four main cusps appear to touch at the center of the tooth, so that the primary grooves form a plus sign.	2. X-groove. The mesiobuccal cusp (cusp 1) and the distolingual cusp (cusp 4) meet at a groove and appear to touch, and the mesiolingual cusp (cusp 2) and distobuccal cusp (cusp 3) do not appear to meet. This is the most common form for M2.
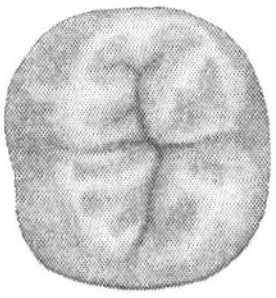	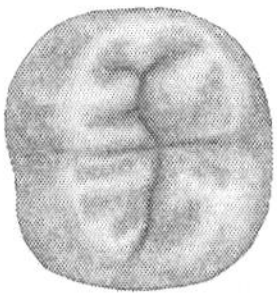	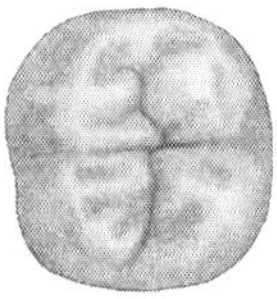
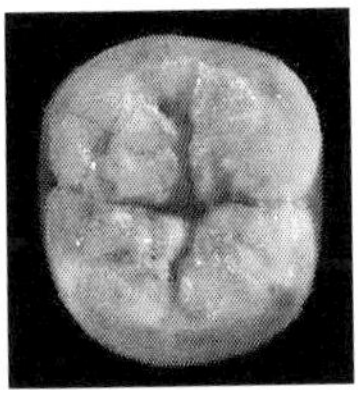	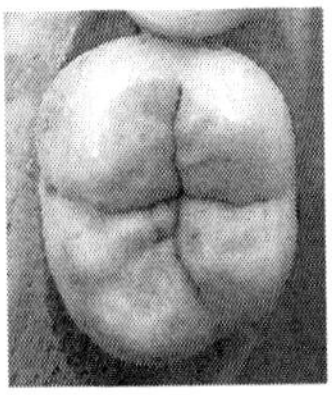	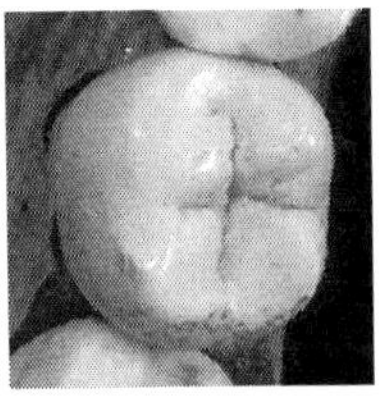
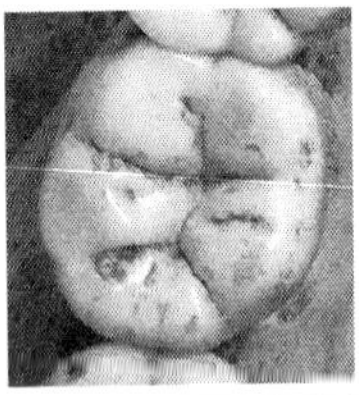	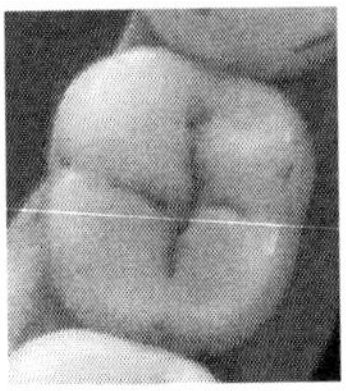	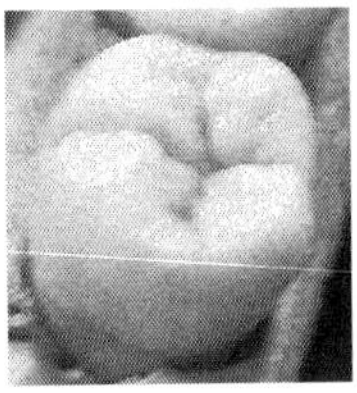

		ASUDAS Plaque: None
		Other Teeth Scored: LM1; LM3

Full Name of Trait (Abbrev.): Mandibular Molar Cusp Number—First (LM1CN)		
Detailed Trait Description: This observation consists of a count of the normally occurring cusps on a mandibular molar. The mesiolingual, mesialbuccal, distobuccal, and distolingual cusps (1, 2, 3, and 4) are assumed to be present. The observation is whether there are only four cusps present, or if five or six cusps are present. Cusp 7 or any additional cusps that may be seen on the mesial margin of the tooth are not included.		
5. Cusp 5 is present.	6. Cusps 5 and 6 are present.	

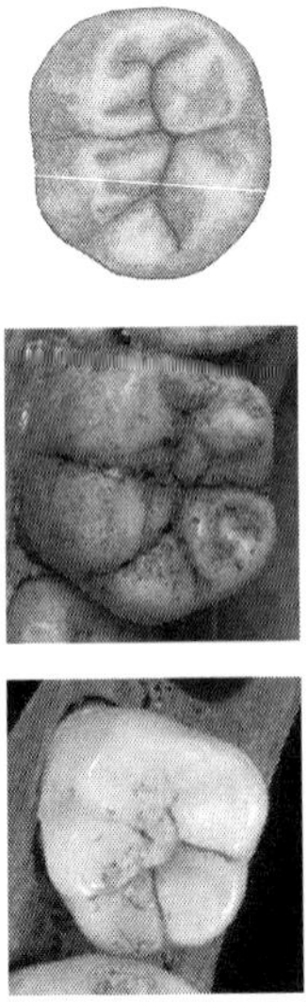

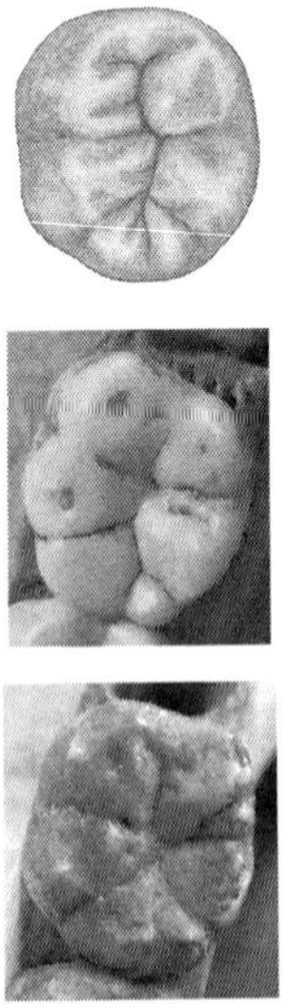

		ASUDAS Plaque: None
	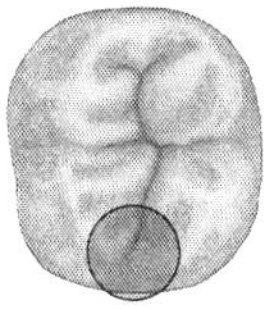	**Other Teeth Scored:** LM2; LM3
		4. Only four cusps are present. 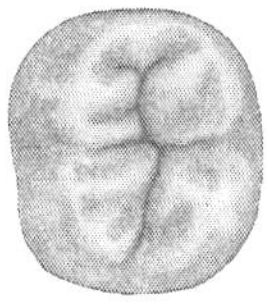 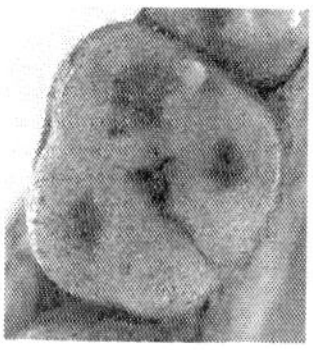 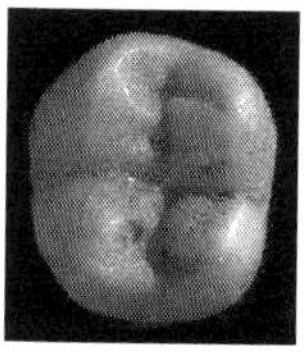

Full Name of Trait (Abbrev.): Mandibular Molar Cusp Number—Second (LM2CN)

Detailed Trait Description: This observation consists of a count of the normally occurring cusps on a mandibular molar. The mesiolingual, mesiobuccal, and distobuccal cusps (1, 2, and 3) are assumed to be present. The observation is whether there are only three cusps present, or if four, five, or six cusps are present. Cusp 7 or any additional cusps on the mesial margin of the tooth are not included.

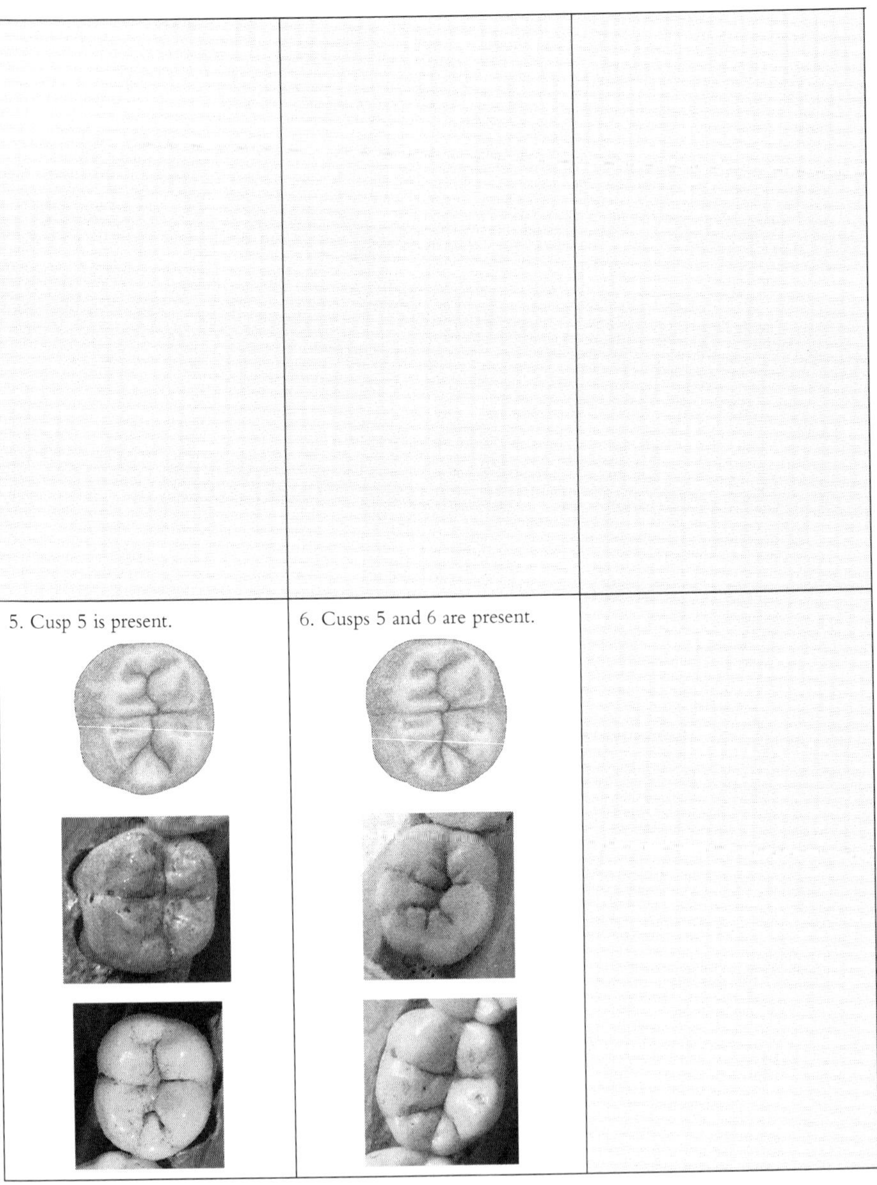

5. Cusp 5 is present.

6. Cusps 5 and 6 are present.

	ASUDAS Plaque: None
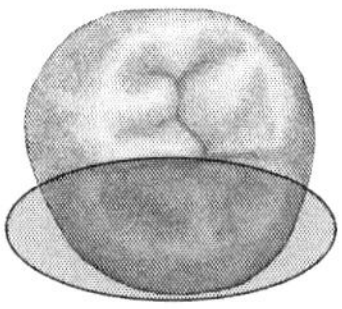	**Other Teeth Scored:** LM1; LM3
3. Only three cusps are present. 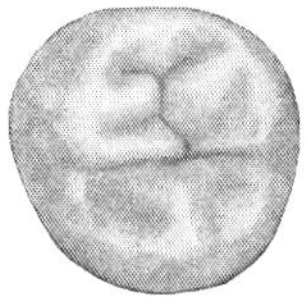 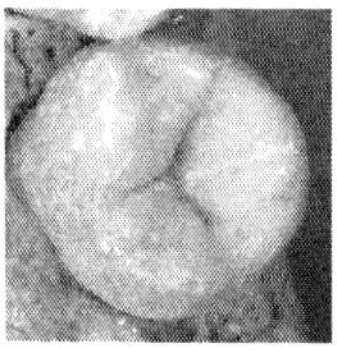 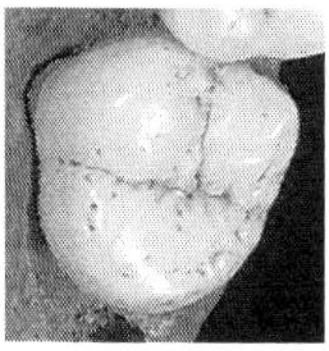	4. Four cusps are present. 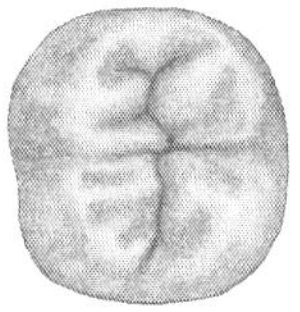 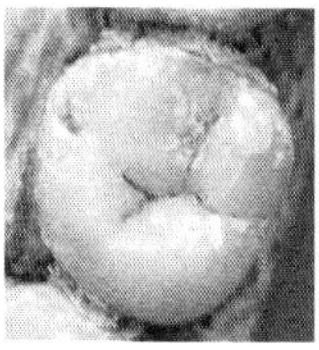 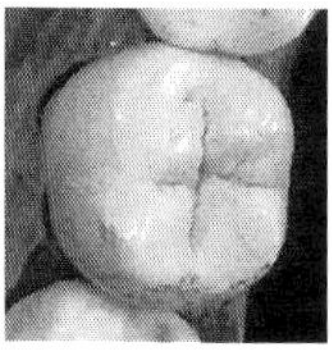

Full Name of Trait (Abbrev.): Mandibular Molar Protostylid—First (LM1PS)

Detailed Trait Description: This trait is a pit, groove, or cusp on the buccal surface of the tooth. The pit form is by far the most common variant, although some observers consider it to be a separate trait.

0. The buccal surface is smooth. 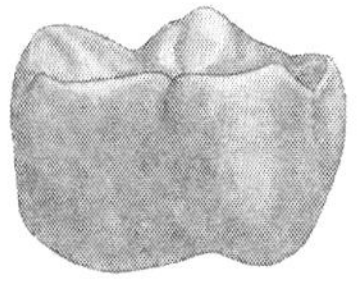 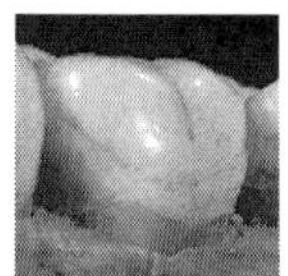 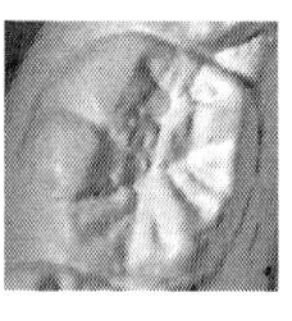	1. There is a pit in the buccal groove. In contemporary samples, there is often a restoration filling the pit. 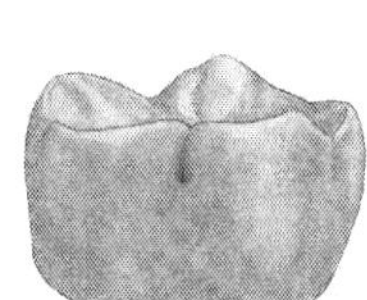 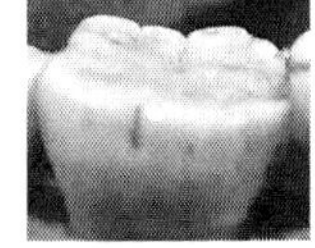 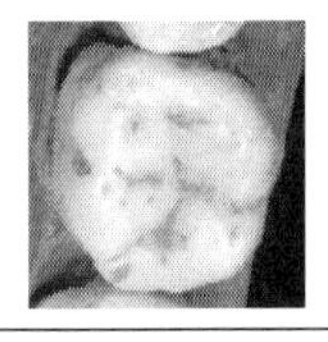	2. The buccal groove curves distally and may make the shape of a faint "Y." 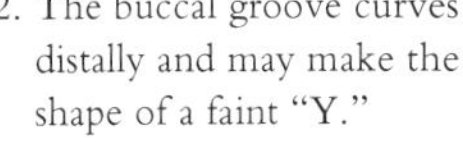  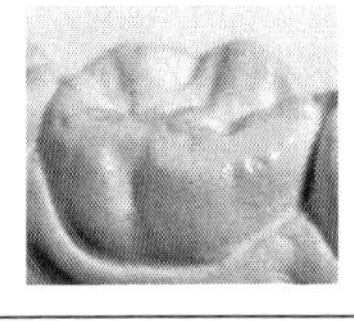
5. The groove extending mesially from the buccal groove is deeper and/or longer, and may extend over half the buccal surface of the mesiobuccal cusp (cusp 1). 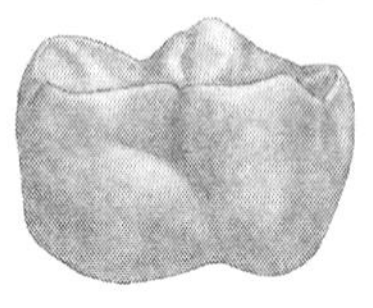 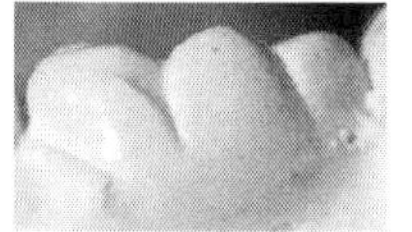 	6. A small cusp with apex attached is formed by the extension of the mesial groove from the buccal groove. 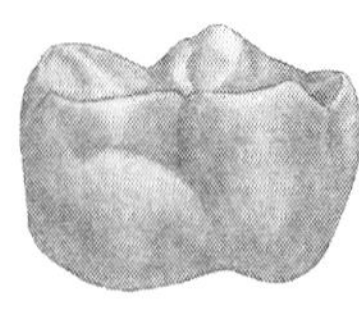 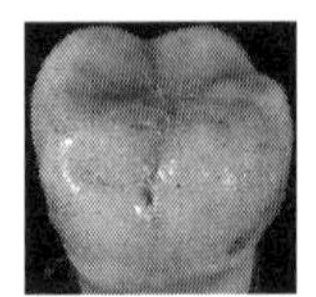	7. There is a cusp with a free apex on the buccal surface of the mesiobuccal cusp (cusp 1). Occasionally, this cusp is very large. When this large cusp is present, it is often unilateral. 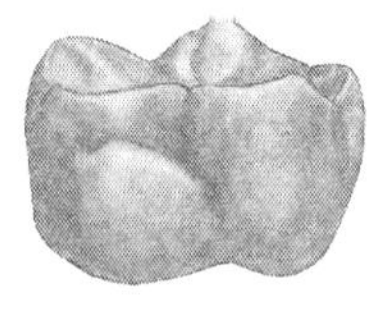 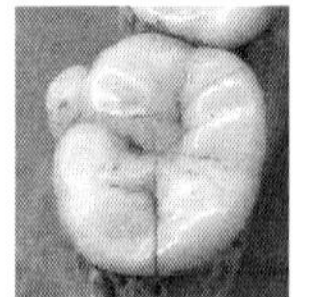

	ASUDAS Plaque: PROTOSTYLID
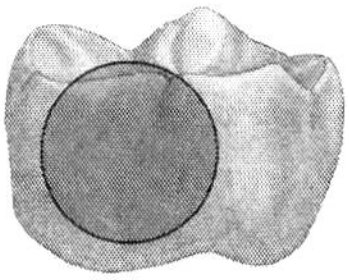	**Other Teeth Scored:** LM2; LM3
3. There is a faint groove extending mesially from the buccal groove. 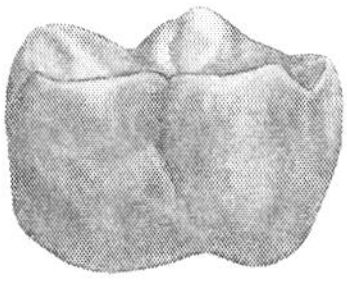 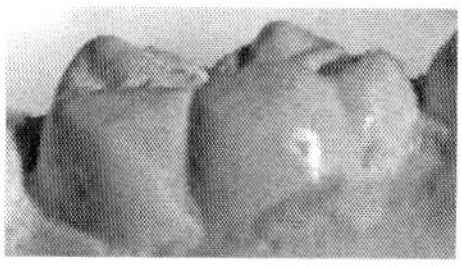 	4. The groove extending mesially from the buccal groove is clearly visible, but extends over less than one-third of the buccal surface of the mesiobuccal cusp (cusp 1). 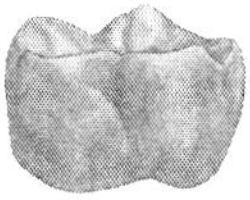 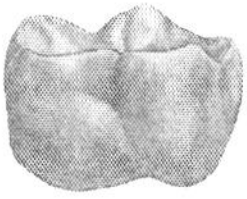 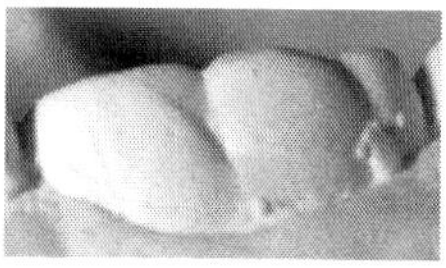 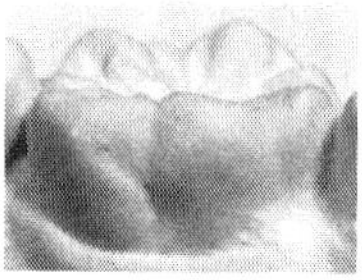

Full Name of Trait (Abbrev.): Mandibular Molar Protostylid—Second (LM2PS)

Detailed Trait Description: This trait is a pit, groove, or cusp on the buccal surface of the tooth. The pit form is by far the most common variant, although some observers consider it to be a separate trait.

0. The buccal surface is smooth.

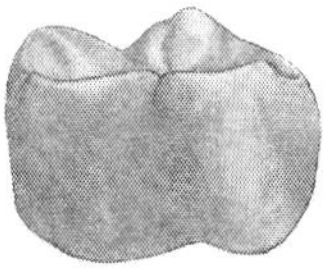

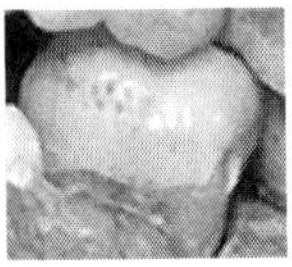

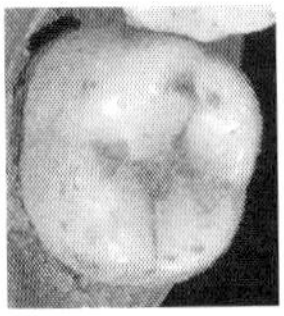

1. There is a pit in the buccal groove. In contemporary samples, there is often a restoration filling the pit.

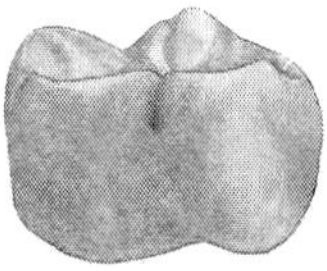

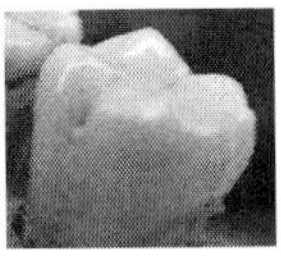

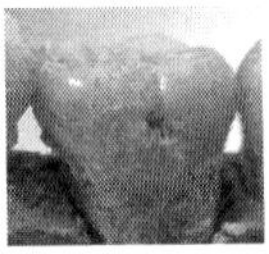

2. The buccal groove curves distally and may make the shape of a faint "Y."

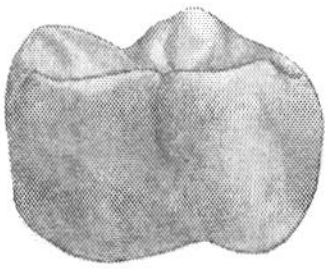

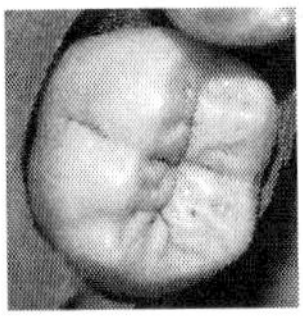

5. The groove extending mesially from the buccal groove is deeper and/or longer, and may extend over half the buccal surface of the mesiobuccal cusp (cusp 1).

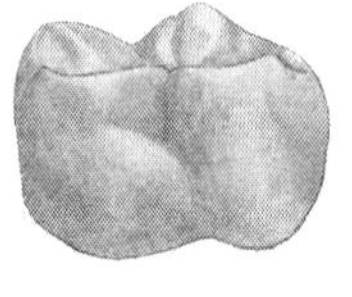

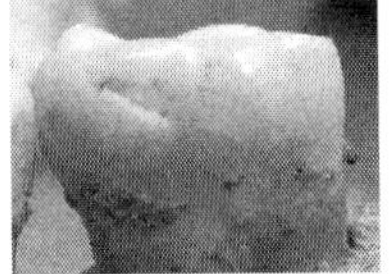

6. A small cusp with apex attached is formed by the extension of the mesial groove from the buccal groove.

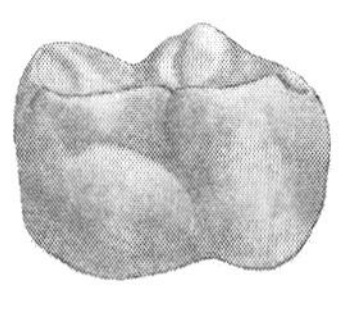

7. There is a cusp with a free apex on the buccal surface of the mesiobuccal cusp (cusp 1). Occasionally, this cusp is very large. When this large cusp is present, it is often unilateral.

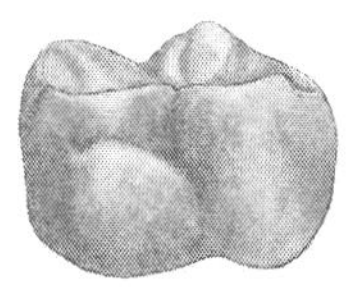

	ASUDAS Plaque: PROTOSTYLID
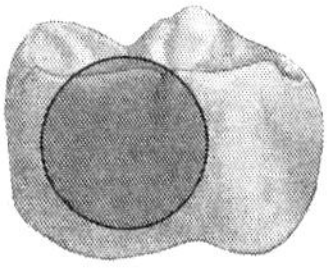	**Other Teeth Scored:** LM1; LM3
3. There is a faint groove extending mesially from the buccal groove. 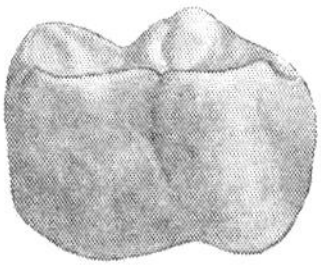  	4. The groove extending mesially from the buccal groove is clearly visible, but extends over less than one-third of the buccal surface of the mesiobuccal cusp (cusp 1). 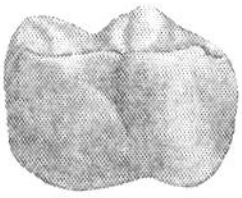  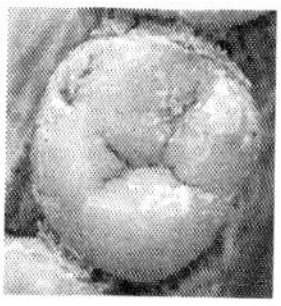 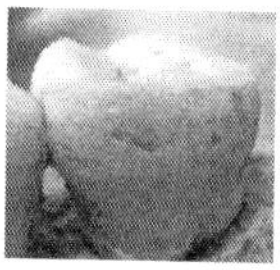

Full Name of Trait (Abbrev.): Mandibular Molar Trigonid Crest—First (LM1TC)		
Detailed Trait Description: This observation is of the presence of a ridge connecting the mesiobuccal cusp (the protoconid, cusp 1) to the mesiolingual cusp (the metaconid, cusp 2) interrupting the groove that separates the two cusps. Some authors describe the placement (mesial, middle, or distal) or angle of this ridge.		
0. The groove between the mesiobuccal and mesiolingual cusps (1 and 2) is continuous. 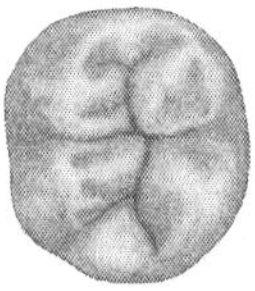 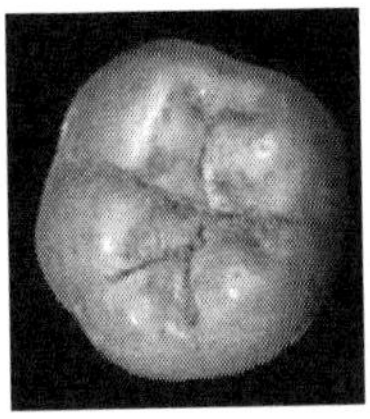 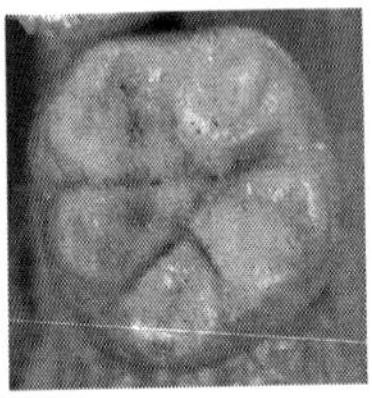	1. There is a ridge of enamel that interrupts the groove that separates the mesiobuccal and mesiolingual cusps. 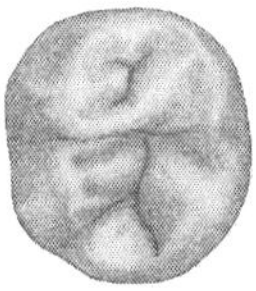 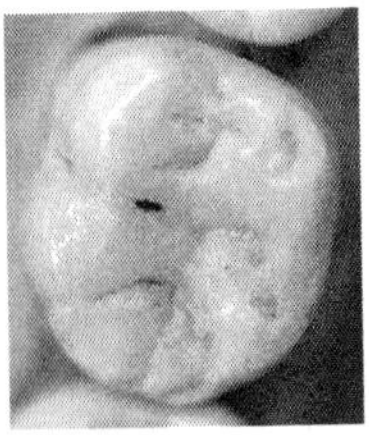 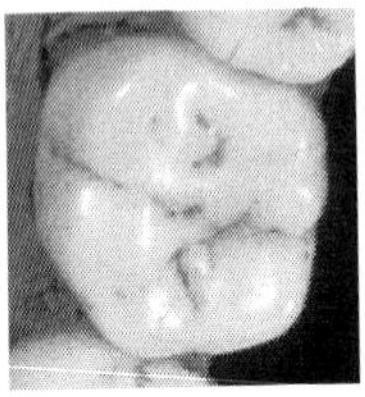	

		ASUDAS Plaque: MID-TRIGONID CREST
	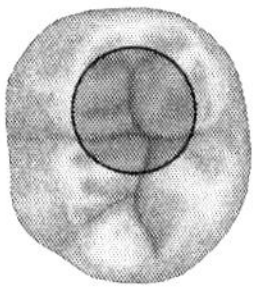	**Other Teeth Scored:** LM2; LM3

Full Name of Trait (Abbrev.): Mandibular Molar Trigonid Crest—Second (LM2TC)		
Detailed Trait Description: This observation is of the presence of a ridge connecting the mesiobuccal cusp (the protoconid, cusp 1) to the mesiolingual cusp (the metaconid, cusp 2) interrupting the groove that separates the two cusps. Some authors describe the placement (mesial, middle, or distal) or angle of this ridge.		
0. The groove between the mesiobuccal and mesiolingual cusps (1 and 2) is continuous.	1. There is a ridge of enamel that interrupts the groove that separates the mesiobuccal and mesiolingual cusps.	

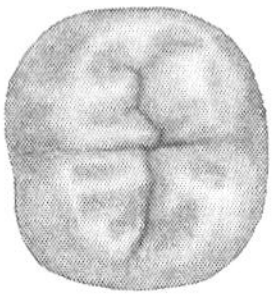

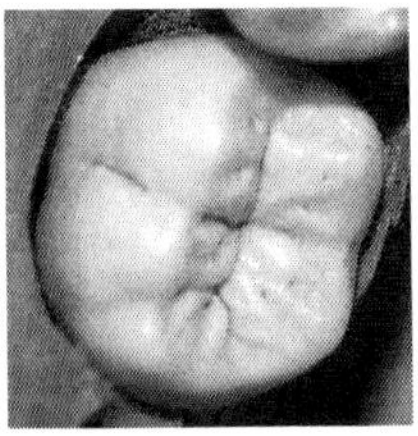

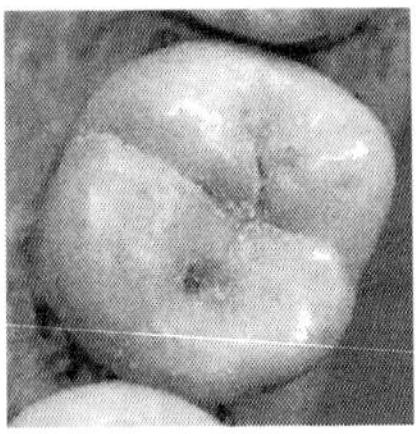

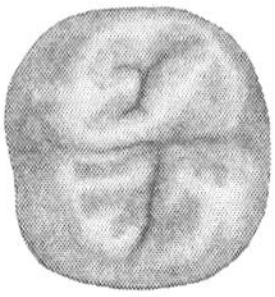

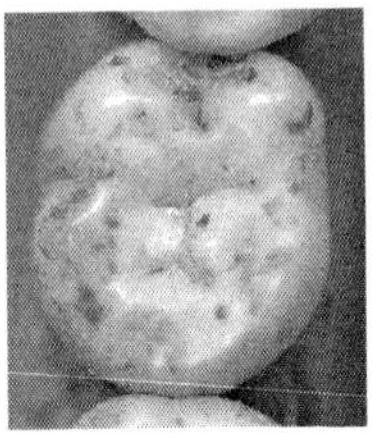

		ASUDAS Plaque: MID-TRIGONID CREST
	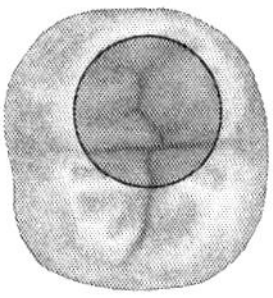	**Other Teeth Scored:** LM1; LM3

Full Name of Trait (Abbrev.): Mandibular Molar Cusp 5—First (LM1C5)

Detailed Trait Description: This observation is of the presence and size of a cusp or cuspule on the distal margin of the occlusal surface of the mandibular molars occurring between the distobuccal (cusp 3) and distolingual (cusp 4) cusps. Sometimes there are two cuspules in this location: cusps 5 and 6. If there is only one cuspule, assume it is five. If there are two cuspules, cusp 5 is the more buccal of the two.

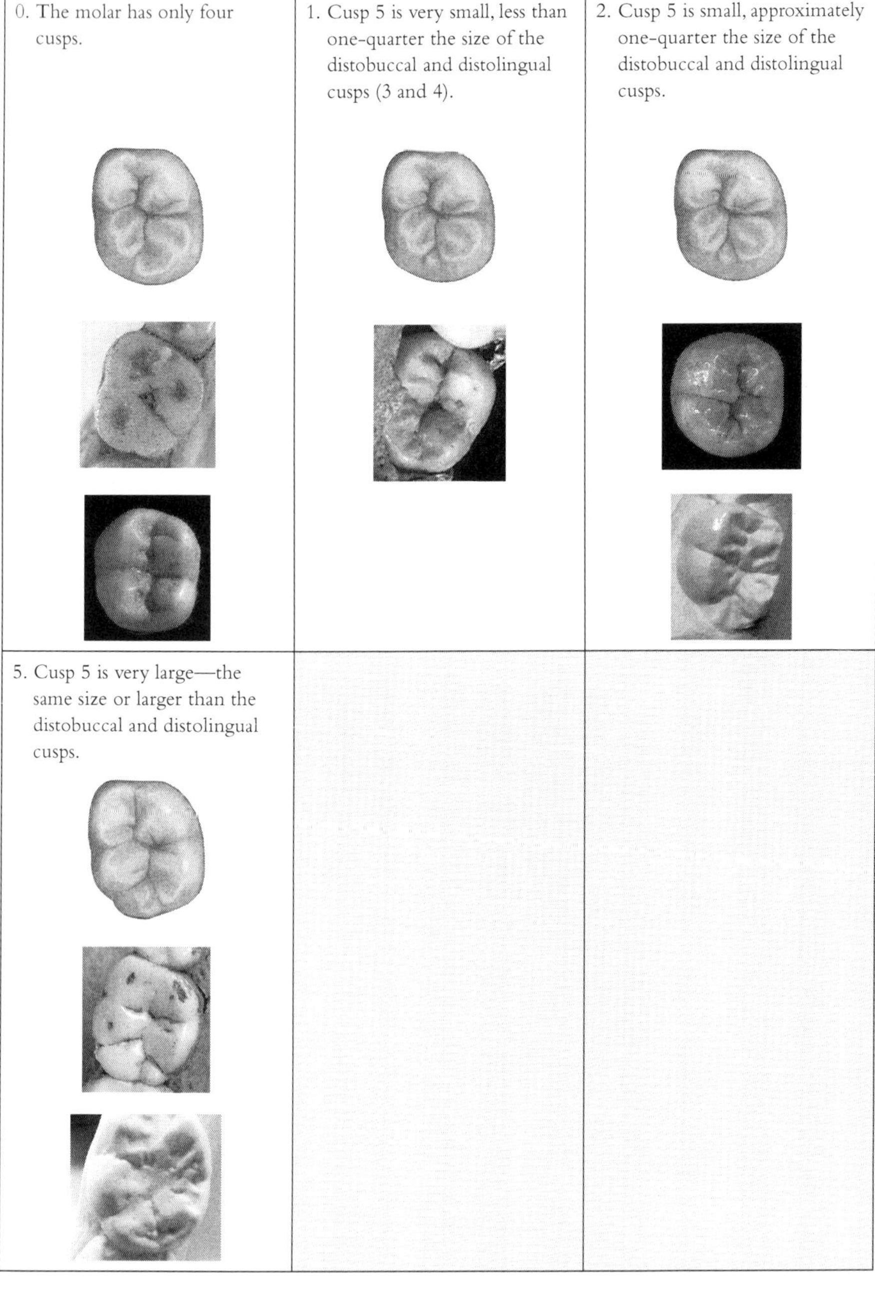

0. The molar has only four cusps.	1. Cusp 5 is very small, less than one-quarter the size of the distobuccal and distolingual cusps (3 and 4).	2. Cusp 5 is small, approximately one-quarter the size of the distobuccal and distolingual cusps.
5. Cusp 5 is very large—the same size or larger than the distobuccal and distolingual cusps.		

	ASUDAS Plaque: LM CUSP 5
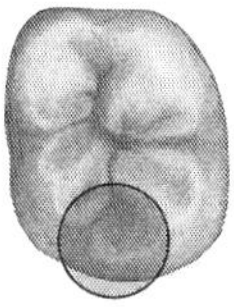	Other Teeth Scored: LM2; LM3
3. Cusp 5 is medium, approximately one-third to one-half the size of the distobuccal and distolingual cusps. 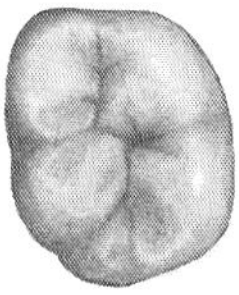 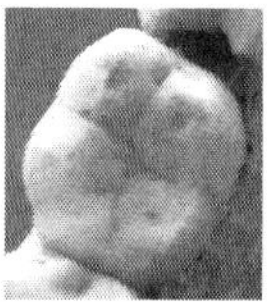 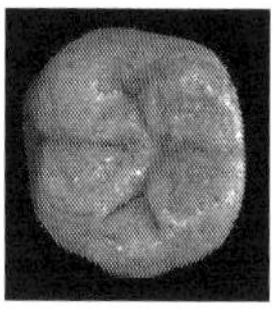	4. Cusp 5 is large, between one-half and the same size as the distobuccal and distolingual cusps. 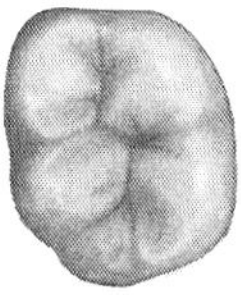  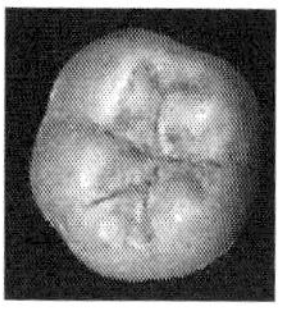

Full Name of Trait (Abbrev.): Mandibular Molar Cusp 5—Second (LM2C5)		
Detailed Trait Description: This observation is of the presence and size of a cusp or cuspule on the distal margin of the occlusal surface of the mandibular molars occurring between the distobuccal (cusp 3) and distolingual (cusp 4) cusps. Sometimes there are two cuspules in this location: cusps 5 and 6. If there is only one cuspule, assume it is five. If there are two cuspules, cusp 5 is the more buccal of the two.		
0. The molar has only the four usual cusps. 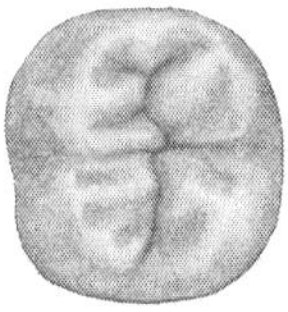 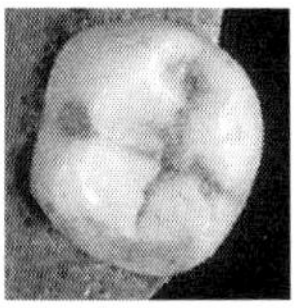 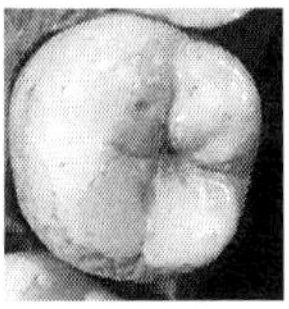	1. Cusp 5 is very small, less than one-quarter the size of the distobuccal and distolingual cusps (3 and 4). 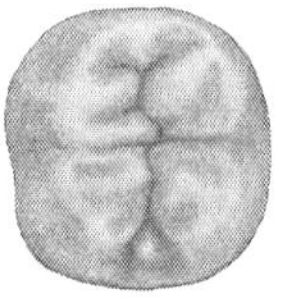 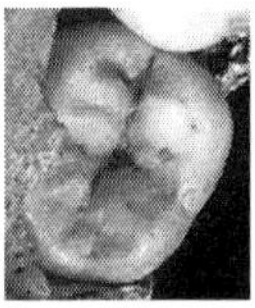 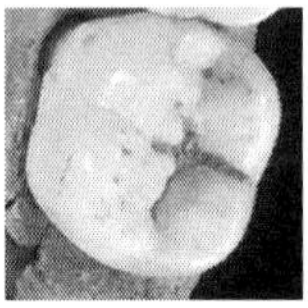	2. Cusp 5 is small, approximately one-quarter the size of the distobuccal and distolingual cusps. 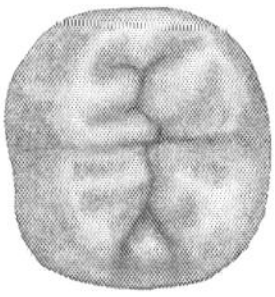 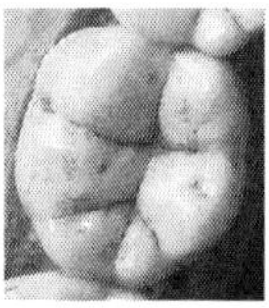 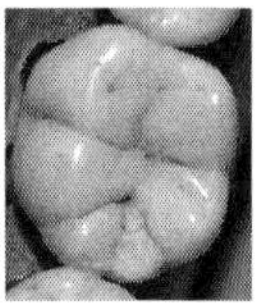
5. Cusp 5 is very large—the same size or larger than the distobuccal and distolingual cusps. 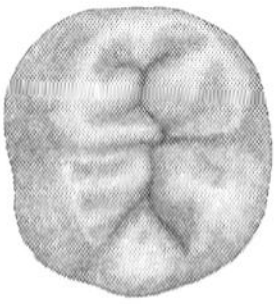 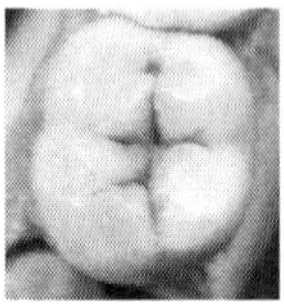 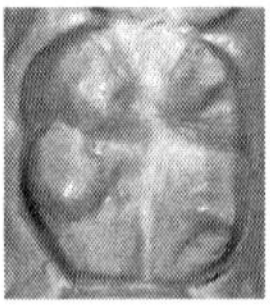		

		ASUDAS Plaque: LM CUSP 5
		Other Teeth Scored: LM1; LM3

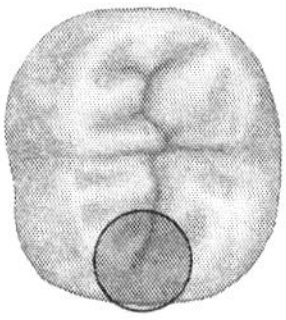

3. Cusp 5 is medium, approximately one-third to one-half the size of the distobuccal and distolingual cusps. 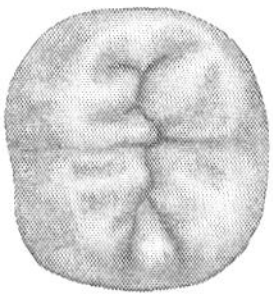 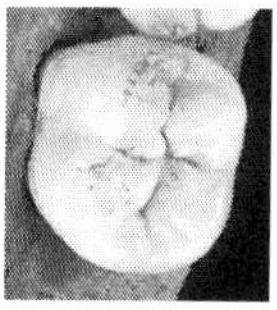 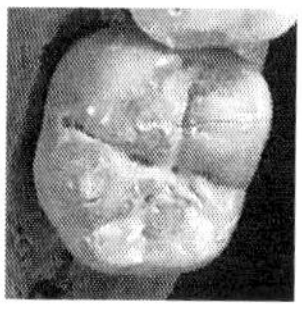	4. Cusp 5 is large, between one-half and the same size as the distobuccal and distolingual cusps. 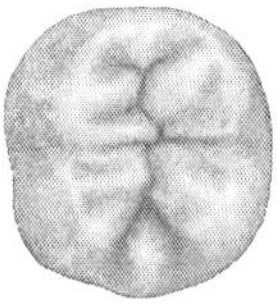 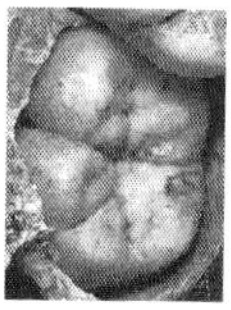 

Full Name of Trait (Abbrev.): Mandibular Molar Cusp 6—First (LM1C6)		
Detailed Trait Description: This observation is of the presence and size of a second small cusp on the distal margin of the occlusal surface of the mandibular molars occurring between the distobuccal (cusp 3) and distolingual (cusp 4) cusps. If there is only one cusp in this location, assume it is cusp 5 and score cusp 6 as absent. If there are two cusps, cusp 6 is the more lingual of the two. If the tooth is worn and it is unclear whether there is one or two cusps, do not score the trait.		
0. The molar has only four or five cusps.	1. There is a cusp lingual to cusp 5. This cusp is very small, one-third or less the size of cusp 5.	2. There is a cusp lingual to cusp 5. This cusp is larger than one-third the size of cusp 5, but not as big as cusp 5.
5. There is a cusp lingual to cusp 5. This cusp is at least one-third larger than cusp 5.		

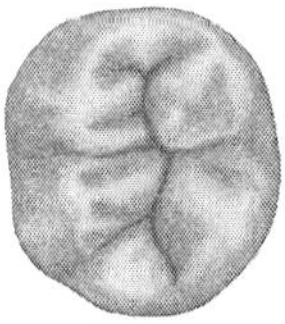

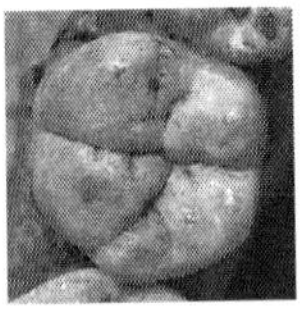

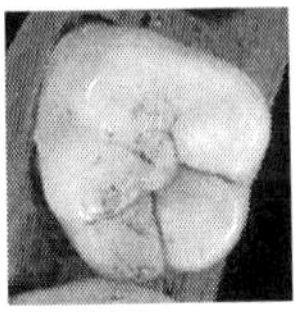

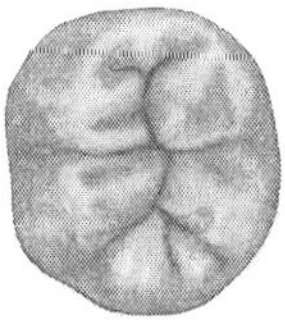

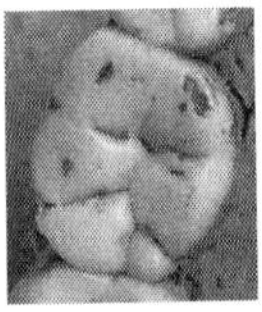

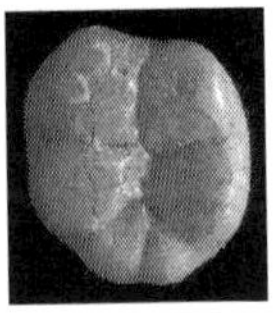

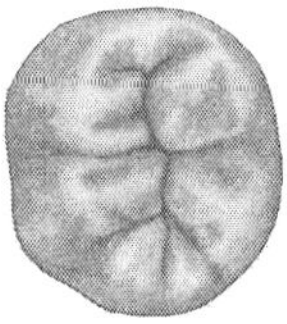

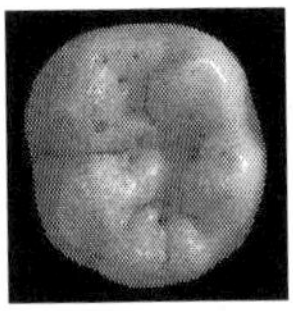

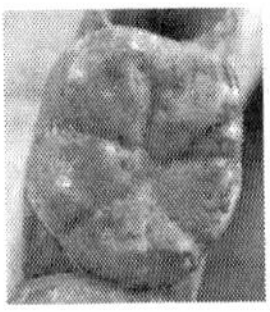

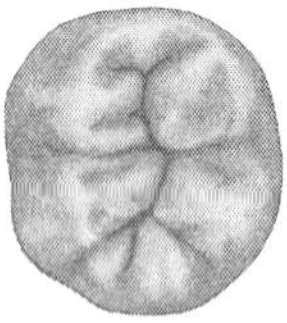

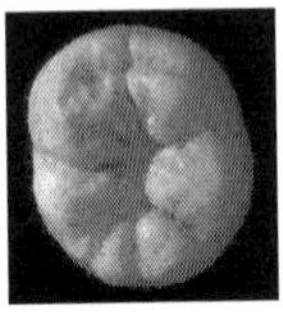

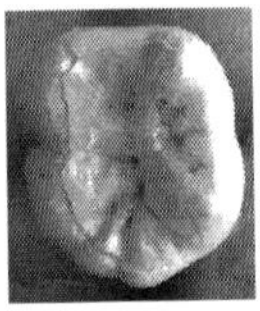

	ASUDAS Plaque: CUSP 6
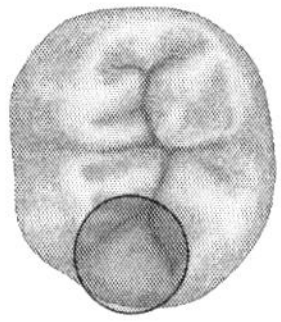	**Other Teeth Scored:** LM2; LM3
3. Cusps 5 and 6 are of equal size. 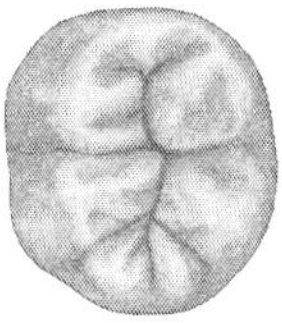 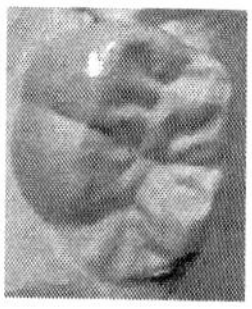 	4. There is a cusp lingual to cusp 5. This cusp is slightly larger than cusp 5. 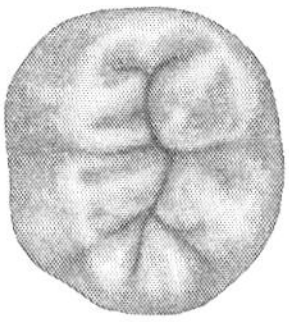 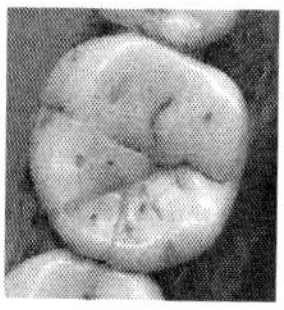 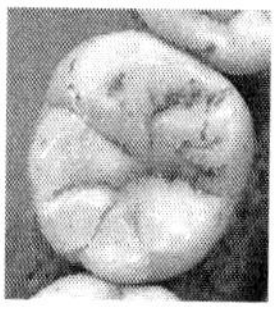

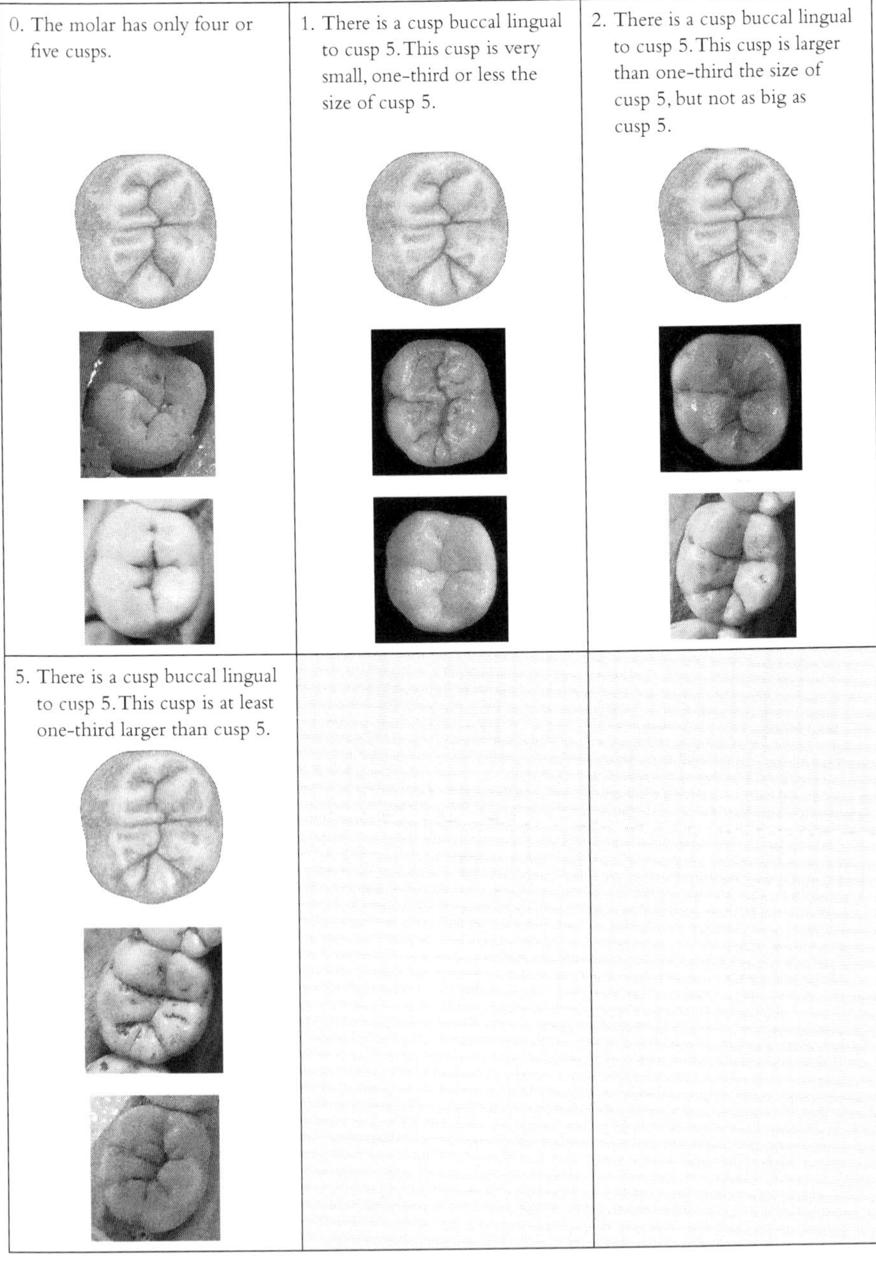

Full Name of Trait (Abbrev.): Mandibular Molar Cusp 6—Second (LM2C6)

Detailed Trait Description: This observation is of the presence and size of a second small cusp on the distal margin of the occlusal surface of the mandibular molars occurring between the distobuccal (cusp 3) and distolingual (cusp 4) cusps. If there is only one cusp in this location, assume it is cusp 5 and score cusp 6 as absent. If there are two cusps, cusp 6 is the more lingual of the two. If the tooth is worn and it is unclear whether there is one or two cusps, do not score the trait.

0. The molar has only four or five cusps.	1. There is a cusp buccal lingual to cusp 5. This cusp is very small, one-third or less the size of cusp 5.	2. There is a cusp buccal lingual to cusp 5. This cusp is larger than one-third the size of cusp 5, but not as big as cusp 5.
5. There is a cusp buccal lingual to cusp 5. This cusp is at least one-third larger than cusp 5.		

	ASUDAS Plaque: CUSP 6
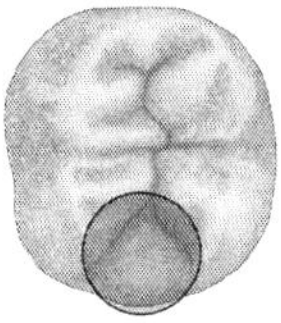	**Other Teeth Scored:** LM1; LM3
3. Cusps 5 and 6 are of equal size. 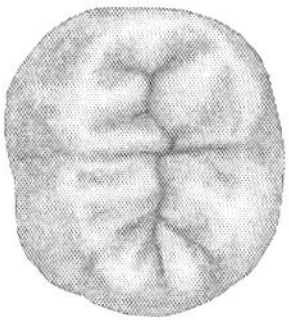 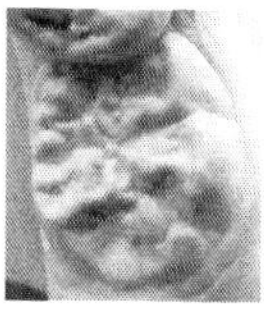 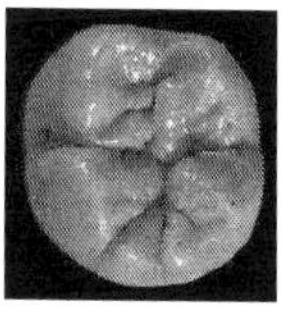	4. There is a cusp buccal lingual to cusp 5. This cusp is slightly larger than cusp 5. 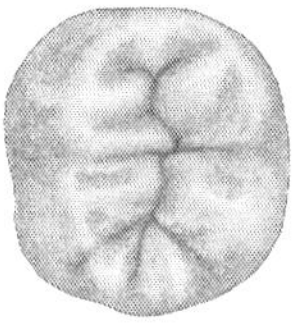  

Full Name of Trait (Abbrev.): Mandibular Molar Cusp 7—First (LM1C7)

Detailed Trait Description: This trait is a small cusp that can occur on the lingual side of the occlusal surface of mandibular molars between the mesiolingual (cusp 2) and distolingual (cusp 4) cusps. M1 often expresses this trait more strongly than M2. Turner et al. (1991) scores 1 and 1A are combined here for ease of statistical analysis.

0. There is no cusp or ridge between the main mesiolingual and distolingual cusps (2 and 4). 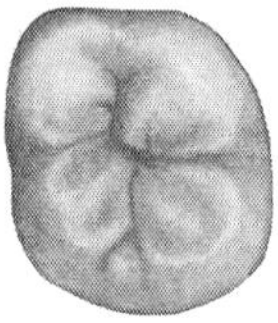  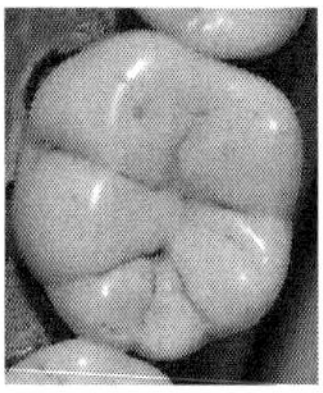	1. A faint cusp is present, demarcated by the presence of two lingual grooves. It may occur as a bulge along cusp 2. 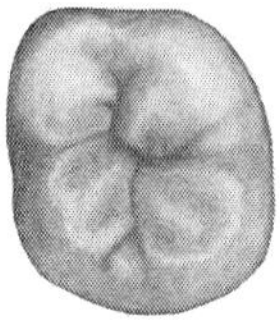 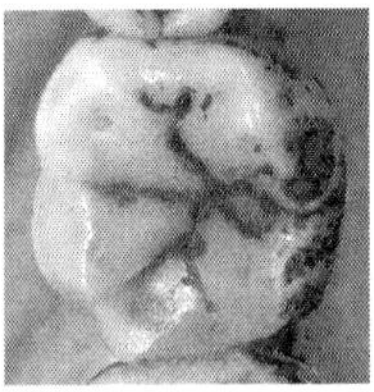 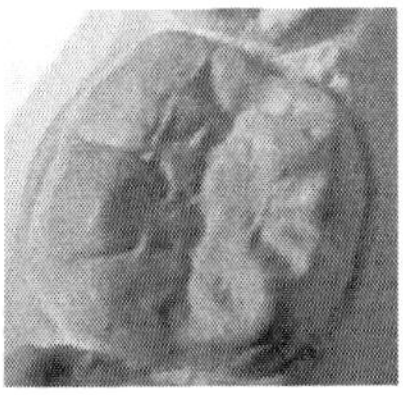	2. Cusp 7 is small and may appear to lean toward cusp 2. 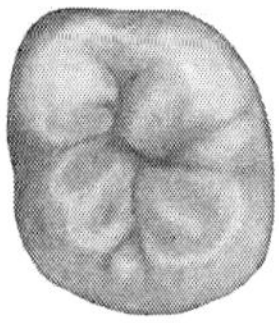  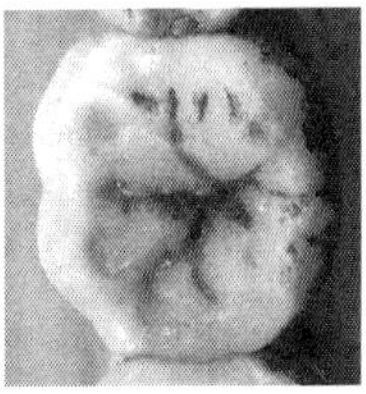

	ASUDAS Plaque: CUSP 7
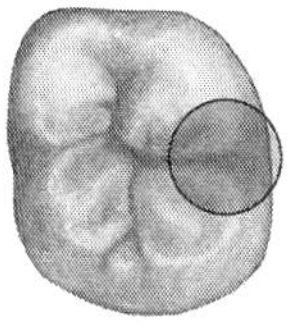	**Other Teeth Scored:** LM2; LM3
3. Cusp 7 is medium and in the midline between cusps 2 and 4. 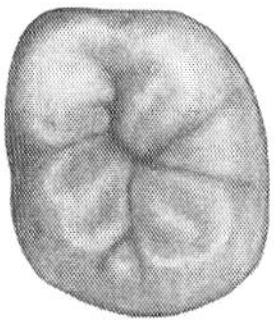 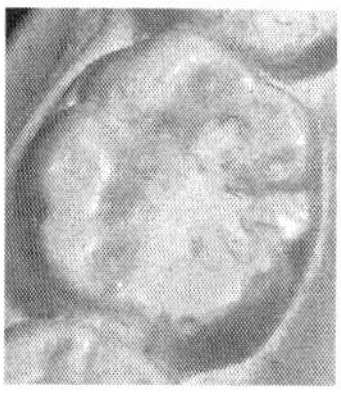 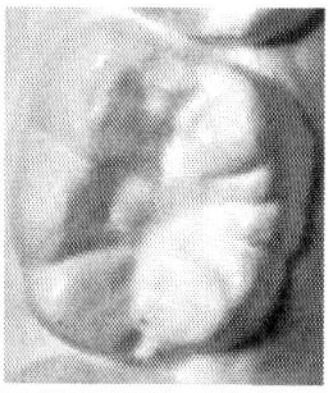	4. Cusp 7 approaches the size of the mesiolingual cusp and lies in the midline between the mesiolingual and distolingual cusps. 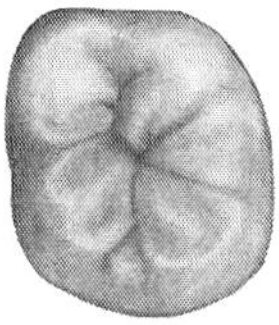 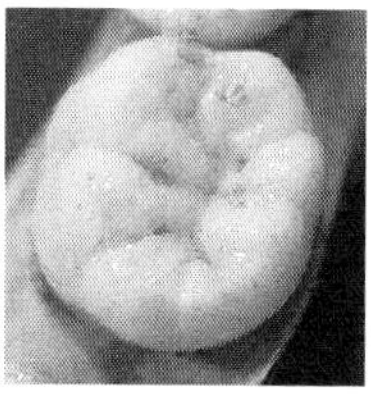 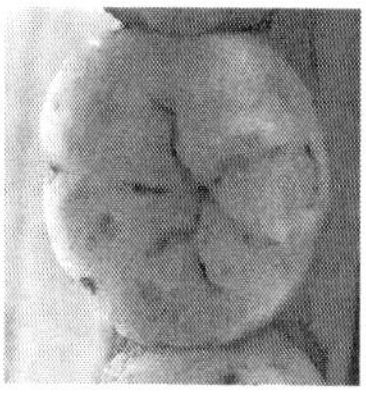

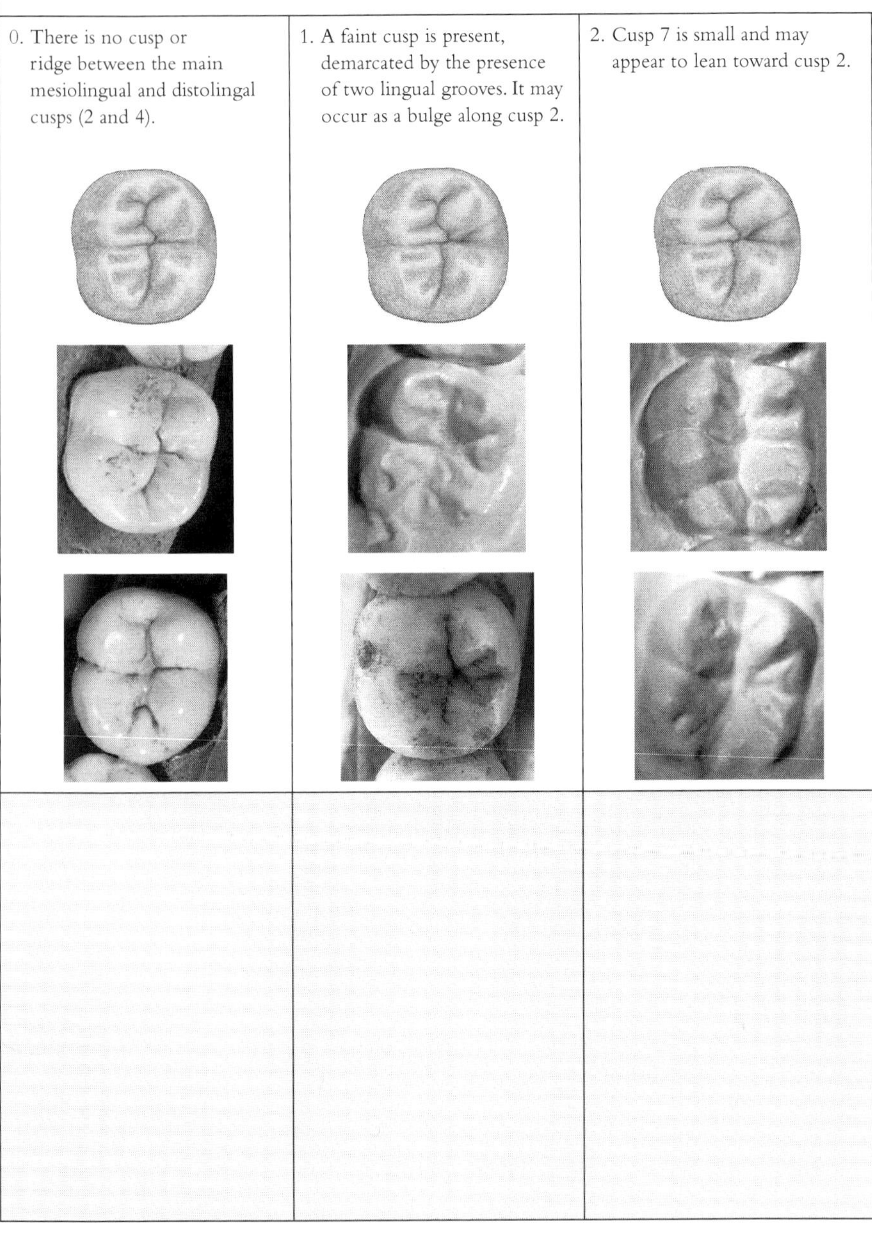

Full Name of Trait (Abbrev.): Mandibular Molar Cusp 7—Second (LM2C7)

Detailed Trait Description: This trait is a small cusp that can occur on the lingual side of the occlusal surface of mandibular molars between cusps 2 (mesiolingual) and 4 (distolingual). M2 often expresses this trait less strongly than M1. Turner et al. (1991) scores 1 and 1A are combined here for ease of statistical analysis.

0. There is no cusp or ridge between the main mesiolingual and distolingal cusps (2 and 4).	1. A faint cusp is present, demarcated by the presence of two lingual grooves. It may occur as a bulge along cusp 2.	2. Cusp 7 is small and may appear to lean toward cusp 2.

	ASUDAS Plaque: CUSP 7
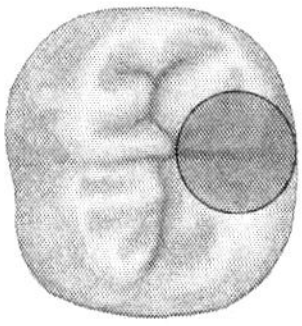	Other Teeth Scored: LM1; LM3
3. Cusp 7 is medium and in the midline between cusps 2 and 4. 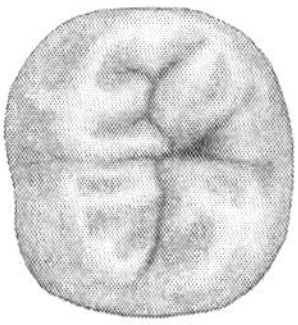 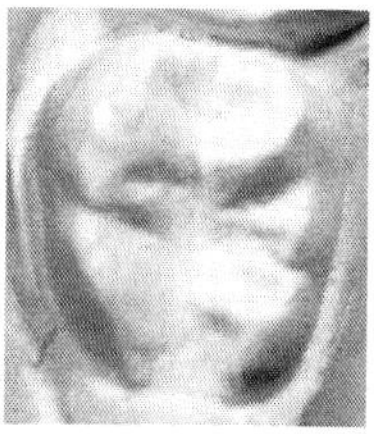 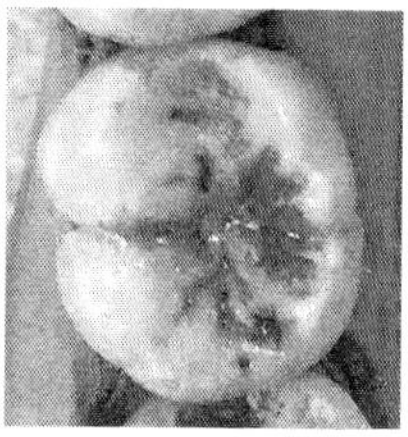	4. Cusp 7 approaches the size of the mesiolingual cusp, and lies in the midline between the mesiolingual and distolingual cusps. 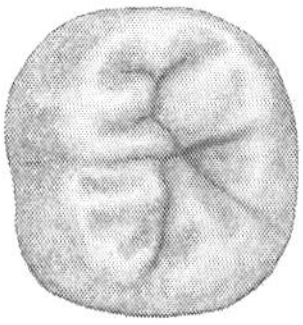 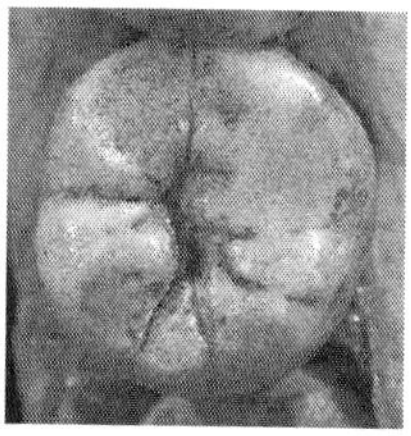 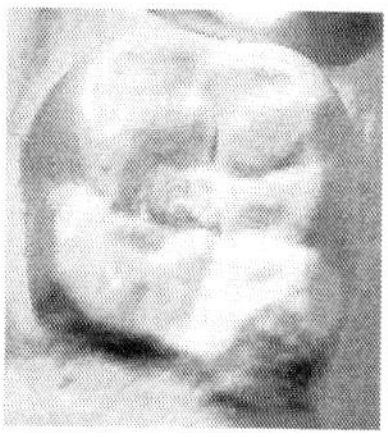

Full Name of Trait (Abbrev.): Mandibular Molar Enamel Extension (LMEE)

Detailed Trait Description: This trait is an apical extension of the enamel from a straight line that is the usual cemeto-enamel junction on the buccal surface, usually in line with the buccal groove. It is more common on maxillary than mandibular molars. Enamel in the buccal groove but not attached to the tooth crown is not considered an enamel extension, but may be an enamel pearl.

0. The enamel margin is straight or curved away from the tooth's apex.	1. There is an extension of the enamel in line with the buccal groove. The extension is less than 2 mm long.	2. There is an extension of the enamel in line with the buccal groove. The extension is more than 2 mm but less than 4 mm long.

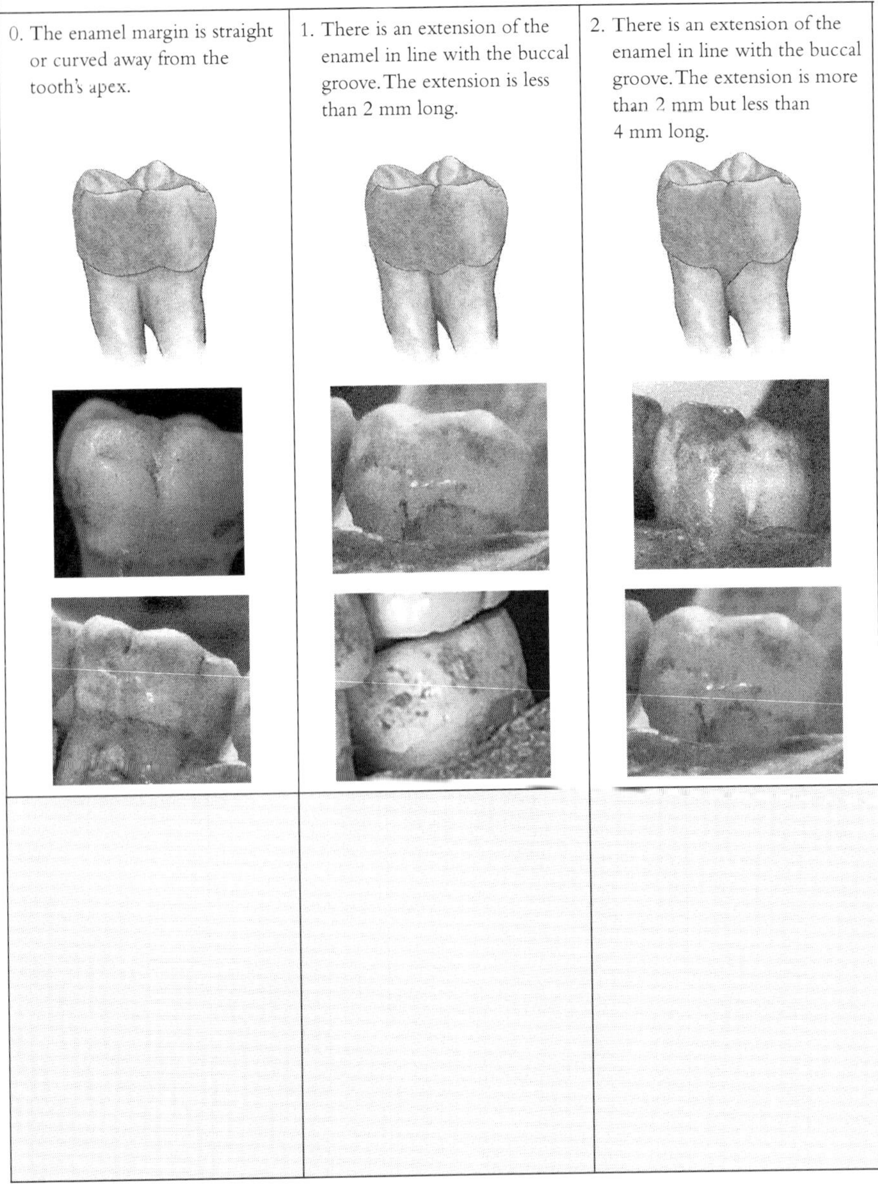

	ASUDAS Plaque: None
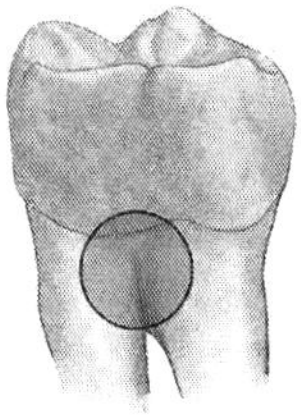	**Other Teeth Scored:** Upper molars
3. There is an extension of the enamel in line with the buccal groove. The extension is more than 4 mm long. 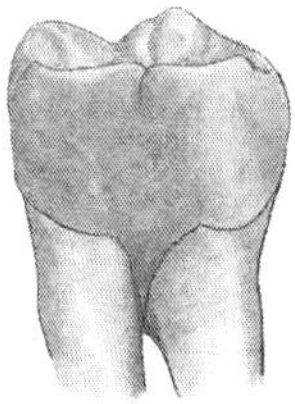 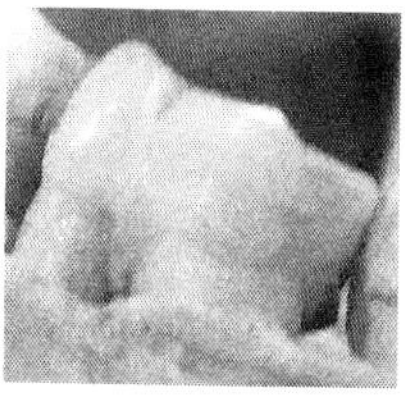 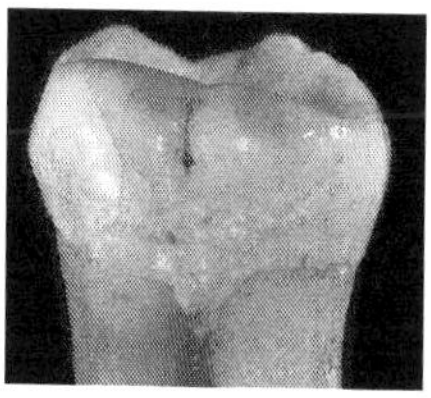	

Rare traits		
Full Name of Trait	*Description*	*Reference*
Maxillary Incisor Talon Tooth	A large accessory cusp extends from the cingulum at least half the length toward the occlusal edge. A ridge of enamel often connects the apex of this cusp to what would usually be the lingual surface of the tooth.  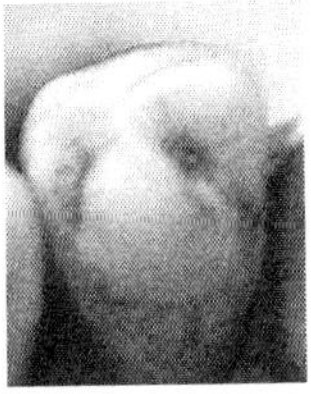	Bailey-Schmidt, 1995
Maxillary Incisor Mesial Bending—Lateral	There is a concavity in the middle of the mesiolingual margin of the tooth, causing the appearance of the tooth to appear to bend toward the midline. 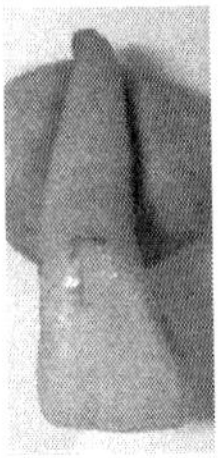 	Pinto-Cisternas et al., 1995
Maxillary Premolar Tri-cusp Form—Anterior and Posterior	The tooth has two lingual cusps, rather than the usual single cusp. 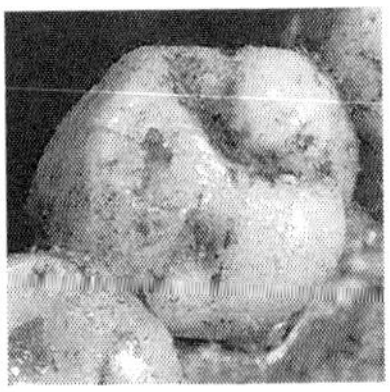 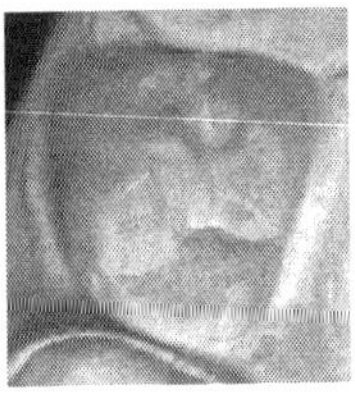	Turner et al., 1991
Maxillary Molar Enamel Pearl and Mandibular Molar Enamel Pearl	There is a globule of enamel on the buccal surface of the tooth root, usually in the bifurcation, that is not in contact with the tooth crown. 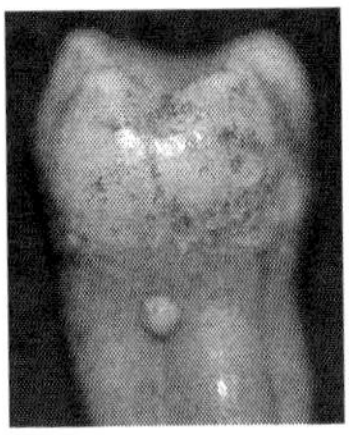 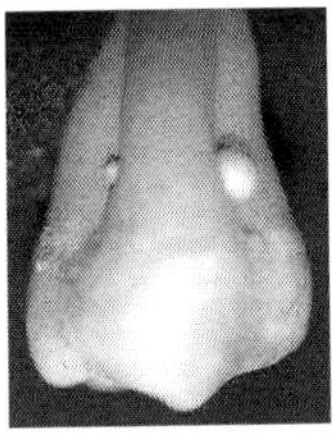	Risnes, 1974

Full Name of Trait	*Description*	*Reference*
Premolar Odontome	A spike or cone of enamel and dentin that projects from the occlusal surface of a premolar, often from the center of the tooth. While they tend to fracture from the tooth, because they have a dentin component, they can be scored if the tooth is not very worn by the presence of a small circular exposure of dentin. 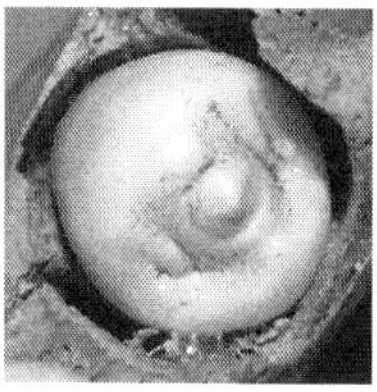 	Turner et al., 1991
Supernumerary teeth	The presence of one or more teeth greater than the number usually seen in any particular tooth class. The tooth may be small, peg-shaped, or of normal anatomy. Record the class of the tooth if possible as well as its location with regard to the dental arch. 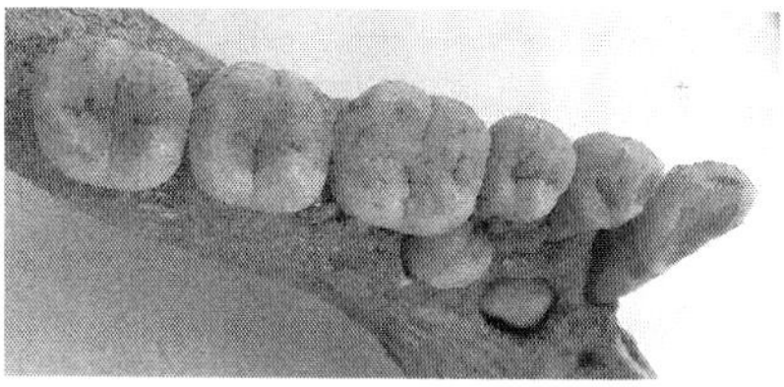 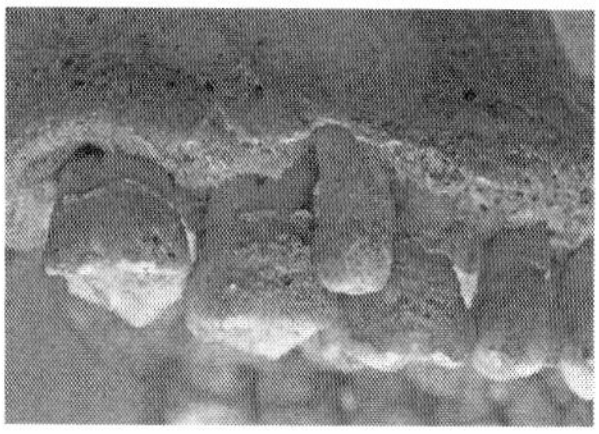	Hillson, 1996

4

DATA COLLECTION PAGES

These pages are based on and updated from similar pages sent out when ASUDAS casts are purchased from Arizona State University. They may be photocopied from this book and used for data collection. Simply record the score for each observation in the appropriate square in the matrix.

Alternatively, data collection can be made directly into an access database custom designed to work with this manual. This database and associated documentation can be found through the author's faculty page at the University of New Mexico, or requested directly from the author.

DATA ENTRY SHEET 1 MAX

Specimen Number		*Data Collector*		*Date*	
Collection		Collection Location			
Other Identifiers/Notes					

	UI1		UI2		UC		UP3		UP4		UM1		UM2		UM3	
Trait	R	L	R	L	R	L	R	L	R	L	R	L	R	L	R	L
Winging																
Diastema																
Labial Curvature																
Double Shoveling																
Shoveling																
Peg/Reduced Tooth																
Congenital Absence																

Specimen Number					*Data Collector*							*Date*				
Trait	R	L	R	L	R	L	R	L	R	L	R	L	R	L	R	L
Interruption Groove																
Tuberculum Dentale																
Mesial Ridge																
Distal Accessory Ridge																
Accessory Cusps																
Distosagittal Ridge																
Mesial Accessory Ridge																
Distal Accessory Ridge																
Metacone																
Hypocone																
Cusp 5																
Carabelli's																
Parastyle																
Enamel Extension																

DATA ENTRY SHEET 2 MAND

Specimen Number					*Data Collector*							*Date*				
Notes																
	LI1		LI2		LC		LP3		LP4		LM1		LM2		LM3	
Trait	L	R	L	R	L	R	L	R	L	R	L	R	L	R	L	R
Shoveling																
Congenital Absence																
Peg/Reduced Tooth																
Distal Accessory Ridge																
Elongated Form																
Premolar Complexity																
Anterior Fovea																
Deflecting Wrinkle																
Groove Pattern																

Specimen Number					*Data Collector*							*Date*				
Trait	L	R	L	R	L	R	L	R	L	R	L	R	L	R	L	R
Cusp Number																
Protostylid																
Trigonid Crest																
Cusp 5																
Cusp 6																
Cusp 7																
Enamel Extension																
Rare Traits																
Talon tooth					Odontome							Other Observations				
Mesial Bending					Enamel Pearl											
Tri-cusped Premolar					Supernumerary											

5

ROOT TRAITS

Many dental anthropological studies have made use of root traits as variables in addition to those observed on the crown (see Table 5.1; Turner, 1990; Irish, 1997). If roots are observable on a high percentage of individuals being analyzed, these traits can add useful information. Most root traits have to do with deviation from the usual number of roots a tooth has. A root is considered present when the bifurcation between it and another root is greater than at least a quarter of the whole root length (Scott et al., 2016). Some researchers also record the number of radicals tooth roots have. Radicals are, "separated rootlike divisions" (Scott and Turner, 1997, p. 22) that are demarcated from each other by developmental grooves. The number of radicals a tooth or dentition has is always equal or greater than the number of roots.

In addition to variation in root number alone, Tomes's root consists of variation of both the number of radicals and the form of the roots. The trait is observed on LP3, and involves the presence of three or four radicals and a second root that does not descend directly in a straight line inferior to a cusp (Scott and Turner, 1997).

A final root trait can be identified with radiographic images. Taurodontism is seen when the pulp chambers of cheek teeth are larger than normal, especially superoinferiorly. This enlargement is associated with shorter roots beyond the furcation. Taurodontism is associated with some genetic disorders and is more common in Neandertals and other hominine groups than in modern humans (Trinkaus, 1978; Zilberman and Smith, 1992).

TABLE 5.1 Usual Numbers of Roots per Tooth and Common Variants

Maxillary	*Number*	*Common Variants*	*Mandibular*	*Number*	*Common Variants*
I 1, 2	1	none	I 1, 2	1	none
C	1	none	C	1	2
P 3	1, 2	3	P 3	1	2, Tomes's
P4	1	2, 3	P4	1	none
M1	3	2, 4	M1	2	3
M2	2, 3	1	M2	1, 2	3
M3	1, 2, 3	none	M3	1, 2	3

6

ARCH AND TOOTH REFERENCE PAGES

The following images are provided as references for where teeth fit in the maxilla and mandible, directions in each arcade, and directions on generalized anterior and cheek teeth. The first image shows a maxilla and mandible with the full complement of dentition. Each tooth class and number is indicated, as are the primary directions of left and right, and mesial, distal, buccal, labial, and lingual. Unlabeled photographs of a maxilla and a mandible, also with all teeth present and relatively unworn, follow these drawings.

Generalized drawings of an incisor and a molar follow the arch images. These images show mesial, distal, lingual, labial, and buccal directions for each tooth. The regions of the tooth, apical, middle, cervical, middle, incisal, and occlusal are indicated. The information shown on the incisor applies to the canine, and the information about the molar applies as well to the premolar.

Next, occlusal views of a maxillary and a mandibular molar are presented with cusp names, numbers, and locations. These are shown with mesial, distal, buccal, and lingual cardinal directions to aid with cusp identification for data collection.

Finally, there are drawings and photographs of a maxilla and mandible with full deciduous dentition. These images are provided to help in the recognition of deciduous teeth. Deciduous morphological traits have been described and standardized (Hanihara, 1963; Grine, 1986; Sciulli, 1998), and they have proved useful for understanding biological relationships at multiple levels, sometimes in combination with data from metric analyses or permanent morphology (Sciulli, 1990; Kitagawa et al., 1995; Lease and Sciulli, 2005; Lukacs and Walimbe, 2005; Delgado-Burbano, 2008; Pilloud and Larsen, 2011; Diaz et al., 2014; Paul and Stojanowski, 2015). However, consistent with previous texts on morphological variation in permanent teeth, deciduous dental morphology is not described here.

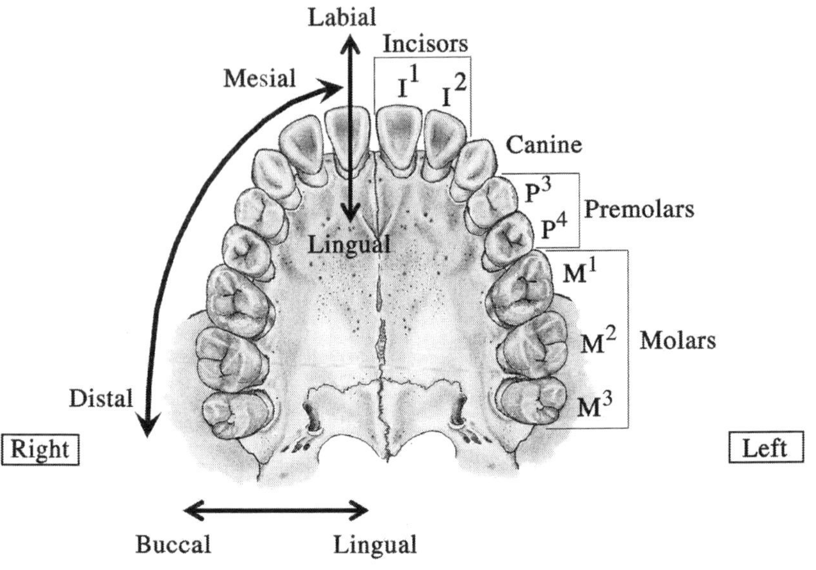

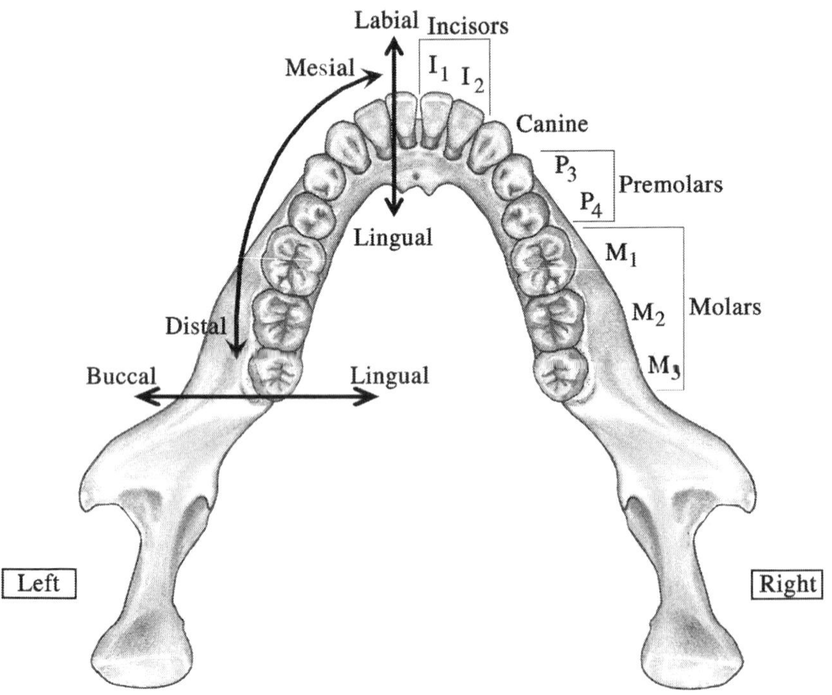

FIGURE 6.1 Illustrations of an adult maxilla and mandible with the full complement of dentition. Each tooth class and number is indicated, as are the primary directions of left and right, and mesial, distal, buccal, labial, and lingual.

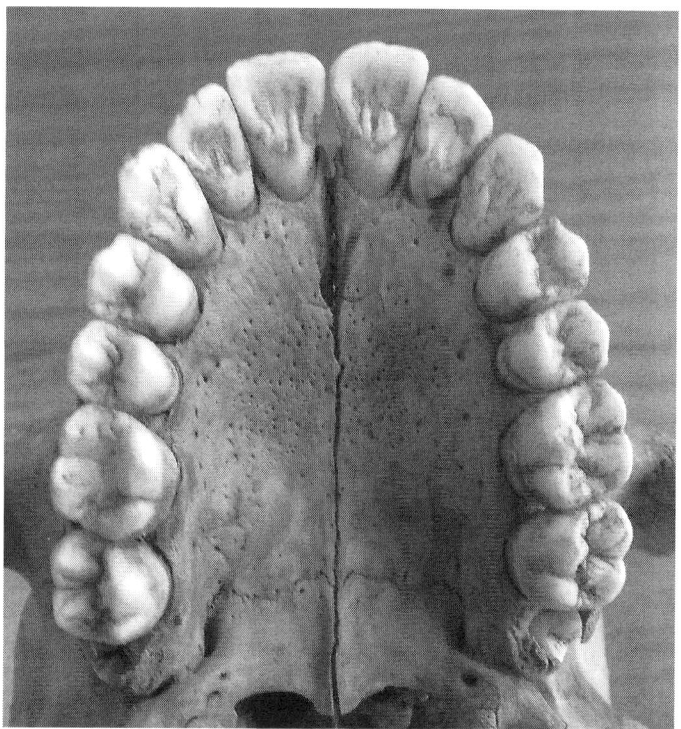

FIGURE 6.2 An adult maxilla, with all teeth present and little wear. Note that the third molars are impacted.

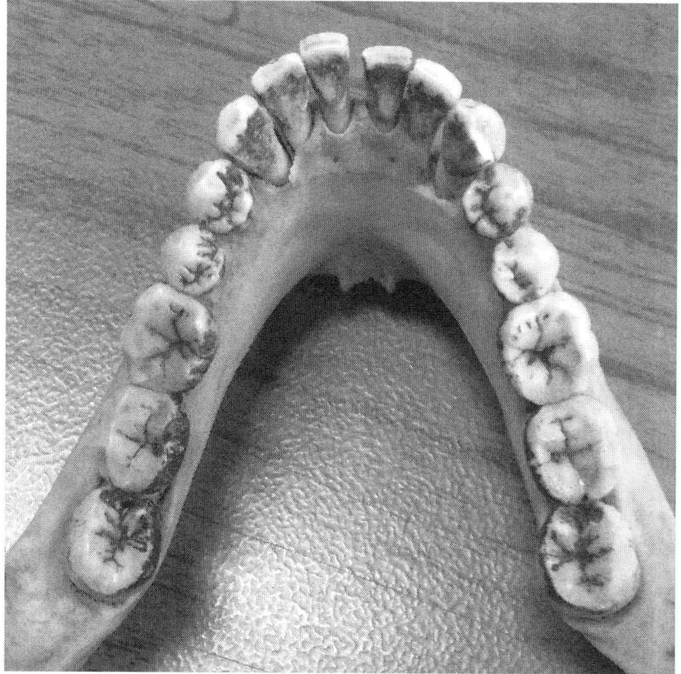

FIGURE 6.3 An adult mandible with all teeth and little wear.

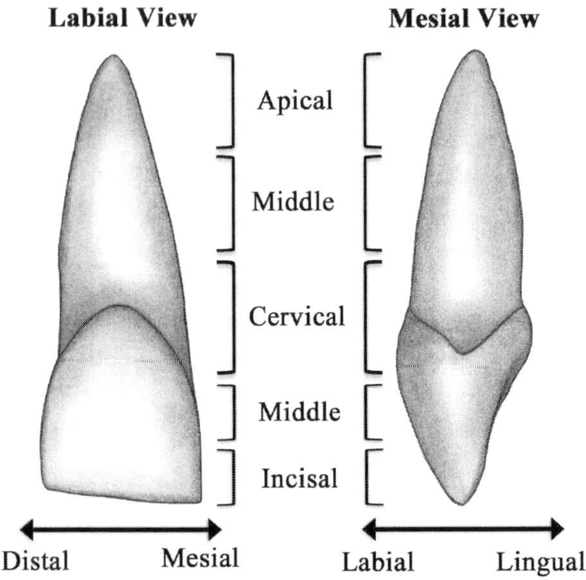

FIGURE 6.4 Schematic view of an anterior tooth (incisor or canine), illustrating directions and portions of the tooth.

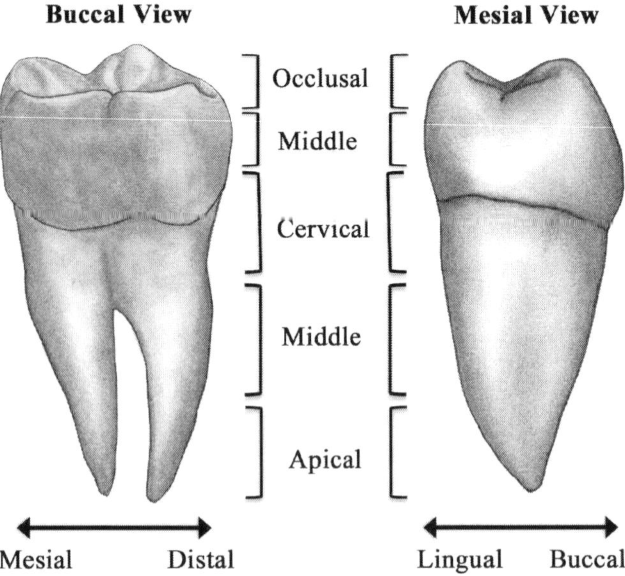

FIGURE 6.5 A schematic view of a posterior tooth (premolar or molar) indicating directions and portions.

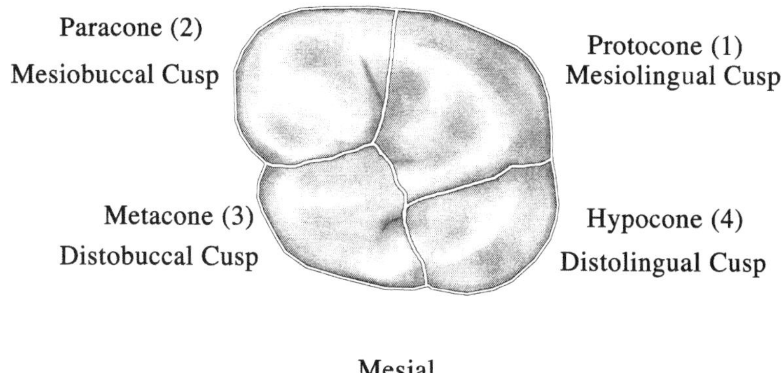

FIGURE 6.6 A schematic of a maxillary molar, indicating directions and cusp names, numbers, and positions.

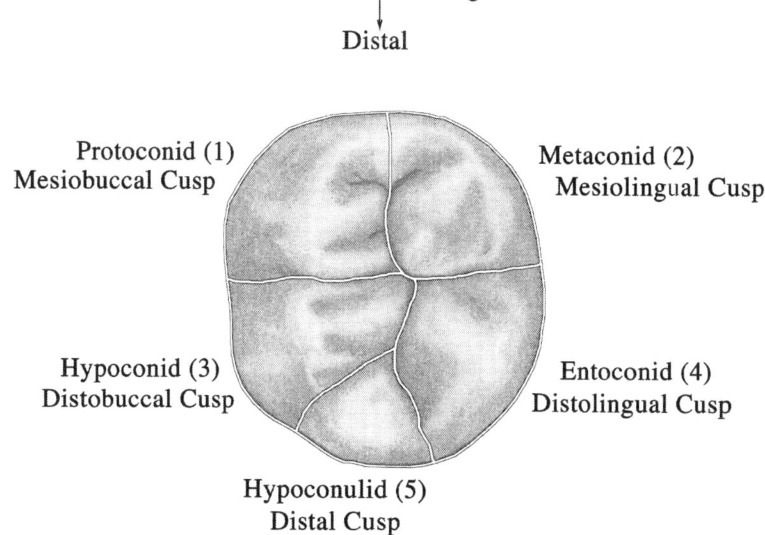

FIGURE 6.7 A schematic of a mandibular molar, indicating directions and cusp names, numbers, and positions.

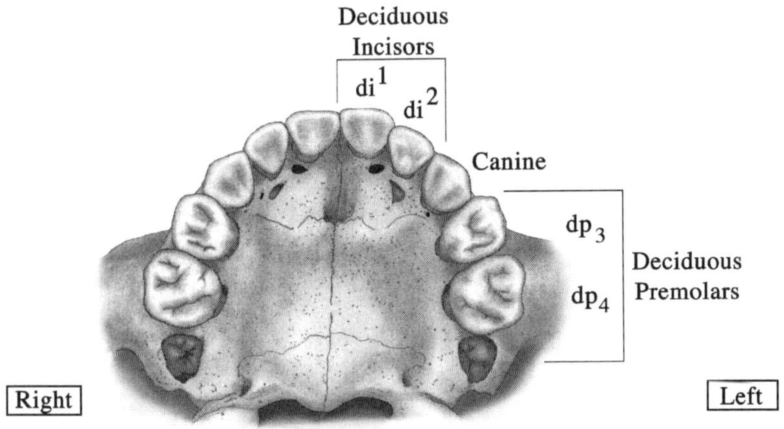

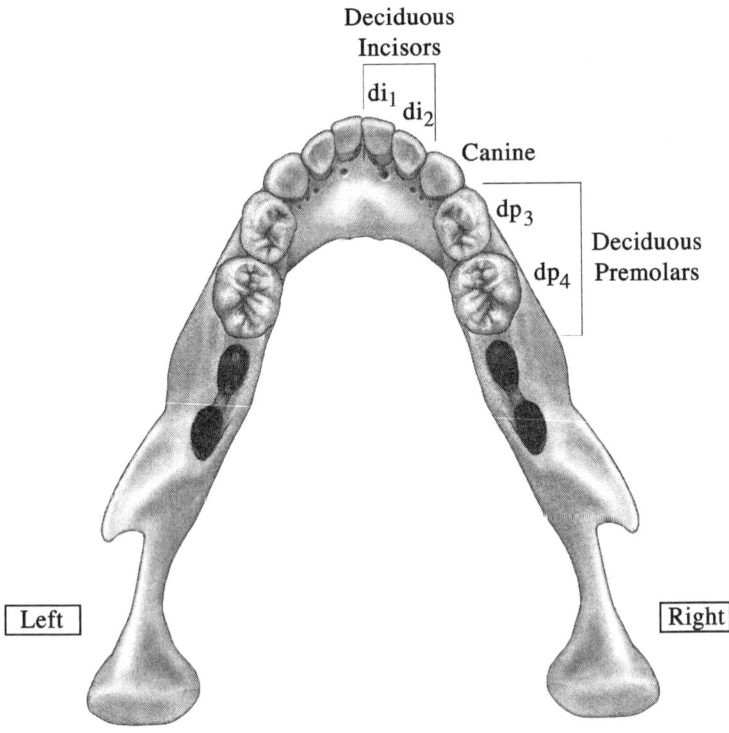

FIGURE 6.8 A schematic of a deciduous maxilla and mandible. Morphological characteristics of these teeth are not included in this manual. These illustrations are provided to help users recognize these teeth, in part to avoid scoring them.

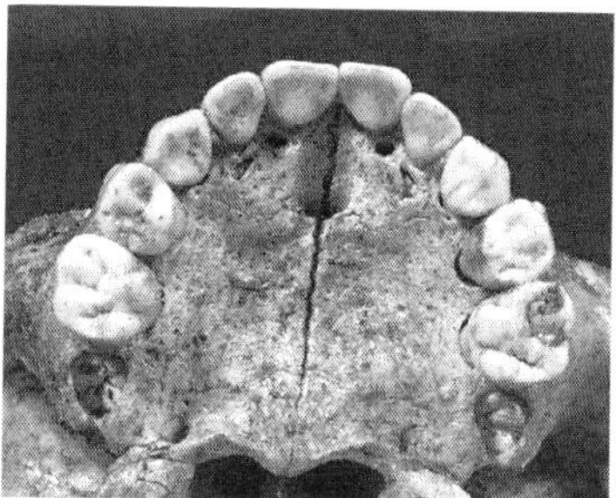

FIGURE 6.9 A deciduous maxilla. These illustrations are provided to help users recognize these teeth, in part to avoid scoring them. Confusion especially arises between the dm2 and the M1.

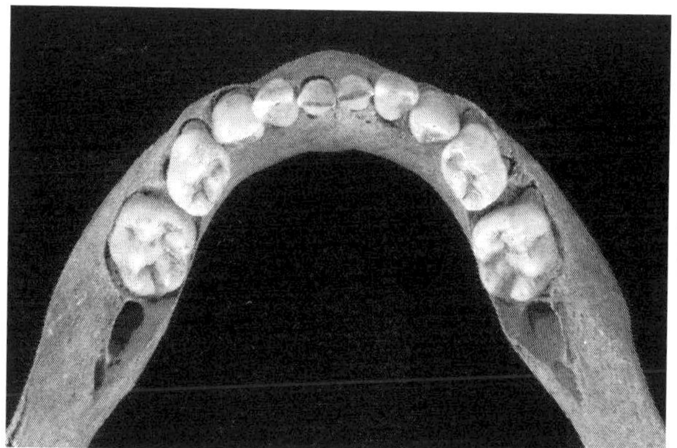

FIGURE 6.10 A deciduous mandible. These illustrations are provided to help users recognize these teeth, in part to avoid scoring them. Confusion especially arises between the dm2 and the M1.

GLOSSARY

Abbreviations: For tooth classes: C = canine, I = incisor, P = premolar, M = molar. For arches: L = lower, mandibular, U = upper, maxillary.

Alveolus: The bone that forms sockets to hold the teeth. It is part of the alveolar processes of the maxilla and mandible.

Antimeres: Teeth that are the same arch, class, and tooth number, but on the left and right sides.

Apical: Toward the root end of a tooth.

ASUDAS: The Arizona State University Dental Anthropology System. This has been the primary guide for collecting dental morphological data since Turner et al. (1991) published their chapter describing standardized observations of most traits. The method consists of using the descriptions in the chapter in conjunction with plaster plaques that represent trait variations to score expressions of dental morphological variants in individual dentitions.

Buccal: The side of a tooth that faces the cheek. Premolars and molars have buccal surfaces, which are equivalent to labial surfaces on incisors and canines.

Calculus: Mineralized dental tartar (plaque) that may cover the surfaces of teeth, obscuring observations of dental morphology.

Canines: Teeth normally found between the second incisor and the third premolar. They usually have a single root and a more or less pointed occlusal margin.

Caries: Dental cavities caused by bacterial decay. Caries will obscure observations of dental morphology.

Cemento-enamel junction: Cervix; cervical line. Where the portion of the tooth root covered with cementum meets the area of dentin covered by enamel.

Cementum: A mineralized substance that covers tooth roots. Cementum is attached to the alveolus via the periodontal ligament.

Cingulum: A bulge on the lingual surface of the base of the crown of anterior teeth.

Crown: The enamel and enamel-covered portion of dentin and pulp chamber that, in life and after eruption, is in the oral cavity.

Cusp: A convex area on a tooth, usually on the occlusal surface. Premolars have one buccal cusp and one to three lingual cusps. Molars have four primary cusps. Cusps are separated from each other by grooves. Additional cusp variations may be found on the occlusal, buccal, and lingual surfaces of molars.

Cuspule: A small cusp that may not have a free apex.

Deciduous: The first set of teeth to develop in humans, which are shed as the permanent teeth develop and erupt. There are 20 deciduous teeth, consisting of two incisors, one canine, and two molars in each quadrant. Some authors refer to deciduous molars as premolars to denote that they are superseded by the permanent premolars and not by molars.

Dentin: The portion of the tooth that forms the root as well as the tooth crown between the enamel and pulp chamber. Dentin is softer than enamel and about the same hardness as bone. As a tooth wears, the pulp chamber can become filled with secondary dentin, which is usually darker than primary dentin.

Distal: Toward the posterior portion of the mouth.

Enamel: The material of the tooth that is visible in the oral cavity after development and eruption. It is the outermost surface of the tooth crown, where nearly all dental morphological characteristics are observed. Enamel is the hardest, most mineralized substance in the human body.

Groove/fissure: A furrow that separates other dental morphological features such as ridges or cusps.

Hypoplasia: A defect of enamel development. Hypoplasia may be evidenced by a single pit, a linear series of pits, a planar area of thinned or absent enamel, or a line of thinned or absent enamel. This last type, called linear enamel hypoplasia (LEH) is most common, and is thought to be evidence of disturbance during tooth development. LEH are most often found on incisors and canines, but it can be seen on premolars and molars as well. Hypoplasia can obscure observation of, or can be mistaken for, dental morphological variants.

Incisal: The cutting edge of an incisor or canine.

Incisor: The most mesial tooth class. Incisors have a spatulate tooth crown and almost always a single root.

Isomeres: Teeth that are the same tooth class, number, and side, but in maxillary and mandibular arches. They oppose each other in occlusion.

Key teeth: From field theory (Butler, 1939). The tooth in a class that most clearly expresses dental morphological variants. These teeth are thought to be the most developmentally and evolutionarily stable in their classes. For incisors, the first incisor is the key tooth in the maxilla, while the second incisor is the key tooth in the mandible. The canine is its own key tooth, as there is only one tooth in the class. The third premolar is key in both arches for the premolars, while the first molar is key in both arches for the molar. Some authors indicate that the first molar is the key tooth for premolars and molars.

Labial: The side of a tooth that faces the lips. Incisors and canines have labial surfaces, which are equivalent to buccal surfaces on premolars and molars.

Lingual: The side of a tooth that faces the tongue. Some authors use the term "palatal" to refer to lingual surfaces of maxillary teeth.

Mandibular: Teeth in the lower arch, situated in the mandible (the jaw).

Margin: The area at the edge of a tooth surface. For example, the margin of the lingual surface of an incisor is the portion of that surface closest to the mesial or distal surface of that tooth. Shovel shaping is observed as variation in the elevation and thickness of the ridges at the margins of the lingual surfaces of incisors and canines.

Maxillary: Teeth in the upper arch, situated in the maxilla.

Mesial: Toward the midline of the mouth, between the central (first) incisors.

Molars: The most distal tooth class. These teeth usually have the largest crowns, with relatively flat, roughly square or rectangular surfaces used for chewing. Maxillary molars typically have three roots (the largest being on the lingual side), while mandibular molars typically have two roots: one mesial, and one distal. Third molars, however, are highly variable with respect to root number.

Occlusal: The chewing surface of a premolar or molar.

Pit: An indentation in a tooth surface with little to no length (not a groove).

Premolars: The tooth class situated between the canines and the molars. Except for the maxillary third premolar, which often has two roots, premolars generally have one root, though Tomes's root is a morphological variant in which the third mandibular premolar has two roots. Premolar crowns generally have one buccal cusp; maxillary premolars almost always have one lingual cusp, while mandibular premolars may have one, two, or three lingual cusps. In humans, premolars are considered a transitional tooth class, serving both biting and chewing functions. Humans almost always have two premolars, but they are often referred to as premolar 3 and premolar 4. This terminology reflects that mammals may have up to four premolars, and humans are thought to have only retained the more distal two through our evolution.

Pulp chamber: The most interior portion of a tooth. In life, it contains nerves and blood vessels. Coronal pulp is in the crown of the tooth; radicular pulp is central to tooth roots.

Quadrant: The left or right side of a single tooth arch. Each quadrant of a mouth normally has eight permanent teeth, two incisors, one canine, two premolars, and three molars.

Radical: Divisions of a tooth root that are separated from each other by a developmental groove.

Ridge (Loph): A raised elevation of enamel, sometimes with a dentin component, that has length and may be separated from other structures by a groove.

Root: The portion of the tooth that holds the tooth in the alveolus. The root consists primarily of dentin. This dentin surrounds the root canal, which is contiguous with the pulp chamber. Incisors, canines, and third mandibular premolars and fourth premolars usually have one root. Third premolars in the maxilla may have one or two roots. Maxillary first and second molars usually have three roots, while mandibular first and second molars usually have two. Third molars are highly variable with regard to root number.

Tooth numbering system: 1 = The most mesial incisor or molar in a quadrant—the first incisor or molar. 2 = The tooth distal to the first incisor or molar in a quadrant. 3 = The molar distal to the second molar in a quadrant; in humans, it is the most mesial premolar in a quadrant, which is denoted as third by convention and to recognize the evolutionary history of mammals having four premolars. 4 = The premolar distal to the third premolar in a quadrant. As there is normally only one canine per quadrant, canines are not denoted with a tooth number.

Wear: The loss of enamel and dentin through attrition or abrasion. Attrition is the result of contact between teeth during chewing. Abrasion results from nonmasticatory uses, such as processing hides with the teeth, tooth brushing, or holding a pipe. Wear can obscure the observation of dental morphological characteristics.

TRAIT EXPRESSION SUMMARY PAGES

Trait Expression Summaries

Trait Abbreviation	Trait Location	Trait Expression Drawings
UI Wing	N/A	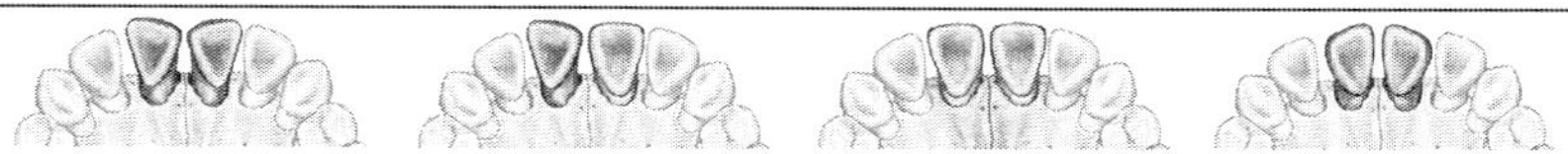 1, 2, 3, 4
DIAS	N/A	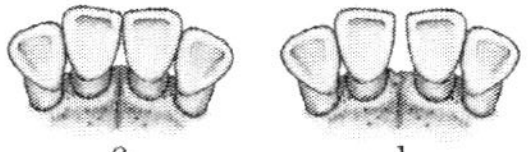 0, 1
UI1LC		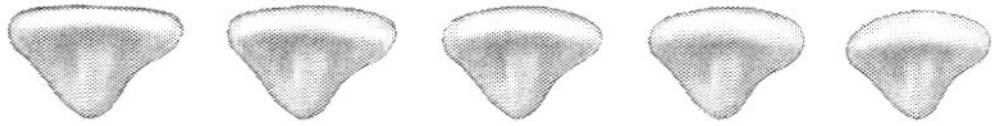 0, 1, 2, 3, 4
UI1DS	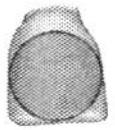	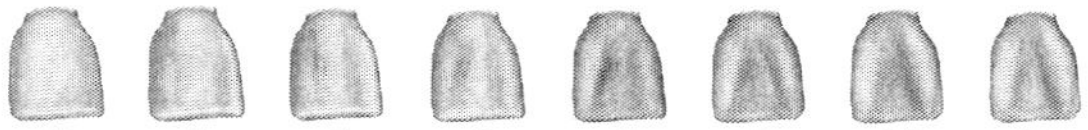 0, 1, 2, 3, 4, 5, 6.1, 6.2
UI2DS	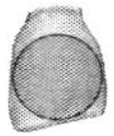	 0, 1, 2, 3, 4, 5, 6
UI1SS		 0, 1, 2, 3, 4, 5, 6
UI2SS		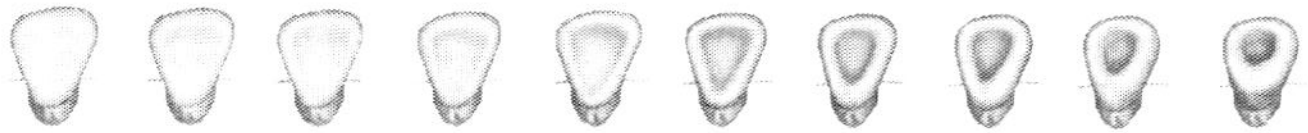 0, 1, 2, 3, 4, 5.1, 5.2, 6.1, 6.2, 7
UCSS		 0, 1, 2, 3, 4, 5, 6

Trait Expression Summaries

Trait Abbreviation	Trait Location	Trait Expression Drawings									
UI2 PEG	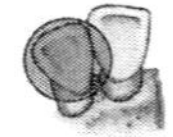	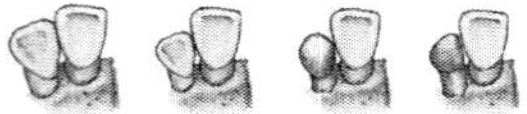 0	1	2.1	2.2						
UM3 PEG		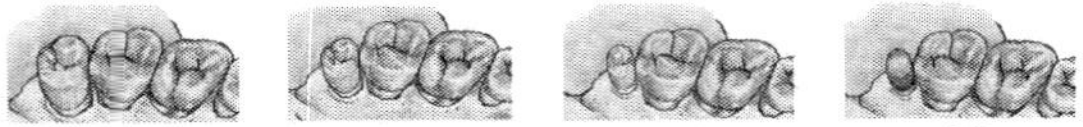 0	1	2.1	2.2						
UI1IG		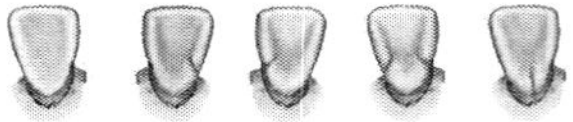 0	1	2	3	4					
UI2IG		 0	1	2	3	4					
UI1TD		 0	1	2	3	3.1	4	4.1	5	6	
UI2TD		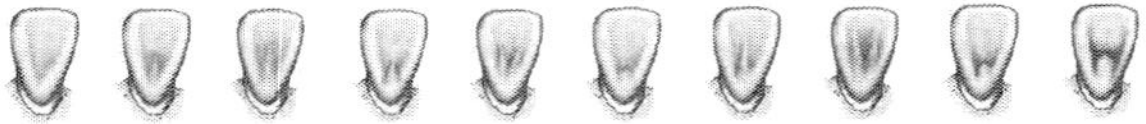 0	1	2	3	3.1	3.2	4	4.1	5	6
UCTD		 0	1	2	3	4	5	6			
UCMR		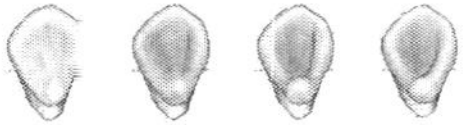 0	1	2	3						

Trait Expression Summaries

Trait Abbreviation	Trait Location	Trait Expression Drawings						
UCDR		 0	1	2	3.1	3.2	4	5
UP3AC		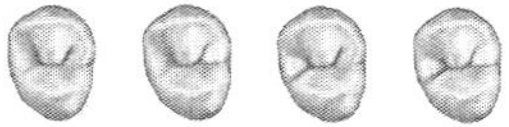 0	1	2	3			
UP4AC		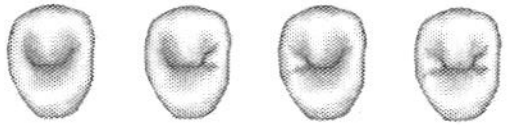 0	1	2	3			
UP3DS	N/A	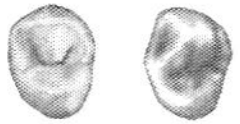 0	1					
UP3M MXPAR		 0	1	2	3	4		
UP4M MXPAR		 0	1	2	3	4		
UP3D MXPAR		 0	1	2	3	4		
UP4D MXPAR		 0	1	2	3	4		

Trait Expression Summaries

Trait Abbreviation	Trait Location	Trait Expression Drawings							
UM1MC		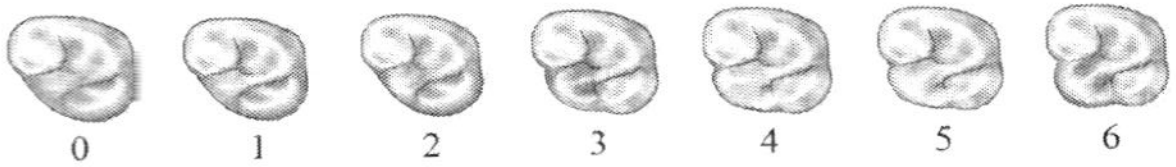 0	1	2	3	4	5	6	
UM2MC		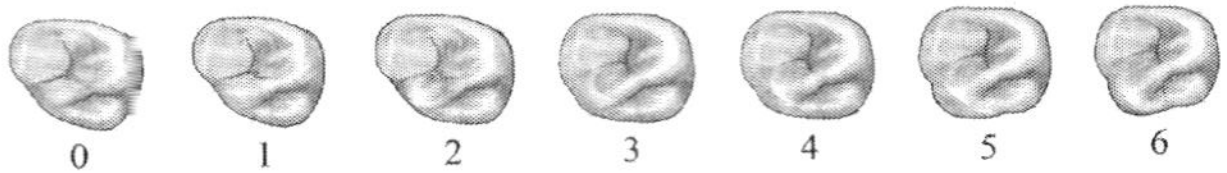 0	1	2	3	4	5	6	
UM1HC		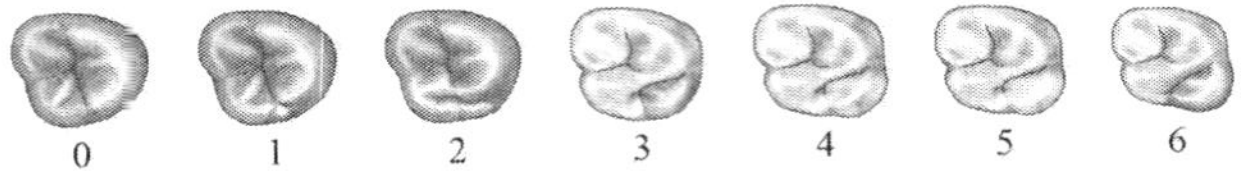 0	1	2	3	4	5	6	
UM2HC		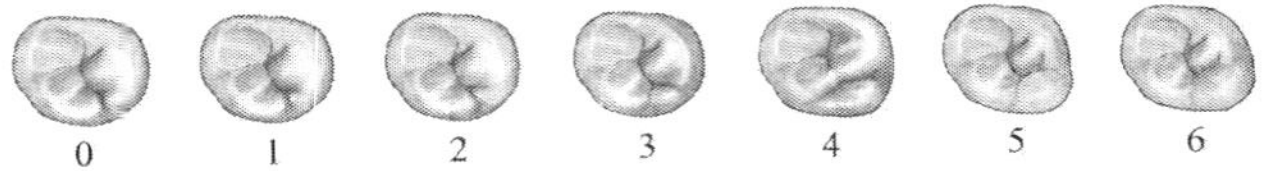 0	1	2	3	4	5	6	
UM1C5		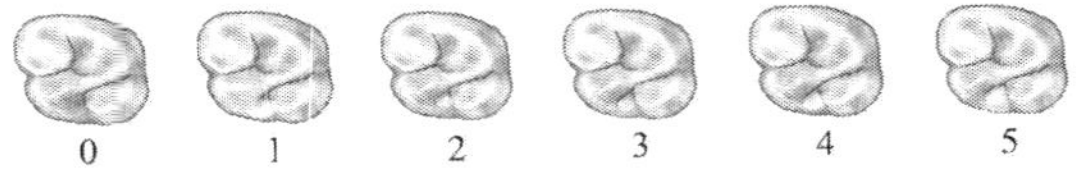 0	1	2	3	4	5		
UM2C5	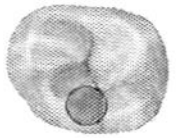	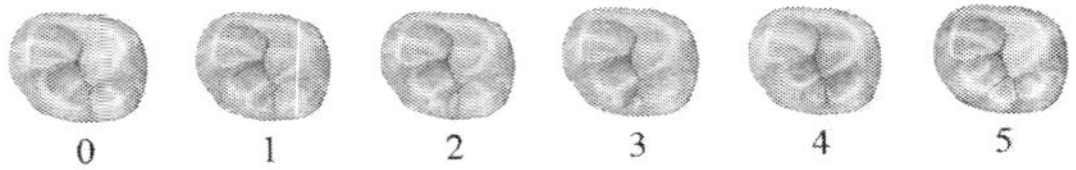 0	1	2	3	4	5		
UM1CB		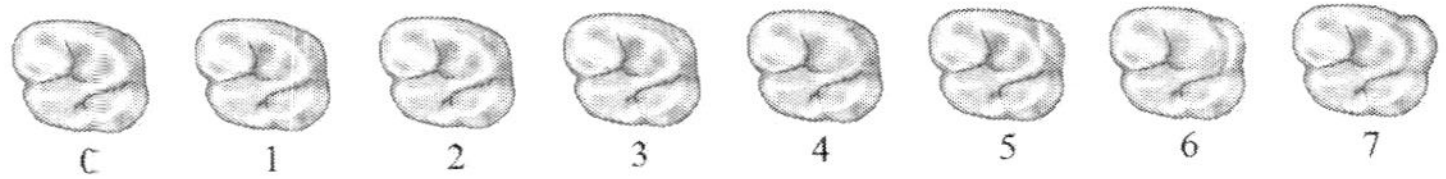 C	1	2	3	4	5	6	7
UM2CB		0	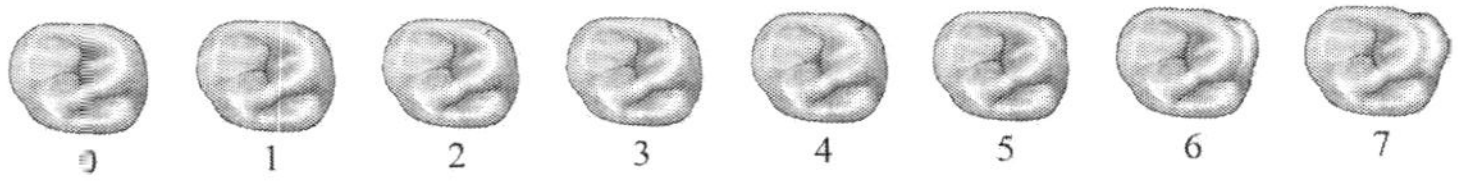 1	2	3	4	5	6	7

Trait Expression Summaries

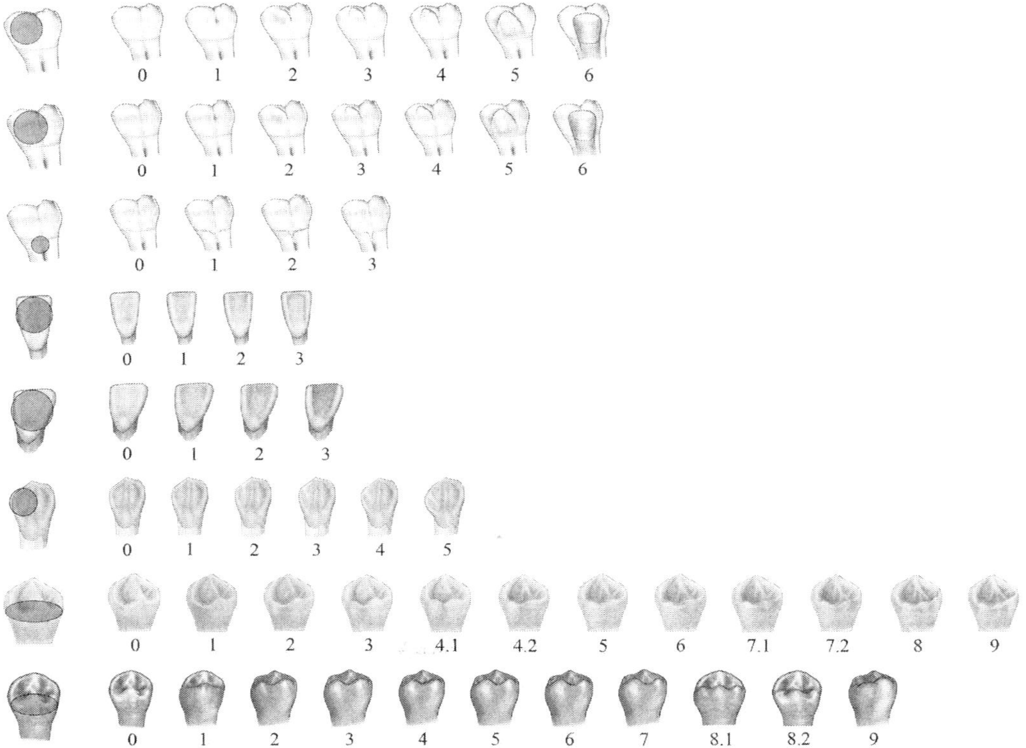

Trait Abbreviation	Trait Location	Trait Expression Drawings
UM1PR		0 1 2 3 4 5 6
UM2PR		0 1 2 3 4 5 6
UMEE		0 1 2 3
LI1SS		0 1 2 3
LI2SS		0 1 2 3
LCDR		0 1 2 3 4 5
LP3LC		0 1 2 3 4.1 4.2 5 6 7.1 7.2 8 9
LP4LC		0 1 2 3 4 5 6 7 8.1 8.2 9

Trait Expression Summaries

Trait Abbreviation	Trait Location	Trait Expression Drawings				
LP3EF	N/A	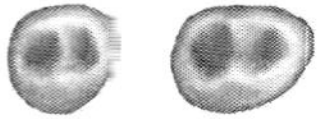 0	1			
LP4EF	N/A	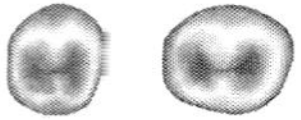 0	1			
LM1AF		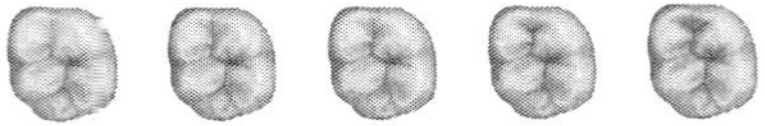 0	1	2	3	4
LM1DW	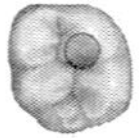	 0	1	2	3	
LM1GP	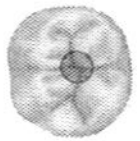	 0	1	2		
LM2GP		 0	1	2		
LM1CN		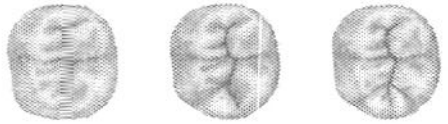 4	5	6		
LM2CN		 3	4	5	6	

Trait Expression Summaries

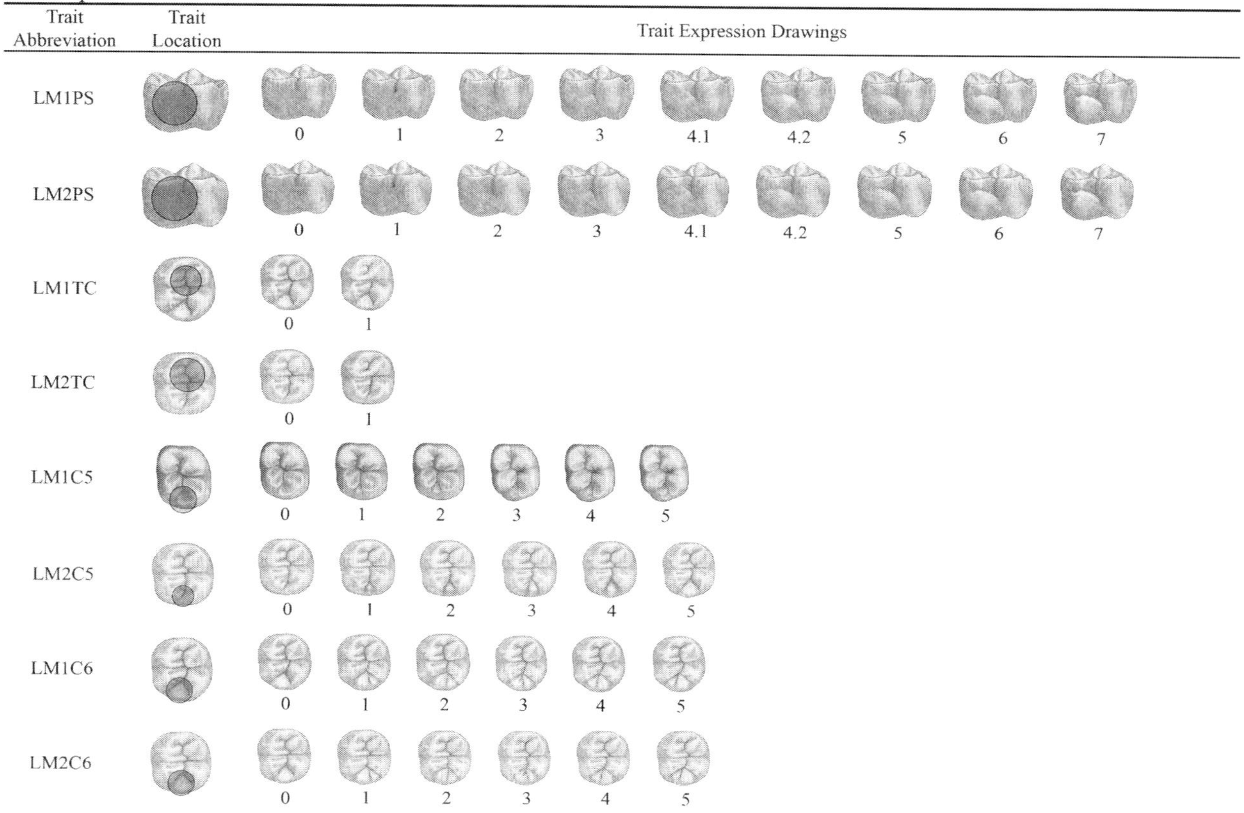

Trait Abbreviation	Trait Location	Trait Expression Drawings								
LM1PS		0	1	2	3	4.1	4.2	5	6	7
LM2PS		0	1	2	3	4.1	4.2	5	6	7
LM1TC		0	1							
LM2TC		0	1							
LM1C5		0	1	2	3	4	5			
LM2C5		0	1	2	3	4	5			
LM1C6		0	1	2	3	4	5			
LM2C6		0	1	2	3	4	5			

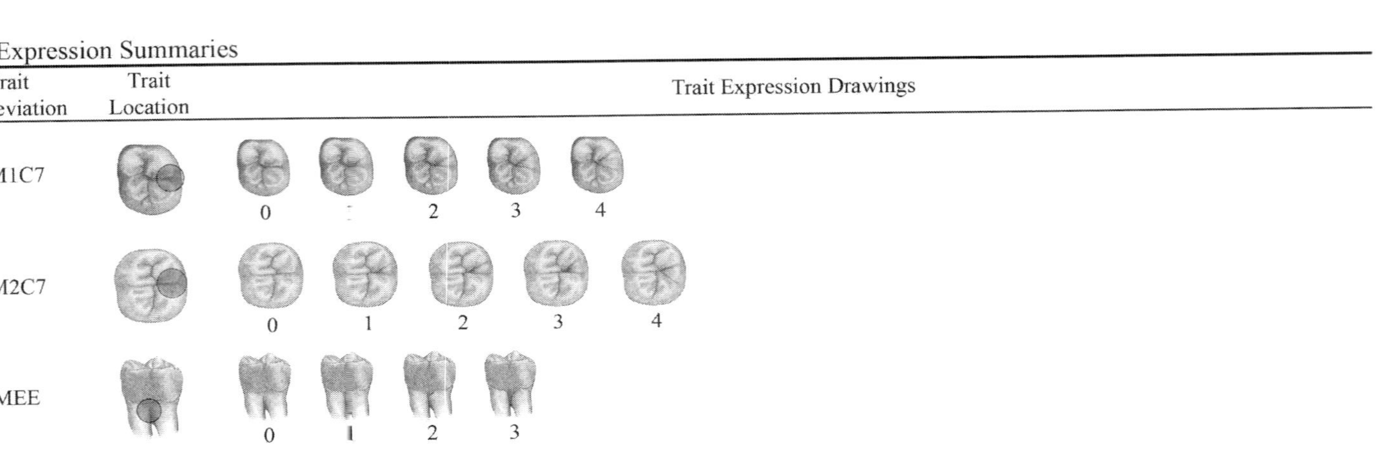
Trait Expression Summaries
Trait Abbreviation
Trait Location
Trait Expression Drawings
LM1C7
0
2
3
4
LM2C7
0
1
2
3
4
LMEE
0
1
2
3

REFERENCES

Alsoleihat F. 2013. A new quantitative method for predicting forensic racial identity based on dental morphological trait analysis. *Int J Morphology* 31:418–424.

Alt KW, Vach W. 1991. The reconstruction of "genetic kinship" in prehistoric burial complexes-problems and statistics. In: Bock H-H, Ihm P (editors). *Classification, data analysis, and knowledge organization*. Berlin: Springer-Verlag. 299–310.

Alt KW, Vach W. 1998. Kinship studies in skeletal remains—concepts and examples. In: Alt KW, Rösing FW, Teschler-Nicola M (editors). *Dental anthropology: fundamentals, limits, and prospects*. Vienna: Springer. 537–554.

Bailey-Schmidt SE. 1995. *Population distribution of the tuberculum dentale complex and anomalies of the maxillary anterior teeth*. MA Thesis, Arizona State University.

Bailey SE. 2002. *Neandertal dental morphology: implications for modern human origins*. PhD dissertation, Arizona State University.

Bailey SE, Hublin J-J. 2013. What does it mean to be dentally "modern"? In: Scott GR, Irish JD (editors). *Anthropological perspectives on human tooth morphology: genetics, evolution, variation*. Cambridge: Cambridge University Press. 222–249.

Bailey SE, Weaver TD, Hublin J-J. 2009. Who made the Auginacian and other early upper Paleolithic industries? *J Hum Evol* 57:11–26.

Berry AC, Berry RJ. 1967. Epigenetic variation in the human cranium. *J Anat* 101:361–379.

Bianchi FJ, Franco de Oliviera T, Borges Pereira Saito C, Rocha Peres RC, Peres Line SR. 2007. Association between polymorphism in the promoter region (G/C-915) of PAX9 gene and third molar agenesis. *J Applied Oral Sci* 15:382–386.

Brook AH. 2009. Multilevel complex interactions between genetic, epigenetic and environmental factors in the aetiology of anomalies of dental development. *Archives Oral Biol* 54S:S3–17.

Brown MB. 1977. The tetrachoric correlation and its asymptotic standard error. *Appl Statist* 26:343–351.

Buikstra J, Ubelaker D. 1994. Standards for data collection from human skeletal remains: proceedings of a seminar at the field museum of natural history. Fayetteville: Arkansas Archeological Survey Research Series No. 44.

Buikstra JE, Frankenberg SR, Konigsberg LW. 1990. Skeletal bioloigical distance studies in American physical anthropology: recent trends. *Am J Phys Anthropol* 82:1–7.

Burnett SE, Hawkey DE, Turner CG II. 2010. Brief communication: population variation in human maxillary premolar accessory ridges (MxPAR). *Am J Phys Anthropol* 141:319–324.

Butler PM. 1939. Studies of the mammalian dentition—differentiation of the post-canine dentition. *J Zool* B109:1–36.

Christensen A. 1998. Skeletal evidence for familial interments in the valley of Oaxaca, Mexico. *Homo* 49:273–288.

Corruccini RS, Shimada I. 2002. Dental relatedness corresponding to mortuary patterning at Huaca Loro, Peru. *Am J Phys Anthropol* 117:113–121.

Cucina A, Price TD, Magaña Peralta E, Sierra Sosa T. 2015. Crossing the peninsula: the role of Noh Bec, Yucatán, in ancient Maya classic period population dynamics from an analysis of dental morphology and Sr isotopes. *Am J Hum Biol* 27:767–778.

Dahlberg AA. 1951. The dentition of the American Indian. In: Laughlin WS (editor). *The physical anthropology of the American Indian*. New York: The Viking Fund. 138–176.

Delgado-Burbano ME. 2008. Deciduous dental morphological diversity in contemporary Columbian ethnic groups. *Dent Anthropol* 21:33–45.

De Souza P, Houghton P. 1977. The mean measure of divergence and the use of non-metric data in the estimation of biological distances. *J Archaeol Sci* 4:163–169.

Díaz E, García L, Hernández M, Palacio L, Ruiz D, Velandia N, Villavicencio J, Moreno F. 2014. Frequency and variability of dental morphology in deciduous and permanent dentition of a Nasa indigenous group in the municipality of Morales, Cauca, Columbia. *Columbua Medica* 45:15–24.

Edgar HJH. 2002. *Biological distance and the African-American dentition*. PhD Dissertation, the Ohio State University.

Edgar HJH. 2004. Dentitions, distances, and difficulty: a comparison of two statistical techniques for dental morphological data. *Dent Anthropol* 17:55–62.

Edgar HJH. 2005. Prediction of social race category using characteristics of dental morphology. *J Forensic Sci* 50:269–273.

Edgar HJH. 2007. Microevolution of African American dental morphology. *Am J Phys Anthropol* 132:535–544.

Edgar HJH. 2008. Dental anthropology of newly excavated human remains: concerns about data collections and consistency. *Dent Anthropol* 21:31.

Edgar HJH. 2013. Estimation of ancestry using dental morphological characteristics. *J Forensic Sci* 58:S3–S8.

Edgar HJH, Sciulli PW. 2004. Elongated premolar: a new morphological variant. *Dent Anthropol* 17:24–27.

Edgar HJH, Willermet CM, Ragsdale CS, O'Donnell A, Daneshvari SR. 2015. Frequencies of rare incisor variations reflect factors influencing precontact population relationships in Mexico and the American Southwest. *Int J Osteoarchaeology* 26(6):987–1000.

George R. 2015. *Non-metric and metric dental assessment of ancestry in contemporary Mexican individuals: an aid to identifying undocumented border crossers*. MA Thesis, California State University, Chico.

Greenberg JH, Turner CG II, Zegura SL, Campbell L, Fox JA, Laughlin WS, Szathmary EJE, Weiss KM, Woolford E. 1986. The settlement of the Americas: a comparison of the linguistic, dental and genetic evidence. *Curr Anthropol* 27:477–497.

Gregory WK. 1922. *The origin and evolution of the human dentition*. Baltimore: Williams and Wilkins.

Grewel MS. 1962. The rate of genetic divergence of sublines in the C57BL strain of mice. *Genetics Res* 3(2): 226–237.

Grine FE. 1986. Anthropological aspects of the deciduous teeth of South African Blacks. In: Singer R, Lundy JK (editors). *Variation, culture and evolution in African populations*. Johannesburg: Witwatersrand University Press. 47–83.

Grine FE, Delanty MM, Wood BA. 2013. Variation in mandibular postcanine dental morphology and hominin species representation in Member 4, Sterkfontein, South Africa. In: Reed KE, Fleagle JG, Leakey RE (editors). *The paleobiology of Australopithecus. Vertebrate paleobiology and paleoanthropology*. Dordrecht: Springer. 125–146.

Guatelli-Steinberg D, Irish JD. 2005. Brief communication: early hominin variability in first molar dental trait frequencies. *Am J Phys Anthropol* 128:477–484.

Haeussler AM, Irish JD, Morris DH, Turner CG II. 1989. Morphological and metrical comparison of San and central Sotho dentition from southern Africa. *Am J Phys Anthropol* 78:115–122.

Hanihara K. 1963. Crown characteristics of the deciduous dentition of the Japanese-American hybrids. In: Brothwell DR (editor). *Dental anthropology*. New York: Pergamon Press. 105–124.

Hanihara K. 1967. Racial characteristics in the dentition. *J Dent Res* 46:923–926.

Hanihara T. 2008. Morphological variation of major human populations based on nonmetric dental traits. *Am J Phys Anthropol* 136:169–182.

Hanihara T. 2013. Geographic structure of dental variation in the major human populations of the world. In: Scot GR, Irish JD (editors). *Anthropological perspectives on tooth morphology: genetics, evolution, variation*. Cambridge: Cambridge University Press. 479–509.

Hardin AM, Legge SS. 2013. Geographic variation in nonmetric dental traits of the deciduous molars of Pan and Gorilla. *Int J Primatology* 34:1000–1019.

Harris EF. 1977. *Anthropologic and genetic aspects of the dental morphology of Solomon Islanders, Melanesia*. PhD dissertation, Arizona State University.

Harris EF. 2008. Statistical applications in dental anthropology. In: Irish JD, Nelson GC (editors). *Technique and application in dental anthropology*. Cambridge: Cambridge University Press. 35–67.

Harris EF, Sjøvold T. 2004. Calculation of Smith's mean measure of divergence for intergroup comparisons using nonmetric data. *Dent Anthropol* 17:83–93.

Hillson S. 1996. *Dental anthropology*. Cambridge: Cambridge University Press.

Hinkes MJ. 1990. Shovel-shaped incisors in human identification. In: Gill GW, Rhine S (editors). *Skeletal attribution of race: methods for forensic anthropology*. Albuquerque: Maxwell Museum of Anthropology. 21–26.

Hlusko LJ. 2004. Protostylid variation in Australopithecus. *J Hum Evol* 46:579–594.

Hrdlička A. 1911. Human dentition and teeth from the evolutionary and racial standpoint. *Dominion Dent J* 23:403–417.

Hrdlička A. 1921. Further studies of tooth morphology. *Am J Phys Anthropol* 4:141–176.

Hubbard AR, Guatelli-Steinberg D, Irish JD. 2015. Do nuclear DNA and dental nonmetric data produce similar reconstructions of regional population history? An example from modern coastal Kenya. *Am J Phys Anthropol* 157:295–304.

Irish JD. 1993. *Biological affinities of late Pleistocene through modern African aboriginal populations: the dental evidence*. PhD thesis, Arizona State University.

Irish JD. 1997. Characteristic high- and low-frequency dental traits in sub-Saharan African populations. *Am J Phys Anthropol* 102:455–467.

Irish JD. 2010. The mean measure of divergence: its utility in model-free and model-bound analyses relative to the Mahalanob D2 distance for nonmetirc traits. *Am J Hum Biol* 22:378–395.

Irish JD. 2013. Afridonty: the Sub-Saharan African dental complex revisited. In: Scott GR, Irish JD (editors). *Anthropological perspectives on tooth morphology: genetics, evolution, variation*. Cambridge: Cambridge University Press. 278–295.

Irish JD. 2015. Dental nonmetric variation around the world: using key traits in populations to estimate ancestry in individuals. In: Berg GE, Ta'ala SC (editors). *Biological affinity in forensic identification of human skeletal remains*. Boca Raton: CRC Press. 165–190.

Irish JD, Guatelli-Steinberg D. 2003. Ancient teeth and modern human origins: an expanded comparison of African Plio-Pleistocene and recent world dental samples. *J Hum Evol* 45:113–144.

Irish JD, Guatelli-Steinberg D, Legge S, Berger L, de Ruiter D. 2013. Dental morphology and the phylogenetic 'place' of Australopithecus sediba. *Science* 340:1–4.

Irish JD, Guatelli-Steinberg D, Legge SS, de Ruiter DJ, Berger LR. 2014. News and views: response to 'non-metric dental traits and hominin phylogeny' by Carter et al., with additional information on the Arizona State University Dental Anthropology System and phylogenetic 'place' of Australopithecus sediba. *J Hum Evol* 69:129–134.

Irish JD, Nelson GC (editors). 2008. *Technique and application in dental anthropology*. Cambridge: Cambridge University Press.

Irish JD, Scott GR (editors). 2016. *A companion to dental anthropology*. West Sussex: John Wiley & Sons.

Irish JD, Turner CG. 1990. West African dental affinity of late Pleistocene Nubians: peopling of the Eurafrican-South Asian triangle II. *Homo* 41:42–53.

Jacobi KP. 2000. *Last rites for the Tipu Maya: genetic structuring in a colonial cemetery*. Tuscaloosa: University of Alabama Press.

Jernvall J, Jung H-S. 2000. Genotype, phenotype, and developmental biology of molar tooth characters. *Ybk Phys Anthropol* 43:171–190.

Kitagawa Y, Manabe Y, Oyamada J, Rokutanda A. 1995. Deciduous dental morphology of the prehistoric Jomon people of Japan: comparison of nonmetric characters. *Am J Phys Anthropol* 97:101–111.

Konigsberg LW. 1990. Analysis of prehistoric biological variation under a model of isolation by geographic and temporal distance. *Hum Biol* 62:49–70.

Konigsberg LW. 2006. A post-Neumann history of biological and genetic distance studies in bioarchaeology. In: Buikstra JE, Beck LA (editors). *Bioarchaeology: the contextual analysis of human remains*. New York: Academic Press. 263–279.

Larsen CS, Kelley MA. 1991. Introduction. In: Kelley MA, Larsen CS (editors). *Advances in dental anthropology*. New York: Wiley-Liss. 1–7.

Lasker GW, Lee MMC. 1957. Racial traits in human teeth. *J Forensic Sci* 2:401–419.

Lease LR, Sciulli PW. 2005. Brief communication: discrimination between European-American and African-American children based on deciduous dental metric and morphology. *Am J Phys Anthropol* 126:56–60.

Luis JR, Rowold DJ, Regueiro M, Caeiro B, Cinnioğlu C, Roseman C, Underhill PA, Cavalli-Sforza LL, Herrera RJ. 2004. The Levant versus the Horn of Africa: evidence for bidirectional corridors of human migrations. *Am J Hum Genet* 74:532–544.

Lukacs JR, Walimbe SR. 2005. Deciduous dental morphology and the biological affinities of a late Chalcolithic skeletal series from western India. *Am J Phys Anthropol* 65:23–30.

Manica A, Prugnolle F, Balloux F. 2005. Geography is a better determinant of human genetic differentiation than ethnicity. *Hum Genet* 118:366–371.

Manly BFJ. 1994. *Multivariate statistical methods: a primer*. London: Chapman and Hall.

Matsumura H, Hudson MJ. 2005. Dental perspectives on the population history of Southeast Asia. *Am J Phys Anthropol* 127:182–209.

Mayhall JT, Saunders SR, Belier PL. 1982. The dental morphology of North American Whites: a reappraisal. In: Kurten B (editor). *Teeth: form, function, and evolution*. New York: Columbia University Press. 245–258.

McClelland JA. 2003. *Refining the resolution of biological distance studies based on the analysis of dental morphology: detecting subpopulations at Grasshopper Pueblo*. PhD dissertation, University of Arizona.

Mizoguchi Y. 1977. Genetic variability on tooth crown characters: analysis by the tetrachoric correlation method. *Bull Nat Sci Museum, Series D* 3:37–62.

Mizoguchi Y. 1988. Degree of bilateral asymmetry of nonmetric tooth crown characteristics quantified by the tetrachoric correlation method. *Bull Nat Sci Museum, Series D (Anthropology)* 15:49–61.

Moormann S, Guatelli-Steinberg D, Hunter J. 2013. Metamerism, morphogenesis, and the expression of Carabelli and other dental traits in humans. *Am J Phys Anthropol* 150:400–408.

Morris DH, Dahlberg AA, Glasstone Hughes S. 1978. The Uto-Aztecan premolar: the anthropology of a dental trait. In: Butler PM, Joysey KA (editors). *Development, function, and evolution of the teeth.* London: Academic Press. 69–79.

Nichol CR. 1989. Complex segregation analysis of dental morphological variants. *Am J Phys Anthropol* 78:37–59.

Nikita E. 2015. A critical review of the mean measure of divergence and Mahalanobis distances using artificial data and new approaches to the estimation of biodistances employing nonmetric traits. *Am J Phys Anthropol* 157(2):284–294.

Paul KS, Stojanowski CM. 2015. Performance analysis of deciduous morphology for detecting biological siblings. *Am J Phys Anthropol* 157:615–629.

Pietrusewsky M. 2014. Biological distance in bioarchaeology and human osteology. In: Smith C (editor). *Encyclopedia of global archaeology.* New York: Springer Reference. 889–902.

Pilloud MA, Edgar HJH, George R. 2016. Dental morphology in biodistance analysis: bioarchaeological and forensic applications. In: Pilloud MA, Hefner JT (editors). *Biological distance analysis: forensic and bioarchaeological perspectives.* London: Academic Press. 109–134.

Pilloud MA, Larsen CS. 2011. "Official" and "practical" kin: inferring social and community structure from dental phenotype at Neolithic Çatalhöyük, Turkey. *Am J Phys Anthropol* 145:519–530.

Pinto-Cisternas J, Moggi-Cecchi J, Pacciani E. 1995. A morphological variant of the permanent upper lateral incisor in two Tuscan samples from different periods. In: Moggi-Cecchi J (editor). *Aspects of dental biology: palaeontology, anthropology, and evolution, Vol. 7, Leonardo series.* Florence: International Institute for the Study of Man. 333–339.

Powell JF. 1993. Dental evidence for the peopling of the New World: some methodological considerations. *Hum Biol* 65:799–819.

Press J, Wilson S. 1978. Choosing between logistic regression and discriminant analysis. *J Am Statistical Assoc* 73:699–705.

Ragsdale CS, Edgar HJH, Melgar E. 2016. Origins of the skull offerings of the Templo Mayor, Tenochtitlán. *Curr Anthropol* 57:357–369.

Relethford JH. 1994. Craniometirc variation among modern human populations. *Am J Phys Anthropol* 95:53–62.

Relethford JH. 2001. Global analysis of regional differences in craniometric diversity and population substructure. *Hum Biol* 73:629–636.

Relethford JH, Blangero J. 1990. Detection of differential gene flow from patterns of qualitative variation. *Hum Biol* 62:5–25.

Ricout F-X, Auriol V, von Carmon-Taubadel N, Keyser C, Murail P, Ludes B, Crubezy E. 2010. Comparison between morphological and genetic data to estimate biological relationship: the case of the Egyin Gol necropolis. *Am J Phys Anthropol* 143:355–364.

Risnes S. 1974. The prevalence, location, and size of enamel pearls on human molars. *European J Oral Sci* 82:403–412.

Roseman CC. 2004. Detecting interregionally diversifying natural selection on modern human cranial form by using matched molecular and morphometric data. *Proc Natl Acad Sci USA* 101:12824–12829.

Schmidt CW. 2008. Forensic dental anthropology: issues and guidelines. In: Irish JD, Nelson GC (editors). *Technique and application in dental anthropology.* Cambridge: Cambridge University Press. 266–292.

Sciulli PW. 1990. Deciduous dentition of a late archaic population of Ohio. *Hum Biol* 62:221–245.

Sciulli PW. 1998. Evolution of the dentition in prehistoric Ohio Valley Native Americans. II: Morphology of the deciduous dentition. *Am J Phys Anthropol* 106:189–205.

Scott GR, Anta A, Schomberg, R, de la Rúa C. 2013. Basque dental morphology and the "Eurodont" dental pattern. In: Scott GR, Irish JD (editors). *Anthropological perspectives on tooth morphology: genetics, evolution, variation*. Cambridge: Cambridge University Press. 296–318.

Scott GR, Irish JD (editors). 2013. *Anthropological perspectives on tooth morphology: genetics, evolution, variation*. Cambridge: Cambridge University Press.

Scott GR, Maier C, Heim K. 2016. Identifying and recording key morphological (nonmetric) crown and root traits. In: Irish JD, Scott GR (editors). *A companion to dental anthropology*. West Sussex: John Wiley & Sons. 247–261.

Scott GR, Potter RHY. 1984. An analysis of tooth crown morphology in American white twins. *Anthropologie* 22:223–231.

Scott GR, Turner CG II. 1997. *The anthropology of modern human teeth: dental morphology and its variation in recent human populations*. Cambridge: Cambridge University Press.

Serre D, Pääbo S. 2007. Evidence for gradients of human genetic diversity within and among continents. *Genome Res* 14:1679–1685.

Skinner MM, Gunz P. 2010. The presence of accessory cusps in chimpanzee lower molars is consistent with a patterning cascade model of development. *J Anat* 217:245–253.

Sofaer JA, Niswander JD, MacLean CJ, Workman PL. 1972. Population studies on Southwestern Indian tribes V. Tooth morphology as an indicator of biological distance. *Am J Phys Anthropol* 37(3): 357–366.

Sokal R, Michener C. 1958. A statistical model for evaluating systematic relationships. *U Kansas Sci Bull* 38:1409–1438.

Stojanowski CM, Schillaci MA. 2006. Phenotypic approaches for understanding patterns of intracemetery biological variation. *Ybk Phys Anthropol* 131:49–88.

Stratford D, Heaton JL, Pickering TR, Caruana MV, Shadrach K. 2016. First hominin fossils from Milner Hall, Sterkfontein, South Africa. *J Hum Evol* 91:167–173.

Stringer CB, Humphrey LT, Compton T. 1997. Cladistic analysis of dental traits in recent humans using a fossil outgroup. *J Hum Evol* 32:389–402.

Tan JZ, Peng QQ, Li JX, Guan YQ, Zhang LP, Jiao Y, Yang YJ, Wang SJ, Jin L. 2014. Characteristics of dental morphology in the Xinjiang Uyghur and correlation with the EDARV370A variant. *Sci China Life Sciences* 57:510–518.

Thesleff I. 2006. The genetic basis of tooth development and dental defects. *Am J Med Genet* 140A:2530–2535.

Townsend GC, Bockmann M, Hughes T, Brook A. 2012. Genetic, environmental and epigenetic influences on variation in human tooth number, size and shape. *Odontology* 100:1–9.

Trinkaus E. 1978. Dental remains from the Shanidar adult Neaderthals. *J Hum Evol* 7:369–382.

Turner CG. 1979. Dental anthropological indications of agriculture among the Jomon people of central Japan: X. Peopling of the Pacific. *Am J Phys Anthropol* 51:619–635.

Turner CG II. 1985. Expression count: A method for calculating morphological dental trait frequencies by using adjustable weighting coefficients with standard ranked scales. *Am J Phys Anthropol* 68(2):263–267.

Turner CG II. 1987. Late Pleistocene and Holocene population history of East Asia based on dental variation. *Am J Phys Anthropol* 73:305–321.

Turner CG II. 1990. Major features of Sundadonty and Sinodonty, including suggestions about East Asian microevolution, population history, and late Pleistocene relationships with Australian aboriginals. *Am J Phys Anthropol* 82:295–317.

Turner CG II, Nichol CR, Scott GR. 1991. Scoring procedures for key morphological traits of the permanent dentition: the Arizona State University Dental Anthropology System. In: Kelley MA, Larsen CS (editors). *Advances in dental anthropology*. New York: Wiley-Liss. 13–31.

Underhill PA, Passarino G, Lin AA, Shen P, Lahr MM, Foley RA, Oefner PJ, Cavalli-Sforza LL. 2001. The phylogeography of Y chromosome binary haplotypes and the origins of modern human populations. *Ann Hum Genet* 65:43–62.

Zilberman U, Smith P. 1992. A comparison of tooth structure in Neanderthals and early Homo sapiens sapiens: a radiographic study. *J Anat* 180:387–393.

INDEX

accessory cusps 58–61, 150, 180; UP3AC 10–11, 58–9; UP4AC 10–11, 60–1
accessory ridges, maxillary premolar 2, 64–71; UP3D MXPAR 10, 11, 68–9; UP3M MXPAR 10–11, 64–5; UP4D MXPAR 12, 70–1; UP4M MXPAR 10–11, 66–7
admixture 6
Africa 176–8, 180
Afridont 6
ancestry 1, 7, 16
anterior fovea 112–13, 151; LM1AF 10, 12, 112–13
antimeres 19, 162
Arizona State University Dental Anthropology System 2, 6, 162; ASUDAS 2, 8, 18, 21–145, 162
ASUDAS *see* Arizona State University Dental Anthropology System

biodistance *see* biological distance
biological distance 5, 14–16
breakpoints *see* threshold levels
BUSHMAN CANINE *see* canine mesial ridge

canine mesial ridge 54–5; UCMR 6, 10, 11, 54–5
Carabelli's trait 84–7; UM1CB 6, 12, 84–5; UM2CB 12, 86–7
congenital absence 11, 36–9, 98–101; LI1CA 10, 12, 98–9; LM3CA 10, 12, 100–1; UI2CA 10–11, 36–7; UM3CA 6, 10–11, 38–9
cusp 5, mandibular molar 2, 120, 122, 132–9; LM1C5 10, 13, 132–3; LM2C5 10, 13, 134–5
cusp 6 13, 136–9; LM1C6 6, 13, 136–7; LM2C6 10, 13, 138–9
cusp 7 120, 122, 140–3; LM1C7 6, 10, 13, 140–1; LM2C7 142–3
cusp number, mandibular molar 120–3; LM1CN 10, 13, 120–1; LM2CN 6, 10, 13, 122–3

Dahlberg, A. 2, 5
decision trees 14
deflecting wrinkle 115–16; LM1DW 6, 10, 12, 115–16
dental complexes 5–6
dental genetics 3
DIAS *see* diastema
diastema 22–3; DIAS 10, 11, 22–3
discriminant analysis 14, 16–17
distal accessory ridge, canine 56–7, 102–3; LCDR 10, 12, 102–3; UCDR 10, 12, 56–7
distosagittal ridge 62–3; UP3DS 10–11, 62–3
DNA analyses 3, 7, 14
double shovel 26–9; UI1DS 6, 10–11, 26–7; UI2DS 10–11, 28–9

elongated form premolars 2, 108–11; LP3EF 10, 12, 108–9; LP4EF 10, 12, 110–11
enamel extension 92–3, 144–5; LMEE 10, 13, 144–5; UMEE 6, 10, 11–13, 92–3

enamel pearl 146
Eurodont 6

F_{ST} 5
forensic anthropology 1, 7, 16
frequency data 9

genetic variability 3
groove pattern 116–19; LM1GP 10, 12, 116–17; LM2GP 6, 10, 13, 118–19

Hanihara, K. 2
heritability 3
hominin evolutionary relationships 4
Hrdička, Aleš 2
human evolution 3
hypocone 2, 76–9, 80; UM1HC 10, 12, 76–7; UM2HC 6, 10, 12, 78–9

identification, tooth 8
interruption groove 44–7; UI1IG 11, 44–5; UI2IG 11, 46–7
intracemetery relationships 6

labial convexity *see* labial curvature
labial curvature 4, 24–5; UI1LC 10–11, 24–5
LCDR *see* distal accessory ridge, canine
LI1CA *see* congenital absence
LI1SS *see* shovel shape
LI2SS *see* shovel shape
lingual cusp complexity, mandibular premolar 104–7; LP3LC 10, 12, 104–5; LP4LC 6, 10, 12, 106–7
LM1AF *see* anterior fovea
LM1C5 *see* cusp 5, mandibular molar
LM1C6 *see* cusp 6
LM1C7 *see* cusp 7
LM1CN *see* cusp number, mandibular molar
LM1DW *see* deflecting wrinkle
LM1GP *see* groove pattern
LM1PS *see* protostylid
LM1TC *see* trigonid crest
LM2C5 *see* cusp 5, mandibular molar
LM2C6 *see* cusp 6
LM2C7 *see* cusp 7
LM2CN *see* cusp number, mandibular molar
LM2GP *see* groove pattern
LM2PS *see* protostylid
LM2TC *see* trigonid crest
LM3CA *see* congenital absence
LMEE *see* enamel extension
logistic discriminate function analyses 14, 16
logistic regression 16
LP3EF *see* elongated form premolars
LP3LC *see* lingual cusp complexity, mandibular premolar
LP4EF *see* elongated form premolars
LP4LC *see* lingual cusp complexity, mandibular premolar

MDS *see* multidimensional scaling
mean measure of divergence 5, 14–15
mesial bending 146
metacone 2, 72–5; UM1MC 10, 12, 72–3; UM2MC 10, 12, 74–5
metaconule 80–3; UM1C5 10, 12, 80–1; UM2C5 10, 12, 82–3
migration 4–6
Moss, M. 2
multidimensional scaling 5, 7; MDS 17

Neandertal 3–4, 153
neutral 3–5

odontome 147

parastyle 88–91; UM1PS 10, 12, 88–9; UM2PS 10, 12, 90–1
peg or reduction 40–3; UI2PEG 11, 40–1; UM3PEG 11, 42–3
phenetics 3, 15
plaques, ASUDAS 2, 5, 8, 18
probability 7, 14, 16
protostylid 6, 10, 13, 124–7; LM1PS 124–5; LM2PS 10, 13, 126–7
pseudo-Mahalanobis D^2 14–16

race 14, 16
root, tooth 153–4, 164–5

Sciulli, P. 2
scoring types 10
shovel shape 4, 10, 16, 30–5, 94–7; LI1SS 10, 12, 94–5; LI2SS 10, 12, 96–7; UCSS 10–11, 34–5; UI1SS 6, 10–11, 30–1; UI2SS 10–11, 32–3
Sinodont 6
size, tooth 3
Standards for Data Collection from Human Skeletal Remains 2
Sundadont 6
supernumerary teeth 147

talon tooth 2, 146
threshold levels 10–11, 13–14
tri-cusp premolar 146
trigonid crest 4, 13, 128–31; LM1TC 10, 13, 128–9; LM2TC 10, 13, 130–1

tuberculum dentale 48–53; UCTD 10–11, 13–14, 52–3; UI1TD 10–11, 48–9; UI2TD 10–11, 50–1
Turner, C.G. II 2

UCDR *see* distal accessory ridge
UCMR *see* canine mesial ridge
UCSS *see* shovel shape
UCTD *see* tuberculum dentale
UI1DS *see* double shovel
UI1IG *see* interruption groove
UI1LC *see* labial curvature
UI1SS *see* shovel shape
UI1TD *see* tuberculum dentale
UI2CA *see* congenital absence
UI2DS *see* double shovel
UI2IG *see* interruption groove
UI2PEG *see* peg or reduction
UI2SS *see* shovel shape
UI2TD *see* tuberculum dentale
UM1C5 *see* metaconule
UM1CB *see* Carabelli's trait
UM1HC *see* hypocone
UM1MC *see* metacone
UM1PS *see* parastyle
UM2C5 *see* metaconule
UM2CB *see* Carabelli's trait
UM2HC *see* hypocone
UM2MC *see* metacone
UM2PS *see* parastyle
UM3CA *see* congenital absence
UM3PEG *see* peg or reduction
UMEE *see* enamel extension
unweighted pair group method with arithmetic mean 5, 14–16
UP3AC *see* accessory cusps, premolar
UP3D MXPAR *see* accessory ridges, mandibular premolar
UP3DS *see* distosagittal ridge
UP3M MXPAR *see* accessory ridges, mandibular premolar
UP4AC *see* accessory cusps
UP4D MXPAR *see* accessory ridges, mandibular premolar
UP4M MXPAR *see* accessory ridges, mandibular premolar
UPGMA *see* unweighted pair group method with arithmetic mean
UTO-AZTECAN PREMOLAR *see* distosagittal ridge

wear, tooth 3, 9, 165
weighted frequencies 13–14
WING *see* winging
winging 20–1; WING 6, 10–11, 20–1